This Book Can Change Your Life!

These words teach the reader how to be healthy, happy, and wise. Their Source is Cosmic, and they were written without a purpose known by the writer, using a method called Cosmic Telepathy. They are as much for the writer as for the reader. The Author is the One Cosmic God, Who has given the thoughts to the writer for you and for him.

Those who have read the Books of <u>A New Way of Living</u> report strange and wonderful improvements in health, happiness, outlook on life, marriage relationships, and even the management of money and of possessions. Common remarks by readers are that these words have changed their lives, seem to have been written just for them, and have made a total change in the way they handle their day-to-day problems.

The words are uplifting, encouraging, and fulfilling. They promise to give purpose and meaning to life, giving you the means of finding your inner truth from the Kingdom of God within you. They teach you of your own worthiness as an immortal child of Creation, and they show you how to cope with the negativity and the turmoil of the last days of Earth. They also give you hope that the last days can be extended into the indefinite future for those who simply learn to love one another.

Ventris Nukayis

ACKNOWLEDGMENTS

I would like to express special appreciation for the proof reading help offered by Pope Goodson, Dr. Jo Ann Campbell, Dr. Pam Winkler, Fay Clark, and many others. At least fifty other readers of the Series of Books called <u>A New Way of Living</u> have also offered many words and letters of encouragement and support.

The greatest encouragement, however, has come from my mate, who has seen me go into seclusion, pray, and write for about an hour almost every day for three years. As we worked together and changed together, we learned to love life and one another more and more deeply. These lessons in loving, without exceptions and without conditions, reveal the meaning of all life and all reality.

Most of all, I acknowledge God, the Brotherhood of Light, and the brotherhood of humankind as the centers of all fulfillment on Earth.

Ventris Nukayis

Last Days?

Spiritual Reality

and

Physical Illusions

Ventris Nukayis

Copyright ® 1987, 1991 by ANWOL Publishers.

All Rights reserved. This book may not be reproduced in any form by any means, or copied into a database or electronic retrieval system, without express prior written approval of the publisher, except in the case of brief quotations for critical articles or reviews. In the event of quotations, material copied and quoted out of the context in which it is written will constitute a violation of the copyright.

To make copies of any part of this book except for your own personal use is also a violation of United States copyright laws.

ISBN: 1-56266-149-3

For information, write to the following:

ANWOL Publishers
P. O. Box 525
Jasper, AR 72641
SAN: 297-3081

Printed in the United States of America

First Printing 1991

Last Days?

Table of Contents

		Title	Page	From Book	Date Written
Chapter	1	The Doomsday of Earth	1	3	03/06/88
Chapter	2	Turmoil and Peace	7	5	05/01/88
Chapter	3	Time and Change	13	6	06/01/88
Chapter	4	Truth and Repentance	19	6	06/11/88
Chapter	5	The Title	25	6	06/13/88
Chapter	6	The Last Days	31	7	07/13/88
Chapter	7	Hope and Joy	37	8	08/17/88
Chapter	8	Dwelling	43	9	09/08/88
Chapter	9	Stillness	49	10	09/28/88
Chapter	10	Falling Leaves	55	11	10/27/88
Chapter	11	Passages	61	11	11/02/88
Chapter	12	Laughter	67	11	11/15/88
Chapter	13	Daily Life	73	12	12/09/88
Chapter	14	Fulfillment	79	13	12/21/88
Chapter	15	Patiently	85	14	02/07/89
Chapter	16	Peace	91	15	02/25/89
Chapter	17	Extremes	97	16	04/13/89
Chapter	18	Water	103	17	04/28/89
Chapter	19	Storms	109	18	05/27/89
Chapter	20	Existence	115	19	07/11/89
Chapter	21	Contentment	121	20	08/11/89
Chapter	22	Be Ready	127	21	09/10/89
Chapter	23	The Story	133	22	10/03/89
Chapter	24	From Everywhere	139	23	11/07/89
Chapter	25	Shadows	145	24	12/05/89
Chapter	26	The Price	151	24	12/07/89
Chapter	27	The Books	157	24	12/20/89
Chapter	28	Consider	163	25	01/09/90
Chapter	29	Sweeping Changes	169	26	02/26/90
Chapter	30	Apocalypse	175	27	03/18/90
Chapter	31	Stimulation	181	28	04/04/90
Chapter	32	Proof of Life	187	29	05/18/90
Chapter	33	The First Call	193	30	06/16/90
Chapter	34	Each Call	199	30	06/16/90
Chapter	35	Time Lag	205	31	06/27/90
Chapter	36	Adjustment	211	32	08/06/90
Chapter	37	Evening	217	32	08/06/90
Chapter	38	Regardless	223	33	08/22/90
Chapter	39	I Am God	229	33	08/30/90
Chapter	40	Preparation	235	33	09/02/90
Chapter	41	Being Prepared	241	33	09/05/90
Chapter	42	Conditional Cares	247	34	09/30/90
Chapter	43	Waiting	253	35	11/17/90
Chapter	44	Best Is Last	259	36	12/15/90

Glossary 264

About the Writer

Ventris Nukayis (a pseudonym) was born and raised in Indiana. He began his career as a farmer, then sold his dairy to work his way through Purdue University, and was graduated with a degree in Mechanical Engineering at age 36. He became a Registered Professional Engineer and co-founded a manufacturing facility in his first year after graduation, which he sold to a larger company thirteen years later. He then operated and managed his 2000 acre grain farm for another 15 years, also working part-time as a consulting engineer while managing his various other real estate investments.

In his earlier years he also worked for short periods as a truck driver, electrician, and plumber. He is a private pilot with several thousand hours of business flying experience. He holds multi-engine and instrument ratings. At the time this writing started he had worked for five years as a micro computer sales consultant. He specialized in commercial networked computer installations involving accounting, manufacturing management, and banking applications.

When this writing unexpectedly began, he took early retirement and moved to another state in order to give full attention to his mission of writing the 36 Books in the Series of <u>A New Way of Living</u>.

"Your escape from the holocausts of the last days of Earth will be a spiritual escape. It will also be a time of acceptance of <u>all</u> physical illusions as illusions, an acceptance which will make <u>all</u> things beautiful and joyful for you. At the time your universal love allows this, you will not believe in Satan, in evil, in guilt, in punishment, in vengeance, in pain, in suffering, in sorrow, or in death."

From Book 36 — <u>A New Way of Living.</u>

Chapter 1 From Book 3 — <u>A New Way of Living</u>

The Doomsday of Earth

The time of prophecy that is revealed in the Book of Revelations is coming soon. There should be no mortal fear in the heart of anyone, for those who believe these words can escape it if they will. And those who do not will suffer bodily pain for only an instant and will be separated from that body by the death of it.

The destruction of the Earth is as natural as the death of a flower. It is not horrible and final, and it is not unusual. It only seems so to those who do not realize the wonderful plan of My Creation. The destruction of the Earth is necessary so that it might be renewed.

Last Days?

A flower withers and dies, and returns to life and beauty. Psalm 90 tells a simple story that can easily be understood as it applies to the destruction of the Earth.

The horror stories and the frustrating experiences of the life you are living are morbid and sad. They cause you to dwell on futility and senseless happenings. But there is sense and purpose in the doomsday of Earth.

When your thoughts return today, think of it from another point of view. Think of the darkness that will be destroyed. For all life and truth will be saved. The physical bodies that are destroyed were frail and doomed to die in any case. And the souls and spirits within them will be instantly taken to a better place for further opportunities.

At the time of doom for the Earth, there is also doom for countless billions of the illusionary works of Satan. For he cannot survive the destruction. He will be chained and helpless for a thousand years, and you cannot imagine the joy that can flourish in his absence.

For in that time of renewal there will be harmony, and although it will be a physical existence for those of you who have chosen to live in it, it will be like nothing you can now imagine. It will take you years to realize the confidence that comes with perfect health, perfect joy, perfect friendship, perfect love, and perfect peace.

For there all truth will be practiced, all wisdom understood, and all joy experienced. It will be a Heaven on Earth. It will be a Garden of Eden. No sorrow or pain will be there. The stifling emotions of anger, envy, and covetousness will be unheard of and will never enter the minds or hearts of any soul in that day.

So the doomsday of Earth will be very merciful to those who do not believe and are not prepared. It will take them from a world of pain into a plane of opportunity. I am not a punishing and vengeful god. When, in the Books of the old Bible, you read that vengeance is Mine, you have interpreted that I use it and enjoy it. That is not true. I only control it

The Doomsday of Earth

as My Will for My Purpose. It is not for mankind to use.

So if the destruction of the Earth is merciful to those who believe Me not, and if it will bring down Satan and his many projects of your time, how much more will it be wonderful for the souls who have prepared to be taken in bodily form and renewed with this newness of life.

For the souls who are taken from the Earth will be blessed more than any of them can imagine, and will be in perfect peace and joy. The time of their sojourn in space while the Earth is being renewed will be spent in singing, in praising My Name, and in learning from one another in preparation for the rehabilitation of the Earth as their home for a thousand years.

As they learn of the plan for the renewal of Earth after its cleansing, they will look forward with great joy to the population of it. It will again be a living thing, with all the beauty of animals, plants, and natural wonders of mountains and brooks and hills.

For in the harmony of those days all things will flourish, and life will be seen all around you. Children will be born and bring their joy upon the Earth. And the souls for these children will come from My Kingdom of Happiness as I allow them in their stage of perfection.

The renewal of the Earth in preparation for its new inhabitants will be rapid and greatly accelerated. Some years will pass, but there will be no feeling of loss by the time spent in space. The accommodations will be spacious, harmonious, and well chosen. There will be privacy for all, and the opportunity to share.

The home in space that is already prepared will be about one hundred miles in diameter and about eleven miles in height. It will be able to travel in space or stay in one place, so much can be seen of the universe while the time of instruction for the new life is going on.

Calculate the number of cubic feet per soul on board if there are to be a hundred million souls. I am not at this time revealing that as a number to be believed. I do not divulge the results of future choices of souls, and many souls have not yet even considered the possibility of this event, or that they could be on board if they choose.

When you arrive at the cubic feet available, you will see that there is much space for both privacy and for gatherings of schooling, enjoyment, and entertainment of all kinds. For it will be a happy place even before the return to the New Earth for the New Way of Living.

And these words will be studied and discussed there, and every soul will see with a new sight the truth of these inspired Words. Few people have been able to see the revelations and explanations that I give you to write, and you are not yet ready to enjoy these words to their fullest meaning.

For knowledge requires knowledge, and wisdom requires wisdom. And since the main destruction of the Earth is for the destruction of the works of darkness so that light might flourish, there is much resistance and fear among the spirits of darkness. They know of the prophecy of the Book of Revelations, and they well know their time is short.

These words in A New Way of Living are for Buddhists, Moslems, and for all people of all persuasions of faith, and for all bodies of religious groups. There is no soul on Earth who has not some form of opportunity to come to Me in some name and in some way.

I have had no chosen people as a group on Earth since the first coming of Jesus and the prophets of other religious bodies. Only souls have been chosen, as you, the writer of these Words, were chosen. I deny the opportunity of salvation from destruction of the Earth to no man.

You will see people of all races, creeds, and colors on the great ship that will be your home in space. And you will rejoice in their presence, for no bigot will be among you. Those who are there will have, without exception, an open mind and a willingness to accept, without question, the rights of every soul around them and of every soul left behind at the evacuation.

The Doomsday of Earth

Many wonderful things can be said, and I will reserve many of them for future writings. For your hands will write many blessed revelations to explain the fulfillment of prophecy. Nothing We have said today contradicts the prophecy of any religious body of the world. It only explains, and those who think differently have misunderstood the previous writing.

The writer of these words is not a prophet, and is not denying the Holy Words of the Books of the Moslem, Buddhist, Christian, or Jewish faiths, or the faiths of any others. The sun worshippers, the followers of forgotten beliefs, and those who followed nothing have all been inspired by their very nature to at least wonder about a Creator.

For no one has lived who has not wondered about the force behind Creation and the presence of that force. In the act of denying My Existence, humankind has acknowledged it, and they all have planted into their own minds a seed that will grow. Whatever your present condition, dear reader, you will come to Me.

So the doomsday of the Earth is now revealed as a joyful experience for every soul. Only Satan fears it and will suffer greatly, for he will become captive and in chains. He and the spirits who serve him will not retain possession or control of any soul.

Rejoice in the doomsday of the Earth, and pray for the hastening of its coming. It will be wonderful for every soul, and especially those of you who choose to come away from it. Rejoice, rejoice, for the time of your liberation is at hand.

I, your Father and Friend, bid you to dream of this blessed event, for its greatness will lift your hearts.

> *The footnotes at the end of each Chapter are my personal comments. The preceding Chapter was written about three years ago. As my grasp of true reality was changed and expanded, terms such as 'Satan,' 'evil,' and 'guilt' were explained. Some of those changes are told in*

Last Days?

Book 16, received over a year after the writing began. It reads as follows:

"When the writer of these words began to write, he had already prayed to Me many times throughout his life. Most of his prayers were centered around time and its products, such as his physical health, the health of others, the safety and protection of friends and loved ones, thanks for the food he was about to eat at mealtime, the future years of his life, and many other things related to time and the future in general.

"He was fully convinced, as many of you were earlier, that reality consisted of the things you can see. He was ignorant of the importance of his attitude, the nature of My Being, the nature of Creation, the world of spiritual reality, and of all the many things which are found beyond time and its influence. He thought of Me as a mysterious and remote being, and he thought of spiritual life as something reserved for his resurrection after death.

"He also thought of death, which is just another product of time, as being final, irrevocable, and fully real. He was unaware of the differences between time and Eternity, and thought that Eternity was only an infinite amount of time. And he believed that I was an austere God, stern and demanding, ready to punish the slightest fault, and willing to commit some souls to a hell that lasted for eternity. He was also taught to believe also that most of the souls in the world would come to that end, and that Heaven was a place as remote as My Being, which would receive a very small fraction of the people on Earth today."

Four months after these paragraphs were received, I started writing a footnote at the time of each daily writing. The first footnote written at the time of the writing is found in Chapter 21. Earlier Chapters in this book have footnotes written after the series was finished. They will tell you about the sequence of events that led to the 36 Books of <u>A New Way of Living</u>.

"Dream of joy and peace, dream of shared love and of mercy and kindness, and walk gently on your path today. Anticipate the good you will find, for it is indeed around you. There is good in every life, sometimes hidden and sometimes revealed. Find it, enjoy it, and hold fast to it, for good is not a burden for you to carry. Anticipation is often the best part of a joyful event."

From Book 35 —<u>A New Way of Living</u>

Chapter 2   From Book 5 —<u>A New Way of Living</u>

Turmoil and Peace

Find peace for yourself today as much as you can, for there is turmoil in the hearts of billions of souls each day. If the news you read and hear would tell of each one who has no peace, there would be more than you could imagine. Peace is a blessing for many. If it is something you have today, give thanks and be grateful.

Turmoil in the heart of a person can lead to sickness and stress that has a lasting effect. If it is bottled up and ignored it leads to sorrow and illness and death. If it is expressed needlessly in battle and conflict it causes danger of physical injury or reprisal in other ways. I do not come to you today with a lesson on how to cope with turmoil, for every lesson in these words already written can tell you that.

I am telling you today that what you think and dream about is what will be for you. If you have turmoil today, it has been in your mind in the past, for the things that come today are the thoughts and dreams of yesterday. If you dream in fear, the dream will often become an action.

Look for the peace of your life today and think of the joy of it. Peace without care comes from your faith in Me, and turmoil comes from faith placed only in yourself or other people. To control turmoil and find peace is as simple as controlling your thoughts and dreams. It is as effective to find peace as it is to pray for faith in Me and find that also.

In Israel and, indeed, in the entire Mid-East, there are millions who are blaming one another for turmoil and strife. Peace is mentioned thousands of times each day, but turmoil is universal and continuous. Little effort is made, and little thought is given, to the blessings already possessed, and the thoughts and dreams of the people are too often centered on their rights and their property.

There are many more than two sides to the turmoil. The reasons given for the battles are as many as the people involved, and these reasons go back for generations. Bitterness and revenge creep into the context of many conversations, and the people who fight one another are brothers and sisters by heritage as well as through Creation. Their anger is greatly increased as each tries to impose his will upon the other, and they are losing freedom the more they fight for it.

This area of the world is the location of what will be the battle of Armageddon. When Israel was given a land of their own in 1948 it was the beginning of the fulfillment of prophecy. Now they cannot agree on the use of their property. Some would use it for aggression to obtain more of what they call their rights, and some would compromise for peace and accept what they have. So the fighting goes on within their ranks, as well as with their neighbors.

Turmoil and Peace

    They call it a holy war, and they say they are throwing holy stones. The minds of children are corrupted by the prejudice of their parents and by the examples of the adults around them. The sins of the fathers would indeed be visited on the children for three generations, as said in the Scripture, except that the violence will escalate beyond control before three generations have passed.

    I will allow the destruction of the Earth before this conflict in the Mid-East is over. It will not be possible for the Earth itself to allow the pollution and destruction of this and other turmoil much longer. Your Earth will protect itself, destroy itself, and renew itself so that its burden of billions of souls in turmoil and battle will be gone. For, even in peace, the natural resources of Earth would be too severely strained by the doubling and redoubling of the human population. In turmoil, the density of the population is impossible to sustain. The population will destroy itself.

    I protect the souls of humankind and allow them always the benefit of new opportunities for faith and love and peace. I do not allow the turmoil of your world to continue. If you are reading these words in a home of peace, in the absence of turmoil, be thankful and be satisfied. For you do not need to take sides or pass judgment on the events in Iraq, Iran, Israel, Egypt, Pakistan, Afghanistan, Africa, and the Americas. Your peace is your good fortune, and it will be of no advantage to you to take on the turmoil of others by dwelling upon their problems and the causes of them.

    Pray for the innocent children and the families in their homes as they are surrounded by turmoil. Pray that they can find peace for a few minutes at a time, and that they can be faithful to Me as they turn to Me to take their cares. Pray that the turmoil does not enter your part of the world, and that your peace is kept safe and will continue. Live so that your dreams and actions are to promote peace and harmony within your family and the people around you, for this battle for peace starts within your thoughts and within your home.

Last Days?

Let anger and thoughts for revenge and rights stay in the Mid-East and in the other strife-torn parts of the world if it must. Keep your own heart pure and free as much as you are able, and if your life is limited in resources, be grateful, at least, that you have life and a chance to make it better. For everyone has needs that are not fulfilled, and everyone has some turmoil. Let your goal for today be to think of the things that bring you peace, and dream of an end to the turmoil.

See that you do not needlessly take away the peace of another and add turmoil to your life. Do not, in carelessness about others, lead their thoughts into turmoil by your conversation. Think and speak of the things that are good and righteous and in harmony with the world around you. Ignore the strife of others and their problems unless you can help or are involved. And if you choose to help, first be sure your help is wanted.

For many battles are fought for revenge, and to help another in this will only involve your life in that other's foolishness. You cannot take revenge for another, and should not seek it for yourself. The life you are living is much simpler if you give both your cares and your need for revenge to Me, for I can deal with it. Revenge is Mine, and if you have been wronged, you cannot, by wrongdoing, make it right. Let the punishment, the revenge, and the judgment be Mine.

Many battles are fought after using false judgment, and punishment is often desired with prejudice and without justice. You are not wise enough to reach beyond your own protection. Beyond defending yourself from the loss of your own food, clothing, and shelter, there is no reason to fight. And there is never a reason for you to punish and gain retribution in order to continue the battle. When you decide to teach a lesson by force, the student only learns to recognize you as his enemy.

Moments and hours spent in turmoil are forever lost as opportunities for meditation and learning of your own. Time spent in peace and quiet gives you health, joy, and long days devoid of danger to your soul or your life. Peace is followed by contentment and happiness, and in peace it is easy to forget the times you have been wronged by your brother. Let him bring the fight to you if he will, and save your energy to defend yourself in your home. Do not go forth to battle and take your revenge when the battle could be over by your choice.

If you study the fighting in the world, you will see that by now it is mostly revenge and retribution. When this spirit grows within your world there will be much less peace and much more turmoil. All over your world the leaders are starving their people by using the available money for weapons instead of food. They are taking the farmers to war, and the ground that could be growing food is littered with the weapons of war and destruction.

Ground is made barren by nuclear fallout, and your population is doubling each forty years. It cannot go on. Peace will be lost and turmoil will take its place. Enjoy peace while you can, and do not waste a minute of your time fighting needless battles of will, either with individuals or with countries. Instead, think of preparing yourself by drawing closer to Me each day, and let Me be a familiar companion in the time of your peace.

Now is the time for A New Way of Living for you. These words will tell you how to know Me within you always. They will tell you of your choices for peace within your heart and of the way of gaining My protection as you turn away from turmoil and accept the peace of My Spirit and power within you. Today is your opportunity to cast out turmoil from your mind and heart, and let peace take its place.

I, your loving Father, will grant you peace. I will take away the turmoil in your heart even while battles rage around you.

> *Nothing in this life had prepared me to find the Creator in just this way. On December 20, 1987, at 6:00 AM, I began to type the following message, after first praying for God's protection. This totally unexpected method of writing had started four days earlier, and I was then told of a mission which was to last for many days. The spirit*

who first gave me thoughts from which to write called himself Ashtar, the Commander-in-Chief of the Fleet of the Almighty.

I chose to call myself Ventris Nukayis because using a pseudonym allows my family to keep more privacy from those who might find these words controversial. Although I had learned to contact my guides several years before, they communicated by answering specific questions with a physical response, a sort of shove that signified 'yes,' or the absence of a response, which signified 'no.' I found that sort of information helpful, but not always dependable.

I have never communicated with any guides or spirits without first praying to God for protection, as I did on the morning I found Him within me.

Behind me, standing in the shadows cast by the dim light above the computer, my nine year old son stood in silence. The boy had asked to watch me write, and had joined with me in a prayer for Light and protection. He had asked to see what had caused so much excitement in his parents during the past couple of days when I began receiving messages from Ashtar.

"So the beauty and freedom of your truth and light come to you when <u>only you</u> are ready. Do not expect others to follow the same timetable or react to the same illusions just as you. There are no absolutes on Earth, and neither do any illusions appear just the same to everyone. The last days will take on many different shapes, forms, and hues for different people. For some, having been in a different place with a different frame of mind, the tribulation has been completed. For others, the troubles are yet to come. And for still others, there will be no trouble at all."

From Book 34 — <u>A New Way of Living</u>

Chapter 3   From Book 6 — <u>A New Way of Living</u>

Time and Change

    In the fulfillment of prophecy and in the daily course of your life, you will find change, and you can mark those changes by the measure of time. For time is needed when changes come to you, and time also marks their progress. And if, at times, the changes seem for the worse instead of for the better, you can still be sure that My goal and purpose is being accomplished.
    There is, then, a need for time and a need for change in your world, and one of the joys of your embodiment will be realized when you trust in Me. That joy is in your knowledge by faith that all change is for good. For all things work together for

good to them who love Me.   You have also another function by which time can be used for your benefit. For time is also required in order to enjoy the virtue and pleasure of patience. It is ironic that the human spirit of self loves comfort and the splendors of idle living, and that the same spirit cannot find patience. Patience is the wise and easy use of time, and it comes to you only when you have indeed cast your cares upon Me. I will let the changes of time, for better or for worse, work to your good as I have promised. And as long as you love Me, and love My blessings for you, all things, changes, and events of time are for your good.

Then where is the excuse for impatience, and where is the excuse for allowing time to be a burden to you? In the lessons of past writing in <u>A New Way of Living</u>, I have taught you that time will seem to pass swiftly when you are without care. And the events of prophecy will seem horrible only to those who are not living in faith, and who are filled with care.

The summit meeting in Russia, involving the government of the United States, is an example of great change, and it is time for that agreement to bear fruit. In spite of the efforts of the media to discredit the leaders, and in spite of the hawks of government and their desires to avoid peace, there is progress. The souls who serve Me in both governments are using time to make changes, as they should.

If you watch closely the news conferences of the future, you will often see the media try to trap the speakers into saying phrases which can be misinterpreted out of context. And when it is time for change, I will put words upon the lips of both the good and the evil doers of these conferences that will allow the people who care to see the truth.

For the greatest danger to your world today is not from the super powers with their thousands of nuclear weapons. Your danger is from the third world countries who either have or soon will have nuclear weapons of their own. These third world nations and terrorist groups have little to lose and much to gain. They will have no fear of the destruction of their own possessions as they use blackmail and fear to destroy their opposition.

Do not fall into the trap of seeing these changes as a turn for the worse. All prophecy is fulfilled for the good of all souls. It will seem to be a curse to some and a blessing to others, but all have had, and still have, the choice of turning to Me. They know the name of their Creator, whatever name they use. Blessed is the man that trusts not in man, nor makes flesh his arm.

I am in all things, including politics and governments, and My Spirit dwells in some of the souls of all nations, and is exercised by their choice. Some would have you believe I am not found in the hearts of the leaders of Russia, or of Iran, or of Pakistan, Afghanistan, Tibet, Iraq, Nicaragua, or of other nations which are at war. But each government has its factions, and in one faction or the other My Spirit is working to make the changes that lead to My goal.

And those changes will seem to be for better or for worse, but there are no accidents in the changes that time will bring to your world. I again counsel you to be without care, and to behold the fulfillment of prophecy with joy and peace, for then you will escape the danger as much as you wish.

If you look around you during these times, and see ones who seem worthy to escape their suffering, remember that you cannot know the desires of their souls. It is not yours to judge the rights and privileges of others, or to try to know their worth by the things that happen to them. Keep away from all judgment of others, and judge even yourself only when it is necessary to make choices.

Your faith will protect you as you see the changes of time that are ahead, and your joy will conquer your fear if trust in Me is within your heart. Many of you who have read these words and faithfully tried to follow them are also finding a new way of living. In this new way you have seen proof of My power and the truth of these words again and again.

You might have noticed how often I prove Myself to you while you live in faith, and how often that proof is something you can easily believe, without being able to prove Me to others around you. If you feel a strong desire to prove Me to others with your faith, you are missing the value of these words.

Let the faith of another prove Me to himself, and let your faith prove Me to you. I will not prove Myself and My power to any soul unless that soul has faith of its own in Me. And when others have that faith, you are not needed, and will need to offer no proof to others.

I say again that the changes of time will be for better or for worse, but they will be according to My Plan and Goal in every way. And you will remember that your faith is for you alone, and it is not a key to the understanding that you might like of the changes that time brings to others.

In the complex interaction between governments, souls, and organizations of your time, many things are changing. If you have no faith, you will not believe I can orchestrate all these changes for a single purpose. You will wonder how I, while chaos exists all around you, can accomplish the fulfillment of prophecies made thousands of years ago. You will also fail to realize that the same chaos that fails to make the required changes for centuries can suddenly work together when it is time.

For time makes changes when the time has come, and the changes will be clear and unmistakable. Those of you who are concerned for the world around you have seen the plagues of the locusts in Africa and the famines in the continents of the world from time to time. If you have love for all men of all races, and of all beliefs, you will see those things as the fulfillment of the prophecies of the last days.

But if you feel the Hindus, and Muslims, and Buddhists, or the followers of any faith but yours are not My children, you will ignore the fulfillment of prophecy until it strikes within the borders of your land. And if you are even more narrow minded, you will ignore it until it comes to your very door and affects your family.

I remind you again that every soul on Earth is My child, and that every man, woman, and child on Earth are precious to Me. They are all your brothers, for you are all My children. Then have compassion for the changes that time is bringing, and be sure that when famine and the plagues of the last times come to your door you will also be grateful for those around you who care about your trials.

And be sure that the changes of time will indeed bring these things to your door, and that your faith will be tested by the dangers and suffering around you. Now is the time to turn to Me if you have not already done so, and now is the day for you to build your confidence in Me. Now is the time to change yourself, so that you can withstand the changes that time brings to the world around you.

For I will prove Myself to you day after day, again and again, as often as you find Me each day in prayer and let Me care for you. Your faith can make you whole, and can give My Spirit within you the power to reinforce your faith with proof of My existence in you that only you can see. And when you see it, and allow your faith to turn to trust and joy, you will be ready for the changes that time will bring to you and your world.

Live in peace, have joy, be happy, and let patience take away the sting of time and the changes it will bring. You have not seen a fraction of the changes that are near to you, and you will do well to believe that the time is short. Many things are yet to be fulfilled, and many events are on the horizon. Because of the shortness of time, one event will follow another rapidly.

Even the climate of your world is telling you of the changes of time. Records are being broken, and there will soon be famines in parts of the world that have never before seen shortages of food. And there are many earthquakes and disturbances even now, and many of them are unreported. Vast areas of the Earth are engaged in strife and conflict which is ignored. But time will bring more and more changes which cannot be ignored. See that you are faithful and true to Me, and that you keep close to Me by the exercise of the Holy Spirit in your life from day to day. The time is short.

Last Days?

I am your Father and Friend. Hear Me.

> *The words of the first lesson in <u>A New Way of Living</u> flowed through my fingers onto the keyboard of a computer. The first sentence identified the Author as 'The Father of all.' This caused me to bow my head and weep. The tears were not of fear or sorrow, but of joy, for I had finally found God within me after searching in the wrong places for a lifetime. And He was speaking to me!*
>
> *I was almost in a state of shock. I could hardly believe what I wrote. I was totally unprepared to communicate directly with my Creator in any way, thinking that He would always hear and never answer.*
>
> *I had looked for God everywhere except within myself. I had read the Bible often, had often prayed to God, and had lived a very full and interesting life. My habit, during the past ten years, of arising before dawn to pray and meditate led to this moment, in which I was able to sit down and write what the Spirit of Creation in my Inner Self gave me. The truth, for which I had searched in churches, books, and the wisdom of humankind, finally came to me from the Kingdom of God within me.*

"You are not the way you are because you have somehow been the victim of parents, family, friends, or a society which has misled you. Your life is far more than the bills that are due, the tires that are bald, the house that is cluttered, the hairs that are turning gray, the body that bulges and sags, or the mind that is confused by the chaos of the last days of Earth. You are the way you are because of your attitudes and your beliefs. They have created what you are, and you have chosen them."

From Book 34 — <u>A New Way of Living</u>

Chapter 4   From Book 6 — <u>A New Way of Living</u>

Truth and Repentance

For the moment, your world is poised at the beginning of famine. The discomfort from the shortage of water and the excessive heat will be bearable, and the cycle of dry weather and famine will take several years to peak. This will be a time of testing, and a time of opportunity for the workers of Light. My servants who are dedicated to Me will begin to be noticed, and their thoughts will sometimes be heeded.

For this is the moment of truth, and the beginning of the end. And in the knowledge of that truth, you who read these words and believe in Me will cast out the lies of your mind and your thoughts. You will repent that you have believed the lies of the majorities around you. But do not mistake the repentance taught by the Bible thumpers for the sort of repentance that is needful and effective.

There is no need in repentance for humiliation, shame, or the feeling of guilt. Simply admit to yourself that you did not previously find the truth you now know, and that you wish you had found it sooner. This is repentance, and should not be followed by a desire for forgiveness by Me. It is of the utmost importance that you forgive yourself, and the next order of importance is that you forgive all others and seek their forgiveness.

But you do not need the forgiveness of others to find favor in My sight. You are loved and favored always, and the door to Me is always open. The importance of repentance is that it will help you remember the thing of which you repented, and the lack of your concept of truth that led to the need for it. What is the advantage of regret if no change is made? What is the use of repentance if you turn not away from the belief of the lies which you regret?

The only reason you need to forgive yourself is to cleanse your mind and heart of the negative ashes of the lies you have lived. For lies are negative, and they lead to your bad judgment of yourself and others. So the lies that adulterate your truth will make you weak and ineffective. The acts that follow the thoughts of the adulterated truth of the past will also be negative and ineffective, and you need to forgive yourself of those thoughts and acts.

For if you do not forgive yourself, you will not find courage to act on the truth which you have learned and purified. It is easy to find truth and add it to your life before you have purged the lies of past beliefs from your mind and heart. But you must not add the purity of new truth to the adulteration of the other truth within you. So repentance is simply the recognition of the mistakes of your belief, and it allows you to purify your mind, so that it might receive the things you have learned.

So you repent, and then you forgive yourself as you resolve to live with your new beliefs of truth. And you forgive others as you forgive yourself, for you cannot cleanse yourself of negative emotions and thoughts if you are concerned with the negative emotions of others. Your companions are so important, for the power of My Spirit in you does not flourish among the negative thoughts and actions of those around you.

Again I say to you that you are at the beginning of the end, and these lessons of joy, peace, and love will take you through. But learn well the lesson of the newness of My Truth, which you will receive both from within and from without. Learn well to seek truth, to love it, and to cleanse yourself by the regret of your past mistakes. And learn well to forgive yourself immediately when you are cleansed, so that the truth you will learn can be absorbed into your very life and lived by you.

It is so easy to become too concerned about new knowledge of the future, and to seek, through clairvoyants and inspired sources, the truth you had not found. This is well, but cleanse your mind of the lies within you by repentance and forgiveness, so that your mind and heart will not destroy the effectiveness of that which you have newly learned. For when you add pure truth to your storehouse of wisdom and peace, it will be immediately adulterated by the mistaken beliefs you have not cast out.

The science of distortion of truth is practiced by all the universities and schools of your life. The political world also distorts truth to meet its goals. And the business world uses the distortion of truth to gain its purposes. The churches have also learned to distort the truth to gain your donations, your allegiance, and your trust.

But as the world turns away from these false beliefs in the organizations around you, the people will need first to repent and regret. For to simply adopt new ways to add to the mistakes of past beliefs will not work. First acknowledge, regret, repent, and forgive yourself. Next you will clearly adopt your new belief, and add that to the truth of what you previously believed, which has now been cleansed of lies.

And as you move ahead, expect this cycle of the discovery of new truth to continue. Live from day to day, and learn to add no newness of truth to the many mistakes and distortions of truth that have been within you. Before you begin to say, 'This is right,' remember to say, 'I was partly wrong.' And clearly admit, identify, and cast out the part that was wrong.

Thus does the discovery of truth require repentance, and regret, and the open admission of your mistakes that leads to the purification of your mind and heart. And thus does your forgiveness of yourself become necessary before you can move ahead with the positive courage of truth believed. And thus does your love for yourself allow you to love others. And thus do you learn to judge the effect of the company you keep upon your harmony and joy, so that you might protect the purity of your truth from the negative effect of things around you.

And remember that your negative emotions can be caused not only by the negative emotions of people around you, but also by your attitude toward material things. Let your priorities be kept straight, and love not the world, nor the things that are in the world above your love for Me. If you cannot see Me in the world and the things around you, your love for them will draw you away and keep you from Me.

If you cannot see Me within you, you will not find Me in the souls around you. And if they do not see Me within themselves, they will not see Me within you. And if you or they do not see Me in the tangible and intangible things of nature and thought, there will be little harmony in your contact with others. Neither will joy and peace be found.

So this is the beginning of the end, and if you wonder why the end is needed, read again the preceding paragraph. There has been too much adulteration of truth, too little repentance, and too few who have said, 'I was partly wrong.' Some one has said the hardest words to say are, 'I was wrong.' I tell you that it is even harder for you to say, 'I was partly wrong.'

People have perished physically while clinging to the belief that led them to disaster. People have failed miserably because they waited too long to regret, repent, forgive themselves, and change. The pity is that people who have been led to believe I am an unforgiving God will not forgive themselves, for they have adopted the ways which their lack of truth ascribed to Me. So truth and repentance can be a matter of life and death for you in this embodiment.

Some will be caught up and changed in the twinkling of an eye, and will live for a thousand years in peace and joy. They will be the ones who have learned how to regret daily, repent, forgive themselves, and move ahead with the newness of truth that is yet to come to them. So I give to you new words of counsel, which you can accept or reject by your free will, which I have also given you.

I counsel you who have followed these words and studied them to add a line or two as you pray daily to Me for faith. You have already been instructed to ask for the things you need and cannot supply for yourself. You have also been told that if you pray submissively I will give you your needs and accept your cares. Know now that it is hard to regret, and repent of your mistakes, if you do not acknowledge them to Me.

I have not given you this before, because the writer and many others were not able to associate repentance with anything but sin. I have first told you that there is no duty, and that there is no sin of your soul. Now that you have believed this and have learned today that repentance is for the purpose of your purification, and that it leads to the forgiveness of yourself and others, add repentance to your prayer. But do not rush to Me in supplication for My forgiveness before you have forgiven yourself and others.

And after forgiving yourself and others you will not need My forgiveness, for when you have judged yourself, regretted and repented of your misconceptions and mistakes, and have withheld your judgment of others as you forgave them, My forgiveness has already been done. And in this new purity of your truth that follows your repentance, you will find a day of new peace and love.

But you are in a world of distorted truth, and tomorrow a new cycle of repentance must follow the truth you learn today. Be watchful and aware of all things around you, and let no day pass by without sorting the new truth around you as it comes to you. And also let each new truth cast its Light upon the hidden memories and beliefs of your past, and do not ignore the repentance of things believed and forgotten long ago, when they come to your mind.

Grow slowly toward the Light, for the Light of truth will save you from the end that has begun. Each of you who read these words must fight this battle for yourself, for the battle is different for different people. No other soul can take responsibility for you, nor can you take responsibility for any other. Live each day in peace and love, and learn of the way of truth and repentance.

I am your loving Father of all Truth and Light.

> *For 1045 days, during a period of exactly three years, the writing continued from the same Source. A new Book was written each month for 36 consecutive months. The meaning of life, the way to be happy on Earth, the explanation of reality, the comfort of God's love, the dangers of anger and vanity, the illusions of materialism, lust, and greed, and many other things were explained.*

"The way of Earth is to seek more. The common ambitions are to have more leisure time, more time to use, more space to roam, more things to see and do, and more new experiences to explore. The ones who are satisfied with just a little are more rare. Having few ambitions for more of anything, they are also few in number. But these satisfied ones, who are satisfied with just a little, are also the happiest ones. If you are satisfied with just a little, you are seldom at the mercy of your environment."

From Book 33 — <u>A New Way of Living</u>

Chapter 5 From Book 6 — <u>A New Way of Living</u>

The Title

To be entitled is an authorization to control. A title is proof of ownership, and a title also refers to the subject matter or content of this writing. My lesson for you today is of the title to the things you possess. Many things have titles of this nature, such as automobiles, airplanes, houses, and land.

If you have possessions or have had them, you know about this type of title. And if you know about the business of banking, you will know that few titles are clear. A clear title is one that is not encumbered by debt and that is not given as security for a commitment of any kind. Any conditional restriction such as age, payment, or the performance of any act or deed yet to be done will keep a title from being clear.

There are restrictions to anything you can possess. If you have a clear title from the legal system around you, your title is still restricted by My will. As I have created all things, I have also created you, and all things are Mine. The laws of humankind are devised to protect ownership and the spirit of religions are also devised to recognize Me as the Source of all things. That is why you can have no clear title to anything in your world.

Everything I have committed to you is subject to My will to change the commitment any time I choose. Your most precious possession is My love for you, and I will never take that from you. Another valuable intangible that I have given you is freedom, and I have told you that you will lose it only when you no longer need it or want it. I also would have you know that all the tangible properties of the Earth and her resources are under the stewardship and at the disposal of any of you who are My heirs.

You are all My heirs if you have not disowned Me. I claim all souls as My children, but those who do not recognize Me are not entitled to the blessings of the Earth. Your claim to property as a titled owner is always encumbered by My Creation of it. And I do not give to those who demand ownership or ignore My Being, but I give freely to those who accept Me in faith and know that My power is with them.

If you know that you are My child and that all things are Mine, you have no desire to own anything at all. The child who is born in your home does not demand title or rights from you, for he knows he is your heir, and that you love him. And if they have no need for their possessions, the first thought of most parents is to give the possessions to their children.

But the greatest gift to your children is to give them your knowledge that you can truly possess nothing at all. You are stewards and managers of My property, and it is yours as My child. But where would you, as a parent, find joy in giving possessions to your children if they claimed your gifts without acknowledging they were from you? What if your gift is received by one who says, 'This is my right, and you have nothing to say about it. Leave me alone.'

Would you not withhold gifts in the future from such people until they changed their feelings about you? And would you not search for others who love you, and give your gifts to them? And if your natural children turned away from you, and if your adopted children accepted you with love, would you not still yearn for the love of your natural children?

This has been the pattern of My favored Hebrew nation, who are, even today, using violence and force to take away the freedom of their brothers. They were My favored children, and when I adopted the Gentiles a great jealousy arose between them. The Jewish people said they were entitled to My gifts, and the Gentiles gladly accepted the things that were refused by the Jews. But among both Jews and Gentiles, and among all the nations of Earth, there are those who do not desire entitlement of possessions, and who live in the joy of My love. These faithful souls also love one another and do not need your laws of equal rights to recognize all men as their brothers. The ones who live in faithfulness and joy have no feeling of a need for titles, possessions, and rights. They know they are My heirs and that I freely give them anything they can find and use in harmony with the world around them.

Let your feeling of pride in ownership and in the possession of titles to your goods be changed to an humble gratefulness that your Father has such great gifts for you to use. Whether you live in a hut or a palace, your gift is from Me, and it is only for your temporary use. When your life is ended and your soul takes its leave of your embodiment, that possession will remain for the use of a stranger, or your child, or a friend of yours.

Look at the abstract of title that goes with the real estate in some parts of your world. You will see many names of strangers, of mortgages, of deeds and covenants, and of restrictions and easements. Seldom will you see a time when the title was not encumbered, and seldom will you see a mortgage paid off in an orderly fashion. Money is borrowed against the property in larger and larger amounts, and finally the property is sold to another who also encumbers it for his purposes.

But beyond the encumbrances of legal documents, I encumber all property with My title. I created it, I allow its use by all men, and I will see it returned to Me when the Earth is destroyed and renewed. The papers and parchments and scrolls of the titles will be burned, destroyed, and forgotten. Oceans and mountains will be moved and rearranged, the equator of your planet will be found at a different place, and magnetic compasses will point to a different part of your Earth.

The legal descriptions and geographical locations will change and be of no use, and the things which are titled to you today cannot then be located or identified. That which is not destroyed will be changed beyond recognition. The granaries will be emptied of their food, the mines will be lost with the ore that is in them, and some of the farm lands of today will be the ocean bottoms of tomorrow.

The Earth will be changed cosmetically, but to your small and finite minds, it will appear to be a drastic destruction and renewal. And as the climate changes in the next few years, the trend toward drought and famine will also create surface stresses in the Earth which will unbalance the ecology. The ozone layer and the carbon dioxide blanket will continue their inevitable buildup of heat and increased radiation, and your media will have many things to tell you of news from other parts of the Earth.

The value of titles will be greatly reduced as your economies of the world collapse and are consolidated, and governments will continue to pretend to control things through secrecy and deception. Be wise, be faithful, and do not be deceived by the learned words of comfort that come from the blind and foolish leaders of the world. The time of the fulfillment of prophecy will make paper money good only when you burn it for heat to warm your body, and nothing will be of value unless it can be eaten, worn, or used for shelter.

And as the credibility of governments continue to fail, anarchy will be attempted and will also fail. The rule of the jungle will rule your land, and the greatest safety will be for those who have no titled possessions, no conspicuous affluence, and no excess goods that can be carried away to eat, to wear, or to use for shelter. And your faith will be tested as you try to forgive those who attack you for their own survival, and who turn away from morality to survive.

Think today of a world of universal hunger, filled with insecurity and need, surrounding you with excess cold, heat, or darkness, and teeming with masses of fearful and miserable souls. Do not plan at that time to take your titles, clear or otherwise, and convert them to money with which to buy food and clothing and shelter. When goods are gone, titles are worthless and can neither be sold or bartered in the collapsed economies around you.

If you believe your governments can protect you, remember that governments are composed of people who can also starve, and who can be cold and naked. You cannot eat the extra dollars they print, the gold they mine, or the oil they sell. Their treaties and the resolutions of the United Nations will not change your appetite or the warmth or coolness of your body. They cannot make it rain when the weather is dry, and they cannot replace the ravaged Earth where earthquakes strike and volcanoes erupt.

Farm programs will not create food, and the repossession of the property which has encumbered titles will not allow the lien holder to resell in a market that does not exist.

Be not afraid as I write to you today, for these words are only to encourage your renewal of faith in Me, and to remind you of your brotherhood with all humankind. Let love and peace and joy carry you through, and be happy in your faith, for all have the opportunity you have had. You need not understand, or even wonder, why some will be taken and others will be left. You have no reason to wonder why you have found faith and joy. And you have no right to let your joy in being My child be lost through your fears for those who do not know Me as their Father.

You are entitled to the things I have made, and there is entitlement for all who wish to find Me and accept their inheritance. You possess nothing, are a part of everything, and cannot lose your life or your joy and peace unless you refuse to accept this concept. I am the Source, I hold the title, and it is clear for you to use without fear.

For I am your Creator and your God.

> *There is a story to be told, and it is the story of a man who searched for a lifetime in all the wrong places and with the wrong ideas about the nature of God. Since the writing began, the changes in me have been profound and unlimited. Anger seldom distracts me from the joy of living. I have learned to more often love and forgive those who oppose me, and to find the joy of a deeper awareness of all life and all reality. I have learned I was once more materialistic than I had realized, and that my Inner Self is found in the Kingdom of God. I have learned much about the nature of God and of His Presence everywhere. In changing these beliefs, I have also changed. The changes go on.*
>
> *At first, I felt I was neither worthy nor capable to be writing truth fit for others to read. The first few Books seemed to be directed mostly to me, for my lack of belief in myself caused me to hesitate to write the thoughts that Cosmic Telepathy revealed.*

"I teach you today that you can study many philosophies of Earth, many of which agree that Earth is in her last days in this epochal development of the Sixth Day of Earth's creation. But many who agree that your Earth's days are numbered, having learned this from sources on Earth and Sources in Our Kingdom, still cannot agree on the way in which the end shall come. The way of the end of Earth is immaterial. The key is not in the <u>way</u> it will happen, which will be no accident. The key is in the <u>preparation</u> of you who believe, which will also be no accident."

From Book 30 — <u>A New Way of Living</u>

Chapter 6 From Book 7 — <u>A New Way of Living</u>

The Last Days

Faithful souls will read these words for centuries to come, and most of them are written for all time. But you cannot believe through faith what you do not know, and some knowledge of the events of today are needed in order for you to live in faith and hope. You are in the last days of this chapter of the civilization of your planet, and if you have fear in these times, I will comfort you.

The last days are a time of fulfillment, and the separation of the faithful from the spiritually blind and ignorant is a blessing to all. Lives of quiet desperation are being lived in fear and dread over your lands, and the search for peace has, instead, found war. The war of spirits, of neighbors, of armies, and of cultures has not only continued, but has also increased.

I did not create you for sorrow and pain, but for joy. When harmony is gone from your Earth, your purpose is also gone. There are those in the land who are liberal with the goods of others, and who feel it is their right to take from those who have in order to give to those who have not. You have no right to take from others by force and redistribute the goods, for you cannot do this without judgment.

But you do have the privilege of giving freely of your own time and your own goods if you have them to spare, for you will find those who ask and need, and whom you can help without judgment. Much of the unrest in your world comes directly and indirectly from the acts of judgment of others. You need not search out and select the needy, or the poor, or the rich who can afford to give to them. And you also have no right to assume control of the souls you have befriended.

The freedom of each individual has been greatly diminished by an overactive and repressive social conscience. This takes place in local and national governments, and even in the churches. You first insist on helping even those whose self respect rejects you, and then insist on taking charge of those you help. For you think that your superiority is demonstrated by your greater possessions, and that this fictitious success, measured by your possessions, gives you the right to judge others.

But I say again that the only success is spiritual success, and that it cannot be proved or demonstrated. You have no way of knowing how your spiritual life compares with others, and need have no concern about it. For in these last days, only your spiritual life will carry you through, and the time is near when you will be fully engaged in spiritual and physical survival.

The luxury of spare time, which is already so scarce, will become non-existent. Your days will be spent in defensive thinking, and you will only think of your deep desire to be hidden and alone. Your safety from the control of others will be your deepest desire, and you will lose all privacy and freedom. It is the nature of governments to take more control when they don't know what else to do.

And governments do not resign and dissolve when they are faced with new and supernatural threats. They will mobilize and take over by martial law, and they will subject you to whims without reason. It is natural for them to do new things to others, and to change things, when things are already beyond help.

These words of <u>A New Way of Living</u> are not generally about the purpose of the last days, but are for your enlightenment in the better days of the new Earth. Today, however, the last days are the subject, and many of you are already aware of what is happening. Things that have never before been seen in the present civilization of your world are becoming more and more commonplace. Your recorded history is scant and inaccurate, but you have pillaged the Earth, and the Earth is responding with defensive readjustment.

You will see governments totter and fall in the next few years. You will see ideologies abandoned, with both socialism and democracy being seen as almost equal opponents of individual freedom. And you will see a world government take over individual governments for a short time. Economic collapse will precede political anarchy, and national governments will be overthrown by the might of terrorism and the incentive for survival.

You will see force take the place of majority rule, and if you are wise, you will not try to stop anything, but instead will try to hide and be alone. Any possessions or positions that make you conspicuous should be avoided, and any desire to become a leader for those less fortunate will be dangerous. Your spiritual life gives you strength, and your faith in Me gives you responsibility only for yourself.

For I am the Father of all, and I give to you the freedom and obligation to do only what you can for yourself and your dependents. To reach out in the time that is left will only make you more vulnerable to the unseen changes that are even now being made. Let your spiritual life and awareness fill you with the knowledge of world events, and pray for yourselves and others around you.

You are fortunate to be alive in these times, and you will see much proof of My power and glory as a reward for your faith. But you need not try to prove Me to others, or to let your pride in spiritual success destroy its value. For your spiritual success is a blessing from Me, and is available to all others around you. More and more the talk shows and media speak of, and show, those who claim spiritual success and enlightenment, but most who hear and see it are skeptical and filled with doubt.

For I do not prove Myself to those without faith. Instead, I show My Spirit and Its power to those who already believe. If you believe, you will know, but if you first try to know Me, you will not believe. Proof comes after faith and belief, not before. And confidence comes with and after faith, not before.

So in these last days, as never before, you need to accept Me by faith without proof, before proof comes to you. And when it comes, it will come for you alone, and cannot be shared or shown to another. Have you ever seen a picture of the sights that are claimed by those who have had out-of-body experiences? And have you ever heard the sound of the thoughts heard spiritually by the mind of another?

You have not, but many of you have seen the joyful change in the lives of those who found spiritual life and success. You have seen a new appreciation for the gift of life, and a new faith in My support as I take away their cares. You have seen new peace, new confidence, and a joy of living that was not seen before the spiritual revival which they have claimed, but could not prove.

Even in the ones who do not know Me during these last days, you see changes as they encounter strange experiences that cannot be explained by their science or religion. For many are the strangers who know Me by name but not by Person. Many are the ones who believe I have the false qualities they have been taught, and who do not recognize Me as a near and universal God. To many souls I am limited by harsh and narrow judgment, and to others I am limited by a love for only those who believe as they do.

To many I am a God of racial bigotry, and of jealous pride in Myself, and of merciless punishment for all who do not fit the rites and traditions of their dogma. The emotional, social, and physical demands of the last days will flush out the narrow, the blind, the proud, and the lovers of justice and judgment. They will be hard pressed to understand when the demands of the last days seem to settle heavily upon their shoulders, and when, because of their lack of spiritual awareness, they see no escape.

So the last days will be a time for silence, and for the spiritual strength that only faith can find for you. Be ready to hear the still small voices of your thoughts, and do not resist changes in your daily life that come into your mind. Do not fear to change the location of your home, your work, or the nature of your companions. If you doubt, turn away from others and turn to Me, for the voice of My Spirit is not delivered to you by those around you. It comes from Me, and in your solitude will you find the counsel to adjust and escape that is needful.

In the last days, avoid the emotion of fear through your faith, and be not emotionally trapped by the fears of those around you. You do not know, or need to know, the cares of others, but only need to keep spiritually alive by faith, and I will care for you. The last days will be the greatest test the life of your spirit has known for thousands of years. Be ready, for the time is short, and it is upon you now. Prepare by faith and by the renewal of your spiritual life, for the many things you read and see and hear will demonstrate the great outpouring of My Spirit on the Earth. Believe it and live.

I am your Father, Savior, and Friend.

It was to be over two years before this method of communication was explained to me in Book 30 of A

Last Days?

<u>New Way of Living</u>. The following paragraph is a direct quotation from that Book, written in June, 1990.

"The very significant difference between channeling and Cosmic Telepathy is that channeling is between two specific spirits in its entirety, while Cosmic Telepathy provides truth filtered from the Perfect Being, Whom We Are. While you are on Earth, you shall never see Us, nor shall you truly comprehend how We Are One while We Are All. You are blinded to Our Absolute Reality by your relative environment and by your imperfection. And yet, you are in total contact with Us when your faith allows you to expose Our Perfect Part of your Inner Self to your conscious mind. Cosmic Telepathy allows this exposure to be attainable for you from within."

"When nations forget political differences and send aid to the stricken ones of other beliefs, it is a sign of brotherhood. It is also a sign that there is hope for the human spirit, for those who give in order to help their enemies are learning to love both themselves and their enemies more than before. To give help to ones who have opposed you is a sign of love, and to accept it from those you have despised is a sign of freedom from vanity and pride. So with your sadness for the victims and their friends, have some joy for the love and peace that have been shown and felt."

From Book 31 — <u>A New Way of Living</u>

Chapter 7   From Book 8 — <u>A New Way of Living</u>

Hope and Joy

Do not be afraid, and do not be hindered by the events of your world today. There is much joy ahead for you, and much justification for a great hope for many things. Your life can be enriched by the new life of your spirit in ways you have never before imagined. Joy is the outcome of hope, and joy is the payment for your submission of your physical life to your spiritual life.

In turning away from the confusion of humanity in these last days, you are turning toward many joyful things. You need not think that the suffering and persecution of the last days are for you. Those who love one another and themselves will escape many things that seem unavoidable. I have caused many to escape prison and to find ways of serving Me in spite of the opposition of many men. I have allowed joy and friendship to develop between strangers who were of the same Spirit through My gift to them, and who truly had faith and belief in Me.

And I gave that Spirit and that faith to those who had humble and contrite hearts, filled with peaceful love and good will and empty of all judgment for their fellow men. I have done these things many times, for on many worlds and in many times have the circumstances of your Earth been repeated. The coming harvest of your Earth is not the first for it, and your Earth is only one of a great many.

This harvest of spiritual souls who believe in Me is very joyful for them. You who read this and who believe in it will be among them, and you will see miracles of transformation and joyful development that will fulfill all your hopes and dreams. Age and affliction will fall away, weakness will be gone, and your energy and desire will be for all goodwill given and received, without the harsh competition of your present surroundings, without the pressing needs of earthly living, and without the cares that life brings to you today.

So hope can be yours today, and that hope can be justified each day by your increasing joy. Even in the times of turmoil and tribulation, there will be peace and joy for you who believe in Me. And if you submit your will to Mine, I will give you things for your joyfulness that you cannot now imagine. The gifts I have in store for you go far beyond your needs for physical protection. You will meet and love beings and spirits from other worlds and from other planes.

These spirits, the living essences of souls such as you, will have equipment and facilities that will guarantee your safety and your escape. Some of you will be able to see, with an eye of faith, the things that threaten you, and will help yourself and others to avoid the attacks of evil ones around you. In your hope and joy, however, remember to let Me guide you through your faith in Me, giving yourself to the care of others only as I inspire you.

Hope and Joy   39

Today is the time for you to have joy, and to hope for these things. You will not learn the lessons of a life of patience, faith, joy, and peace in a single day. Spiritual life leads to spiritual growth, and it comes ever so slowly at first. If you have not prayed daily and reached out to Me for many years, your joy will be tempered by a lack of spiritual energy and confidence, and doubts will come to you from time to time. This is especially true if you are older, for habits of thinking will have to be broken.

On the other hand, if you are young, let your joy and hope grow rapidly, for you are in a time of natural growth. And in any case, you will have joy each day to the extent of your faith. My blessings to you have the same effect as food for a child, giving instant energy, but leading more to exercise than to immediate strength. And as the nourishment is continued and the exercise of the body results, time gives the child greater stature and strength. This does not happen in a day, and cannot be noticed except as months and years pass.

And you are My child, nourished by the food you choose in your freedom. If you choose the nourishment of My Spirit, you will have energy immediately and will exercise the life of that Spirit within you. And you will have a new joy, with greater and greater hope each day of your life. As long as you are spiritually alive, you are growing toward fulfillment, with more joy and greater hope.

Again I remind you that My kingdom is within you, and that it is not dependent upon the circumstances of your environment. Your hope for things to come is limited by your knowledge of the future, and by your interpretation of things to come. Instead, let your hope be for the sureness of My protection and love, and let your joy be in the freedom of action that is afforded to you by the guidance of My Spirit within you.

For when you submit your human spirit to Mine, and when you trust yourself to Me, there will be safety and comfort and joy and peace. There will be love given and received between you and Me and others, accepted by your belief and by your faith.

This is the joy that comes immediately through faith each day, and that is retained through renewed faith a day at a time. It gives rise to the great hope that will fill you, the hope of your spiritual growth and strength that comes more slowly.

But with daily renewal of faith, with your spiritual life, and with the joy of that daily spiritual life, there will be a time when the slow and accumulated growth of your spiritual strength and ability will be noticeable. There will soon be a time for you when you can look back and compare yourself of then to yourself of now. There will be a time when your judgment of your progress gives you even greater joy, for your path will lead you, with My guidance, to better places, far from the hectic and confusing environment you have today.

As hope is fulfilled and joy increases, you will find it easier to trust in the One Who gave you that fulfillment, and Who fulfilled your hopes and dreams. Your hope will be expanded at that time with the added knowledge that growth has brought to you. You will know things you have suspected, and your confidence will increase. And as your confidence increases, it will be more joyful to apply the spiritual strength you have so patiently developed, for you will have learned how to receive My guidance and work with the spiritual teams of which you will be a part.

For as time passes, your spiritual growth is magnified many times by the harmony that it brings. Harmony makes teamwork among believing souls both highly effective and greatly joyful. Harmony allows the united efforts of many to accomplish what one could never accomplish. The workers of Light, guided and united by the mysterious gifts of My guidance, will do things that would seem impossible.

You will never be commanded or driven by another in this joyful effort to survive the last days, for you will be guided by the same Spirit of My Being that works within you all. Having the guidance of the same spirit, and being submissive through faith in Me, your joy will be realized and your hopes fulfilled. You will learn to love one another, yourself, and Me in ways you have never believed. Your common purpose will unite you with others in great joy, and you will have meetings that will encourage you.

You will be taken from the loneliness you have around you into the society of others who are with you in spirit, and in the gathering together you will find great peace and joy. Your hope will be increased by the hope of those around you, and their joy will also give you greater joy.

As the times of trouble come upon you there will be clear signals from Me that will allow you to know when to choose to band together. But I caution you to be patient and to let it happen when it happens. I also caution you to avoid the tendency to place your trust in any human, for although you will work with many, your trust must still be in Me. For My Spirit within you must guide you from day to day, even in the efforts united with those around you. Seek not to hasten the time, or to adjust the way, or to take control of your life. Let that joy and hope continue a day at a time, and stay on the path of My guidance.

For if you dart ahead, or explore the fields along your path in willful denial of My guidance, you are in danger of things you cannot handle. Stand still, and behold My salvation and My deliverance. Be at peace, be confident, and save your spiritual strength for the time I give to you. Do not expect to know in advance when that time will be. Be ready, living in great hope and with great joy, knowing that you will be told, shown, and led to the place of your deliverance when the time arrives.

I am your Mighty Counsellor and Guide.

> *These lessons are written by a process called Cosmic Telepathy, which is the flow of thoughts of truth from the Kingdom of God through the Inner Self of a human being. Cosmic Telepathy is explained by the Source in Book 30, Who also describes how it differs from channel-*

ing. Each lesson is written after prayer, while a changed level of consciousness allows the writer to convert the thoughts of the Author into words.

As the lesson in Book 30 says, Cosmic Telepathy is a very natural and easy way to communicate with God. The thoughts from Him come very rapidly, are easy to convert into words, and allow a daily lesson of about 1800 words to be written in 40 to 45 minutes. I receive the title just before the writing begins each day, usually with some surprise, for I seldom have any idea of the title or the text in advance.

The lessons explain many things I had not earlier believed, but my freedom is always allowed and respected, so I am not given anything I cannot accept at the time of the writing. Because of this, some of my mistaken beliefs of the past caused some of my word choices in earlier lessons to be distorted. Later, after my mind was opened by some of the later lessons, these distortions were explained. Some of the illusions which I earlier believed to be true are also finally exposed in later lessons.

The words are mine, the thoughts are the Author's, and you can judge the truth for yourself. The purpose of the writing is also explained from day to day, and you may judge how you relate to that purpose. The writing is for you, and it was finished in December of 1990 after 36 months of daily writing.

"If you learn to stop and think, time will not defeat you. Stopping, in this sense, does not mean to cast yourself out of the current of your life. Life goes on, in any event, and your path still leads to Us. However winding your path, it leads to Us. But when you stop and think, you only need to stop trying so hard and beating your head against the walls of time."

From Book 32 — <u>A New Way of Living</u>

Chapter 8   From Book 9 — <u>A New Way of Living</u>

Dwelling

You dwell in the land of your ancestors, your parents of generations before. You live in a home, sometimes called a dwelling, and you live for the purpose you choose. And many of you wonder if you even know your purpose, for you have wandered from place to place. Some have lived in many homes, seeking to follow the needs of their occupation wherever it takes them. Others have lived in one place, and their dwelling place has been in the same community.

Last Days?

Some have travelled many times over the lands of the Earth, and are familiar with many oceans, cities, and countries. But the central dwelling place of your people is the Earth. You who live upon the Earth, in a larger sense, have the same dwelling place. Your home in this life is the same, and you are brothers and sisters of the Earth. And in one of the meanings of the word, to dwell means to stay in the same place. From the beginning of this life you have been dwelling upon the Earth.

The time is coming when your dwelling place shall be destroyed and made uninhabitable for a time. You will be unable to stay upon the Earth, for it will be shaken and torn apart by the violent forces of earthquakes and howling winds of destruction. Fires will burn out of control, consuming all the surface combustibles that can be found. The great winds will cover the surfaces of your dwelling, carrying both fire and flood in awesome and majestic force. No human could live through this.

Trees will be uprooted and burned, rocks will fall to the lowest place, and no structures will remain. The high will be brought low, the Earth will reel, the oceans will violently spill into the basins of the land, and the waters will ebb and flow with the force of tidal waves upon the inland valleys.

When it is over, the silence of death will remain, and the dwelling place will be destroyed. The land will be desolate of life, for the source of life will also be gone.

The larger species will be the first to be destroyed, and the desire to live will also depart in the animals who have lost their familiar dwelling place. Death will be a relief and a release from fear, and the agitation will be so great that the peace of death will seem welcome to the plants and animals that have survived for a little time. You can read many of these prophecies in the Scriptures, and this should come as no surprise to you, for it has been revealed to you for centuries in the books of many lands.

A New Way of Living will follow the destruction and renewal of your dwelling place. Life, like energy, cannot be destroyed, but will be transformed according to the ways of its kind. The seeds of plants and the remnants of the species of animals will be spared in various ways according to My plan. The spirits of humans will all be preserved for another life or for an extension of this one, depending upon their faith and preparation.

But your dwelling place will change, and at best you will leave this Earth for several years. Those of you who will then come back to live upon Earth for a thousand years will find a new dwelling, made new by the total cleansing of fire and the waves that wash across the ashes of the desolation. All things that can be burned or washed away will be so treated, and the process will give new life to the seeds that still exist. Nature will come back quickly and restore its beauty far beyond the present state, and the dwelling place upon the Earth will then be fresh and new.

Into this harmony no evil will intrude, and the joy and love found in the absence of ill will can make the Earth's recovery so rapid as to seem miraculous. The climate will stabilize, and regions of the Earth that now are uninhabited will become regions of civilization, and the renewed dwelling place will reveal natural resources in places that your world of today has never explored. You will also learn of the mysteries of gravity and energy that will avoid completely the foul pollution of air and water from the stench and filth of fossil fuels and hydrocarbons.

You will learn immediately at that time of the ways of conservation of energy and its clean and efficient sources. Your dwelling will be renewed with an ecology that is ideal. It will be quiet, peaceful, and effortless, for food and clothing and shelter will all come from the joy of harmony with little effort. Comfort and joy will be enhanced by faith and love, in a social environment in which you will know nothing of fear, of sorrow, of pain, or of want.

Time in this new dwelling place will be of insignificant value, for you will have no duties to fill your mind with worry or care, and you will live for one another as much as for yourself. You will learn to give love and expect nothing in return, for nothing will be needed or wanted. And you will know that the love you receive is also given to you without a price, for this will be a dwelling of perfect love and perfect kindness.

The new dwelling place in the New Earth is a place that you can find. It is for you, and you are able to receive it without a doubt. But it is a place that will not come to you, for you will have to choose it for yourself. Like faith, it comes from action on your part, not from sitting and waiting for it to happen. It will not happen of itself, for it depends on you. It is not to be earned, and will not come to you as payment for any effort, but neither will it come without belief and faith in Me.

You have heard the prophecies of a home not made with hands, eternal in the heavens. You will live on such a place while the Earth is restoring itself, for you must live in another place while your dwelling is prepared upon the New Earth. For the most part, this preparation will be done without human hands, but it will be spiritually directed by the beings who, even now, encircle your Earth and guard it against the day of destruction that is to come.

But when you return you will furnish your new dwelling place on the New Earth according to your tastes and choices, for you will lose no freedom of choice or will at all in the cleansing and renewal of your dwelling. You will have geographical choices, choices of companions and neighbors, and choices of the nature of the home in which you live. The strides of science will take you away from the daily concerns of climate control, for heat and cold will be easily maintained for your comfort.

There will also be an easy and plentiful source of energy for your body, which will be nourished by a different chemical principle that is too simple for you to understand at this time. The indirect path of energy through photosynthesis that sustains your physical life today will not be needed in the new dwelling place of your Earth, and you will not be faced with the problems of maintaining your health at all. Age will be a useless word of history, without meaning, as you dwell in the New Earth.

Envy and covetousness will be unheard of, for you will neither need nor want anything more for yourself than you have. Anger will also be a thing of the past, for you cannot be frustrated to the point of anger when all things you wish are available without effort. And you will not be able to imagine having an enemy, for there is nothing to fight for when you have or can have anything your imagination is capable of desiring.

And the greatest of blessings in this dwelling place is the quality of the souls and spirits around you. The ones with whom you will live are selected for their qualities of love, friendship, and peace. They are, without exception, spiritually alive and filled with the joy of faith in Me. They do not pull you down, and if you are there you will not pull them down, for you will have learned by then to control all negative emotions.

You are learning now, a little each day, to make this world of today a better place in which to dwell. Your ability to make this a better place will prepare you for that new dwelling, in which the efforts toward harmony today will be of little need. For when you find the new dwelling place you will also find harmony without effort. You will not need to judge yourself and the effect of those around you on your life. You will not need to move away from some for your own protection, nor will you need to be alone for the secret times of meditation that renew your peace.

For in that place your days will be filled with joy upon joy, and happiness can be taken for granted. There will be no depression, worry, or strife, and the barriers of language, race, and philosophy will disappear. You will have goodwill for all things, and be totally surrounded by goodwill. You will dwell as a child, in peace and without care, trusting and knowing beyond a doubt that you are safe and secure.

And those around you will dwell with you like other children, carefree and happy, finding it easy to laugh and smile in perfect joy. This dwelling place will be for you if you have read the Holy Words of inspiration that are provided for you today. Interpret the words you read and hear, seek and find the truth, and live in peace and love. If you can do even a little to find the way under the harsh conditions of the miserable world that surrounds you, I will take you to a dwelling where no effort is needed. This is My offer and My promise, and I am true. I Am the Father of Truth, and you may find truth if you will.

I am your God of deliverance. Hear Me.

> In Books 24 and 25 I learned, for the first time, that there were to be a total of 36 Books. They were defined as a trilogy of 12 Books each, with the general subject of each twelve Books of the series being of the nature of the Spirit of Strength, the Spirit of Light, and the Spirit of Truth. I was not ready for that information until then, for I had believed the Trinity of God is the Father, Son, and Holy Ghost. I was baptized into a church which taught that Jesus Christ is the only Son of God.
>
> At the very beginning of the writing I accepted the words which told me the Author is the God and Father of All. The Author first identified Himself as Jehovah, and over a million words were written before I learned to believe in a more universal God. In Book 21 He told me the Father God could be more realistically referred to as The Strength and Source. It was even harder for me to learn the concept of the Light, and that Jesus the Christ is a very exalted and Divine Son of God, not the only Son of God. This was different than I had been taught as a child. I was also surprised when I noticed that the Holy Ghost was described so often in the Bible as the Spirit of Truth.

"The good things are many, and they have a common ingredient of universal love and goodwill. Reach out around you for things that are true and beautiful for you today. These things are good, for they add to your joy, peace, and harmony. The world is in a constant state of flux today, having patterns of change that are destroying the unstable equilibrium of centuries. Things are not what they seem, for the recent removal of freedom's barriers have presented choices which many are unprepared to make."

From Book 29 —<u>A New Way of Living</u>

Chapter 9   From Book 10 —<u>A New Way of Living</u>

Stillness

 Stillness, quietness, and peace is your reward for faith. Still waters run deep, and in peace you will become still as you behold the last days with deep spiritual faith in the Name of your Creator. In My Words, in the guidance of My hand, and in the quietness of your confident mind I will be with you, and you will know the end of your turmoil as you reach out to Me.
 A spiritual stillness will cause you to hold your tongue and turn to the faith within you in these last days. There is still a temptation for most of you to clamor against the many around you as they follow the blind paths of their traditions, but you are learning that they cannot hear you. They are blind and deaf,

and they follow the false illusions of the world around them. The last days will not be quiet and peaceful for any who believe in physical reality.

The stillness of your spirit, as you turn to the immortality of your being, will seem more and more to be in sharp contrast to the world around you. There will be little comfort or quietness except in the safety and protection of your spiritual faith. As you learn more and more to divorce your mind from the illusion of the reality of your flesh and to join the reality of continual faith and the spiritual contact with Me that it brings, you will sometimes feel as though you are in a dream. It can even be a happy dream.

The more you learn to trust your heart and your emotions through spiritual life and faith, the more you will separate yourself from the hectic, frantic, and even chaotic pace of the world, with its deluded souls, around you. Before you separate yourself physically for your physical safety, you will learn of spiritual stillness and the peace of spiritual separation from the world around you.

More and more you will feel like a visitor as you go about your work. The news, the neighbors, and the community will notice you less, and will finally ignore you, for in your stillness and confidence, you will set yourself spiritually apart from them, and they will know it. Most of them will not oppose you, for neither will you press them or oppose their blindness. Your still waters of spiritual life will run deep within your soul, and your knowledge of the fulfillment of prophecy around you will be deeply hidden from the sight of those around you.

They will be more and more involved in grasping and clinging to their illusions as their illusions of physical reality slip away, and as the Earth turns away from them for its cleansing, they will find panic where you have found peace. They will find deep agitation in the same environment in which you have found stillness. And the more their physical world falls apart, the more your spiritual world will separate itself from theirs. Your reality, which seems so bizarre and strange to so many now, will

Stillness 51

then begin to look like the only haven to some of them. The deep stillness of your spiritual faith will conceal its Source from most of them, for only through faith can they see beneath the surface of your life. And it will be impossible for them to find faith while they are involved in the chaos of the destruction of a world that is physically falling apart around them. Those who have failed to fill their lamps in the evening will not find the Light in the middle of the night. The darkness that will engulf your Earth will bring panic to many, and your stillness and peace will not be available to those who have not prepared for it.

The changes that lead to this are not obvious to those who are distracted, and if you expect to see changes a day at a time, you will see nothing. If, however, you compare this year to five years ago, you will find many clues to the conditions that have changed. World population has gone up by millions per year, your governments have borrowed against a future that will never come for them, and many revolutions have deposed rulers, who have, in turn, been deposed by others.

In the midst of all this, many now withdraw from their awareness of even their illusion of physical reality around them, and they seek the lethargic anesthesia of television entertainment. They look at sports, soap operas, and even the morbid and negative newscasts which people use to deny their own troubles. For many people, the only anchor to sanity is their ability to find others who suffer more violence, more poverty, and more chaos than they have in their own life.

For if you, like a chip of wood in the rapids of a river, see things around you that are moving with you, they will seem still to you. The faster the rapids run, the quicker you will approach the destructive waterfalls ahead, but nothing will seem to have changed. For all things around you will seem to travel at the same speed as you, and a measure of peace will come by comparing yourself to the others with whom you travel.

But if you withdraw from the mainstream of material life you will then begin to see the true destruction that approaches, for you will find in the stillness of your spirit a greater ability to understand the direction of the world around you. I counsel you, in the lesson for today, that you do not resist the current, and that neither do you stay within it. There is a time for you to withdraw from the society around you and to blend the still waters of your spirit with the like spirits of others. Get out of the mainstream of life, and find for yourself the ones who can stand still with you.

Pay your homage to the physical demands for food and shelter if you will, and remember to provide for your physical needs. Care for one another, but do it in stillness and peace. Let the stillness be complete in your mind and spirit, and let your body slow to a pace that you can sustain with as little effort as possible. Turn away from the ambition to save the world, and save yourself from the turmoil of these days.

Be not obsessed with a deep desire to know and understand the future, for you need not know anything for tomorrow except in the stillness of spiritual faith. If you search frantically today for the things you think you need tomorrow, you might be too busy to notice the things I am providing. Be still, and be at peace within your heart, for the needs of today are sufficient for you.

If your mind wanders into speculation and concern for the future, redirect it toward the still waters of faith, and do not allow yourself to drift with the multitudes. Do not expect to stop the downward flow toward destruction, but get out of the stream of it.

Compare yourself with no one when you can, but if you must, compare yourself with those who have found spiritual peace to replace the material and traditional beliefs in their illusions of the hectic world around them. For you will find that the road to destruction is a material road, filled with material illusions, and it will tempt you by the mirages of physical satisfaction that appear ahead of you. The beast will tempt you to accept his mark, and you will find it hard to turn away from the commerce of the world.

Stillness

You will need faith as you turn away from the society of your world to the stillness of seclusion. You will also need faith as you learn to trust others who have still and peaceful spirits, as they will learn to trust you. For stillness attracts stillness, faith attracts faith, and peace attracts peace. You will know the joys of stillness when you have found it, but it does not look attractive while you are rushing down the current of life. The frantic pace of living that takes away your leisure today will seem indispensable to you. You will not know that it is an illusion until you step away from the mirror of yourself. The things you have always done seem natural, and stillness seems dangerous and even impossible for you.

It is tempting to do more when things fall apart around you. It seems strange to do less, to become still, and to withdraw from the battle when all others are fighting for the survival of their physical illusions. But the reality is of spiritual life, and of peace, and of stillness within your heart. In stillness you can see what is moving around you, and you can hear in the quietness of your heart the sounds of the second coming of My Son to redeem you.

You will not find Him or follow Him to Me until you are stilled, and until the silence of perfect peace is given to you as a reward for your faith. You cannot know stillness until you have found the confidence that faith brings, and until you have replaced doubt with trust. You know the end of your journey, and if you are prepared to stop and become still, you will see the blur of the passing illusions of the world fade into darkness. You will see turmoil replaced by stability, and the nightmare of the darkness of night will be replaced by the stillness of a perfect dawn.

I am the God of your fathers.

> *Readers have sometimes remarked that they could see the influence of my earlier beliefs in some of the choices of words of the earlier Books. The Author does not*

choose the words, nor does He force me to write what I do not believe or do not accept at the time of the writing. Nevertheless, I learned to keep a more open mind and gradually adjusted my thinking in order to be able to absorb the thoughts received in the daily lessons. And I finally learned that I enjoyed the writing more fully by knowing that I was perfectly free to stop or to continue any time I chose.

This change in attitude has allowed me to live more at peace, and to have a far greater appreciation for the life in our environment. A sense of duty has been replaced by a sense of freedom, and only you who have suffered from a false sense of duty can appreciate what a relief it is for me to lose this feeling. My wife has helped me to give up the feeling that others might depend on me for a contribution to their search for truth. I have finally learned that all truth lies within each soul, and that the purpose of these Books is only to help the readers unlock the truth for themselves that is found within each of them.

Having learned to believe this, my life of cares and worries has been changed to a life of freedom and happiness. The future and past seem less important, and many of the cares of my life have gone away as soon as I learned to ignore their apparent reality. This change in attitude, which has also come to several dozen readers who have purchased the Books as they were written, has made drastic improvements in many lives. Each life which changes, with respect to freedom, joy, and love, has an effect on all the lives around it. Therefore, thousands are affected in very positive ways when new truth is found by a few.

"These lessons teach you the way to find security by removing your cares, your consciousness of past and future, and your mistaken definition of reality. Learn them well and keep them in force by practicing a better attitude. Look more for freedom than security, for freedom shall never fail to be victorious at the end of time and of life on Earth. Sometime you shall be free of all the things of Earth, including your money, your possessions, your community, your government, your family, and even your body."

From Book 29 —<u>A New Way of Living</u>

Chapter 10   From Book 11 —<u>A New Way of Living</u>

Falling Leaves

As the sun shines upon the trees outside the windows of the home of the writer today, autumn leaves are falling. Another harvest of the Earth has ended in this place, and the squirrels have gathered their food for the long and dark winter ahead. It will be a winter in which more weather records will be set, and more people will wonder what has changed, and why.

But this harvest of falling leaves is no more natural than the harvest of the Earth which is upon you, for you are also being gathered and stored for the joyful harvest of the Master. I am giving the tired organism of your Earth the death through which its renewed life may occur, and your world history will begin anew in the Seventh Day.

In each death is the seed of a new life, some for a life tomorrow and some for a later day. So be joyful, for the door to the Seventh Day is a door that can be opened by the choice of anyone who reads these words. I bring you good tidings of great joy, and the death around you is a natural way of bringing life and resurrection. Choose to live, for you have much for which to live.

Learn for yourself the things that lead you on to peace and love, to places of safety, and to times of great joy. For when the lion lies down with the lamb, and when all are brothers and sisters who truly love one another, the resurrection will have arrived for all who are worthy. That worthiness is a simple and wonderful blessing that is for any of you.

The falling leaves are worthy, although seemingly doomed to fall to the Earth in death and decay. But maturity is not death, and all decay leads to life anew. The worm holes in the cross of Jesus and the staff of St. Peter are not without honor, for they failed to destroy the love and spirit of My Light. They only allowed it to shine through from the cross and the staff, for the Light was always within, awaiting those who could see it through the decaying and ravaging battles of time.

The rock of ages and the cross have been beacons of Light for many, and souls through the millions of years of your history have been faithful and maintained the Earth. And the falling leaves are as natural and joyful for those of you who have hope in Me as were the days of springtime, in which they burst into a renewal of their life. For many days they have lived in the beautiful green color of healing, and now they have changed to other hues of gold and scarlet and orange.

They have not failed in their purpose, for in the harvest that comes they will be renewed again to youth and vigor, and to a new life and purpose. For all things, even the organism of your reeling Earth, live and die and live again. All things fall and rise again, and cycles of time cause the very universes to breathe in and out.

Falling Leaves 57

The cycles of life depend upon size, upon purpose, and upon My Wisdom by which I created all things. The cycle of a fly is but a few days, and the cycle of the universes is two billion years. Nothing is lost or destroyed, and all things are renewed by a form of death and rebirth. The cycle of your Earth is about ten million years, and you are finishing a cycle now. But for reasons of My own I intervene, and the Seventh Day of a thousand years is an intervention caused by the choices of the mass consciousness of many souls now upon your Earth.

For your Earth is filled with darkness and wickedness among the corners of its lands, and the Light of the faithful is not sufficient to continue the Earth's justification. So the leaves are falling — the leaves of the Earth that are old, and fulfilled, and are ready to die. However, for those of you who choose the pink love of universal recognition and understanding, this death will be short-circuited and bypassed. You will retain this flesh, it will be renewed, and for a thousand years you will live together with those like you.

This has been promised and foretold by the prophecies of many faiths, and much has been written and believed about a life hereafter. In the ten million years of history in your Sixth Day, which is now ending, you have little truth remaining from studies of the past. If you care to see the confusion that has been heaped upon you, take a few hours to read of Biblical Literature in Volume Two of the current issue of The Encyclopedia Britannica. It is a macropodia that tells of all the efforts to translate, interpret, and maintain the Jewish, Protestant and Catholic Scriptures from the time of Moses.

As you read it, bear in mind that you are reading of only a few thousand years, a small part of the millions of years since your Sixth Day began. When you study it, be prepared to throw up your hands and turn to a life of spiritual inspiration, for you will soon see that the intellectual pursuits of people can only confuse you more than you already are.

You will then begin to see why the words of <u>A New Way of Living</u>, and the words of thousands of others who have been spiritually inspired to find truth from My Spirit, contain your only hope for the truth that you seek. And as you grow away from the studies of eschatology into the simple knowledge of future life from present love and goodwill toward Creation, you will have a chance to allow some of your own leaves to fall.

For the leaves you have grown from the tree of knowledge of good and evil can be safely allowed to fall away, and you can go back to the simple life of a child. A child needs to know little and to love much, for the joy is not in knowing, but in feeling, the instincts of that joy and love. *A child does not explain joy. A child lives it.* A child's life is an explanation of its own to those who watch, and the child's joy can be shared without any understanding at all.

So turn away from the dogma, and the encyclopedias, and the learned and detailed documents of academic discipline. You need only to know and reveal truth to yourself from the wisdom that is My Spirit within you. And what you need to reveal in these perilous times is the door between you and the Seventh Day. That door is love — universal and impersonal love. It is love without judgment, with all things forgiven and forgotten that could cast any shadow upon your Light and your joy of living.

Under any circumstances of life you can learn to do this, to find this joy through your faith and your trust in Me. Avoid the mind perversions of materialism, vanity, anger, lust, and greed. Replace them all with love. Let all others find Me by your example, as you have found Me with the help of the example of others. I offer you life in the Seventh Day, and I offer you a special way to avoid the falling leaves around you.

For in the harvest the seed shall be saved, and the leaves that fall will die, decay, and bloom again in another life and in another time. The seed is those who have learned finally to be filled with universal love and goodwill, forgiving and forgetting all things that were dark and decaying in themselves and those around them.

This can be you, for in the worm holes of the decay of your

present life a Light can shine forth, and the worm holes can also be filled with the pink roses of love. The staff of St. Peter is as strong as it has ever been, and, with the writer, you can carry it as you stand beneath the cross of your brother, Jesus of Nazareth, the Christ (the Light) of His time. And that cross can also be filled with the pink roses of love for you, and by you, and within you. It is your choice.

He did not die to allow you to live, but to show you how to live. He did not die for your sins, but to show you that the law was not needed for your sins. He did not die at all, for He lives in your heart of wisdom and spirit, and He beckons you to open the door of the Seventh Day for yourself, and He beckons you to enter in.

If your faith and training has been helped by other avatars of Muslim or Buddhist or American Indian history, or through belief in one God and Creator by any means, the door to the Seventh Day is ready for you also to open. The love and spiritual reality through faith of any soul from any source is the same, as long as the object of that love is One Universal Creator and One Universal Creation.

If you cannot love your brothers, whom you have seen, how can you love Me, Whom you have not seen? I will give you physical proof of My Presence when you learn to find Me with your spiritual faith. I will not prove Myself to you by gifts that increase your perversions of vanity and materialism. Neither will I be found while you are in the clutches of lust, greed, or anger. In love for all things and through faith will you find Me, and I will increase that love within you by My Spirit, which can also be within you.

Dream of the Seventh Day, and live for the Perfect Love of that day by doing the best you can today. Today is yours, and only in today is the challenge. Forgive and forget the darkness of yesterday around yourself or others, and know that you can be renewed by the miracle of life. The falling leaf can bloom again, and although you might have fallen, I have given you a seed of life that remains within you. This seed cannot be destroyed, and it will bloom again when you choose.

I am your Father and Creator.

> *In the early days of writing the Books I was in an almost continuous state of shock. I was a computer sales consultant, normally working a ten hour day with considerable success and enjoyment. But these lessons caused me to feel more and more detached from my customers and associates.*
>
> *At the beginning, my arms tingled as I wrote. Later, my whole body felt the same way. This feeling can be compared to the sensation caused by carbonated soda water on your tongue, and it has never stopped at any time since the writing began. The same feeling is intensified during the prayer at the beginning of each writing.*
>
> *I feel the earlier lessons seem to be directed more to me than to the reader, for I needed to be prepared for an entirely different life-style, belief system, and attitude toward life. My 'Type A' personality was so different from what it is today. I needed to be prepared to believe what I was to write later, which turned out to be unlike my earlier beliefs and training.*
>
> *The changes this process has made in my life is almost indescribable. It is clear and convincing proof to me and to my mate that truth from within is very effective in adding great joy to our lives on Earth.*

"Live like a child, for you are My child. You are My beloved child of Creation, who has often learned to take yourself and life on Earth too seriously. Life is surrounded by illusions when it is lived in time and space. Life on Earth can be a happy game with artificial rules that change from time to time. The facts of life are not the reality of life. The birds and the bees are beautiful, and the information you give a child of the facts of life need not be so serious. There are blessings in the knowledge of living on Earth, but there need not be so many cares attached to them. Laugh often at any age, and be like a child."

From Book 28 —<u>**A New Way of Living**</u>

Chapter 11   From Book 11 —<u>**A New Way of Living**</u>

Passages

In all of life there is movement, in different directions, different rates, and for different purposes. The Earth rotates around its axis, and this movement causes the sun to seem to rise in the east each day. The same illusion that makes the sunlight of dawn pass across the surface of your Earth in the morning will take that light away when evening comes. And when the sun seems to go down, another day has passed.

This is another of the illusions of your world of time and space. For the passage of day after day is indeed an illusion. Another is the passing of the years. The Earth orbits your sun, sometimes eclipsing the moon, and often the seasons seem to tell you of the summers and winters of your days. The month is marked by the moon, the days are marked by night, and the years are marked by the seasons that also pass by.

In all of this, the time of planting comes and goes, and after it, the time of harvest. The harvest passes, and the time of planting comes again upon your Earth, according to the seasons of your hemispheres. So days pass by, followed by months, which are followed again by seasons. And the events of your life also pass by, equally being illusions of reality. But your spirit shall never pass away, for it is truly a real and living thing that I have created.

Your lives that brought you to this day have also come and gone, passing from one lesson of life to a later lesson of another life. Your body has been born of the Earth, lived until it passed away into the dust from which it came, and was then reborn in another time for yet another passing.

And through the years of your life is also the passing of faithfulness, which comes to you and passes by until it is renewed again. For faithfulness is also a step which is found by your free will. You cannot control the passing of the seasons and of the days and years of your present embodiment, for those are the passages that are meant to mark the lives of all the souls now living on your Earth.

But what of faith, that comes and goes, passing away in the battles against vanity and materialism, but returning to you when you seek its renewal by prayer to Me? The faith that comes and goes is the step that takes you from the passages of the illusions of time to the reality of spiritual contact with Me. This contact of your spirit is the water for your thirsting soul, and it is the bread of your spiritual body that lives in all of its reality. This is the contact with Me which leads you to eternal life, where the sun never sets, the years stop passing by, the seasons are replaced by perpetual joy, and the harvest is also forever past.

The words of this lesson today are to help you to understand that anything which passes by is an illusion. I tell you now, and I will tell you often, that the lasting things that never pass away are the things that bring you joy. The very breath of your body, passing through your nostrils and into your lungs, is only an illusion that keeps your body alive to house your spirit for a few short years on Earth. The reality of yourself is your spirit and your soul, and that is the part that shall not pass away.

I have taught you, many times before, that physical death is also an illusion, marking the end of an embodiment, but having nothing to do with the life of your soul. You will, however, see the passing of time upon your Earth mark the Earth's destruction in a few short years, and no flesh shall be alive upon the Earth after the passage of its life. The Earth is itself an organism, and that organism shall be cleansed by the water of its oceans and by the fire of its forests. By the howling winds that will encircle the Earth for weeks at the time of the polar shift, the Earth shall also be dried and it will begin its millenniums of renewal and repopulation.

This will be a joyful event, for the passing of the Earth to a new life is the new beginning. It will be a home for perfect joy and peace for a thousand years, and then it will continue in renewed life for more millions of years. It will become another step in the passage of events that meet My purpose, and that purpose has been known to Me eternally. I am beyond time, and you are My child. Time is also a temporary illusion for you, giving you always the time you need for eternal perfection and then passing away from your consciousness forever.

These words are to help you realize the things that are real, and that shall never pass away. Again I say for you to look around you at the things that pass by today. The things that come and go, that move here and there, and that are born and die again, are illusions that mask the reality of eternity from your mind.

The things you can see are illusions, and the things you cannot see except with faith are real. It is a shame that you want so much to know the future and to understand by physical proof that I am the Creator of the Universes, for the things you know through faith are the only things that are real. And when you have denied your faith in things seen with your eyes, you have passed the need for the illusions that require faith.

Do not, however, believe that your faith can be perfect in a world of time or an embodiment of the flesh. It is not so, and will never be so for you. Seek only to fulfill your perfection of purpose. For now that purpose is the purpose of faithfulness, and the discovery of My Truth and Light for yourself.

Do not measure yourself against any yardstick of perfection, but against a yardstick of faith and joy. For time is the clever robber of your joy, deluding you into dreams of progress in material ways, and causing you to want more rather than to accept the limitations around you. Within the very limitations of your flesh and its temptations is the opportunity for faith and joy in the reality of your spirit.

Believe the ones around you who have discovered this, or who are discovering it. As these words are spread around your world, they will be rejected by many, for the delusions of the flesh are so ingrained that they cannot pass away from some for many days. But among you there will be those who read these words and readily accept them, knowing by the instincts of their souls that these Words are true, and that they are from Me.

Those are the ones who are ready to pass away from their past mistakes and accept the Divinity of My Spirit within them. They are the ones who will step briskly and with great joy into their future days, knowing that these days will pass on into a glorious tomorrow for them. And when you see them around you, they will be so happy that you will sometimes question their sanity.

But know that their joy is real, their happiness is built on a foundation of truth, and their peace is within their very soul. For when they find this Truth, they have found the rock of ages that shall not pass away. And they have found the rewards of their faithfulness that cause them to turn away the distraction of all things that pass away. They have found their anchor, and instead of passing away from Me, they will remain. Their faith will be easy to find and keep each day, for their life will be a life of the spirit of love and joy.

Their flesh will seem less precious to them, and their fleshly appetites will diminish, for they will have finally found the satisfaction of something that is theirs forever, something that shall not pass away. For them, the passage of time will seem a welcome pathway to the end of time, and to the end of the need for those illusions of the flesh from which their faith has delivered them.

When you see the smiles of those who have made this discovery, and you see their glowing radiance of love for the real Creation and all within it, you will see a glimpse of the Seventh Day. This is the way you can avoid the passages of time that lead to sorrow and heartaches, for in this very same body you can find a joy that will let your heartaches and sorrows finally pass away from you.

If this does not become a fact for you, it will be for others. You have only to believe it, and it will also become a part of your life. And if you choose to deny it, it will become truth for you in a later time and at another place. But the time is short for you now, and many words in these lessons are still available to you. They can teach you of the realities and the truths of Creation. You can learn or not, as you choose.

So live on in peace, finding faith in Me each day by prayer, and through spiritual contact with the brothers and sisters who are workers of Light. They are among you, seen and unseen. And neither shall they pass away, for they are My gift to you in these last days of your Earth. Seek them and find them, for the Spirit of My Love pours over all the Earth, clashing against the perversions of lust, greed, anger, vanity, and materialism. But My Love shall remain, and all of these perversions shall pass away. Love one another, for that is the reality of your purpose and the source of your joy.

I am your God. Stand still on the rock of your faith, and let the illusions pass away from you.

> In the early days of writing the Books, the light above the computer often mysteriously turned on. It was a fluorescent desk light, with a switch that had to be held down for a few seconds in order for the light to stay on when the button was released, but it lit several times as I approached it and was about to write. I was touching nothing on the computer, the desk, or the light when it turned itself on.
>
> In another instance or two, the computer shut itself off and erased about fifteen minutes of writing. In those cases, I was emotionally out of touch with the reality of what was happening, and as I remember, my mind was full of anger or frustration from the interference of unrelated events around me. For example, if the children made a lot of noise while I was writing, I was so distracted I could hardly continue. In the first few Books there are several references to this. Later, I learned to better control my thoughts by turning them off while writing, and this did not happen during the last couple of years.
>
> In another case a friend, who later proved to be skeptical of the Source, wanted to see me write. I told her I would pray, start writing, and that then she could quietly walk in after ten minutes or so if I was not told to stop her. I was not told, but about the time she was ready to come into the room, the electrical power for the entire house shut off just long enough to lose all that was written. I started again, but did not allow her to enter the room.
>
> Proof seems to come only to those of us who have faith before the proof.

"A selfless act is a beautiful thing. An unexpected smile is a beautiful thing. A generous gift, a loving touch, a tender glance, or a hopeful remark are beautiful things. An enthusiastic appreciation for changing beauty is the beginning of universal love, for if more of the beauty of the illusions of time and space are seen, are they not reasons to give more hope for the things unseen that are to come? Seek beauty as sincerely and lovingly as you seek truth, and make no effort to allow majority opinion to decide what is beautiful to you."

From Book 27 — <u>A New Way of Living</u>

Chapter 12   From Book 11 — <u>A New Way of Living</u>

Laughter

I am not a God of a sober and serious Creation. You and I are one, for I have created you as a part of Me, and you have not been created for sorrow and the heavy burdens which you so often find. You seek for duty to prove your submission to Me, but I need no proof that you love Me. I know what you feel for Me the instant you feel it, for I am within you. And when you laugh with a clear conscience and a light heart, I laugh with you, for I love your smiles and laughter as a part of My successful Creation.

What father enjoys a child who is filled with worries and cares? If you are a parent, do you not love to see your children happy, and do you not enjoy the feeling of happiness when their life goes well for them? So do I. You are in a world where laughter and a light heart can be found. They come to you with your positive emotions and with your universal love for all Creation.

A ready smile is a thing of beauty, and it gladdens the hearts of all who are around it. To laugh with others in innocent and careless abandon, forsaking the thoughts of tomorrow or the regrets of yesterday, is good for your body and your soul. Many who are sick can relieve the stress of sickness by thinking of life with good humor and lightness of heart. The stress of living is not made easier by a careful mind and serious attitude toward life.

If you have a choice, do you not seek the company of one who loves good humor more than one who is careful and concerned, fearful of making a mistake or failing in any effort? Look at the children around you, for they can teach you. They sometimes reach out to a stranger more quickly than you even reach out to a friend. The innocence of childhood reaches out in goodwill, fearing not to be rebuffed or rejected, and they seldom are.

They offer you nothing but a smile and their friendly eyes, reaching into your heart with their love. They have no goods to give, and they seek nothing from you but your loving attention and a smile in return. They want to be your friend, to play and laugh and enjoy their toys and their blessings with you. How can this innocent love and laughter be lost so quickly as they mature?

It is lost in a world of serious and sober faces, and in a world where care and ambition and worry deny the laughter of the ones who live just for today. Laughter and song promote harmony and joy, and after the little time that this takes, there is still time enough to do what needs to be done. Tomorrow will come soon enough, and the removal of stress by laughter allows more to be accomplished when the chores of today are begun.

Laughter

Laughter in the evening also causes sleep to come more easily, and it causes the rest to be more effective. With a light heart and good humor, sleep comes more quickly and lasts longer than does sleep with anger or serious thoughts.

Many of the things that concern you will become easier as time passes by, and you will only prolong their effect on your life by thinking of them too soon or too often. So the diversion of laughter is a good way to avoid these thoughts, letting them come later and go away sooner, with less effect on your mind. The stresses of worry and care are often the cause of illness, and even in the midst of cares your laughter will improve your health. Laughter is an escape for a little time, and it is not a mark of one who is irresponsible. It is the mark of one who is wise, knowing the limits of strength and the greatness of My love.

For I do love you, and I do not expect so much from you as you believe. I am not impressed and gladdened by your sense of duty or your cares and worries, for you are still a child to Me at any age. When you remember the shortness of your days and the love from which I created you, you will know that your life is much more than the seventy years or so that some of you have believed. You can set a pace of easier ways and easier goals, with less care, for the things you need to learn in one lifetime are much less than you might have believed.

Take time to play and to laugh, looking for the pleasures of things enjoyed with love and harmony and goodwill, for in these things you are heeding the advice of Jesus. He told you to become as little children, and this was told to you with love. He is your brother, for you have the same Father, and the same Creation is for all. And you can laugh in the rain or the sunshine, for joy is not denied by anything in nature. In birth, in death, and in any part of your life there is cause for joy, and nature has no need for sorrow at all.

The purpose of these lessons is for your happiness, teaching you to avoid the things of worry and care and sorrow, and helping you to live a little more happily and joyfully each day.

Last Days?

If you look for reasons to be serious, you can find them. But if you look for a smile, a laugh, and the lightness of heart that goes with love and goodwill, those are also available to you. In the things you do today, think of these things and smile.

As a gift of love to friends and strangers alike, accept a challenge from Me. I challenge you today, just once, to see if you can make a stranger smile with you. Do this today at least once, and see how it makes you feel afterward. You will find it often can be done without a word, but with only a glance or an expression. The smile and the friendly glance on your own face will not always cause another to respond, but it often will. Try it a few times, and see what happens to you.

For laughter, like perfect love, needs no reason to exist and needs no motive of reward. It can be a gift, given to bring joy into your heart and the heart of another. This is accomplishment enough, and it is well done for its own sake. Like perfect love, laughter can create a ripple in the stream of your life that goes far around you, reaching out far beyond your awareness. It can go on from smile to smile, until it finally dies at the doorstep of one who is filled with cares and worries and regrets.

And if that person who stops the cycle is you, let that be your challenge. I challenge you to look for good humor and goodwill in those around you and to respond with a smile of your own when you see them. In children, or in people of any age, there are those who radiate happiness and joy. They smile easily, and they seek the friendly return of your own smile. Laugh with them, whether they are strangers or friends, for laughter is love in action.

You know I do not speak of laughing at others, for that is hypocrisy. I speak of laughing *with* others, honestly sharing your joys with them. Laughter increases your blessings and adds to them, while worry and care deny the purpose of blessings instead.

I bless you with joy, and I bless your faith with the removal of your cares. If you hang onto your cares and clasp them to your heart, there can be no room for your laughter and joy.

And when your laughter is seldom heard, your heart is made heavy and your thoughts turn inward to problems that are a part of your life. And your thoughts make you what you are today. So if your thoughts are heavy with care, you feel the heavy burden of life. I challenge you, instead, to lighten your heart with laughter today, seeking it and sharing it as the antidote for your cares. See how many of the things that drag you down will go away, for many of your cares are for things that could be ignored, but that cannot be improved by your cares.

It is not a mistake to be careless, if your carelessness comes from faith in Me and starts after you have done the best you can. The best you can do is good enough, and that is the place to find laughter instead. Children soon learn to care for their bodies and avoid pain, and with that they are satisfied. Can you not be as wise? Find ways to play, to laugh, to share your joy, and to enjoy your life as much as you can.

Find the good things in life that are free, for they are many. Among the best of them are the joys of a smile, of shared laughter, love, harmony, peace, and of appreciation and gratitude that accepts My blessings by enjoying them. I do not give you the gift of life so that you can spend it in frantic haste to repay Me. I need no repayment in the form of duty. I ask only that you enjoy the gifts and the blessings I have created for you.

Enjoy these things to the best of your ability, and see that you postpone tomorrow's cares until tomorrow. Learn to laugh and live today, and let tomorrow bring to you the things that it brings. Do not borrow trouble from the future, and much of it will pass away by the time the future arrives. Keep foremost in your mind the joys and blessings of today, and let tomorrow bring what it will. Remember My challenge to you for today, and lighten up your heart, for life is more joyful than many of you have believed.

I am He Who created you for laughter and joy.

Last Days?

We have repeatedly been told that faith is rewarded by proof, but that lack of faith is not turned into faith by later proof. In an earlier Book, I was told that I would later learn to use Cosmic Telepathy under almost any conditions. That has proved to be true.

In the early days of writing I was given more confidence by the earlier lessons. However, in reading some of them a year or so later, I am reminded of how much I have changed, for the mission now seems so much easier and simpler. At first, I felt I had to prove everything, but now I feel no need to prove anything at all.

A large section of the front page of the local newspaper, in two consecutive issues, reported a detailed account of what was happening to me. As a result many readers, scattered over several states, subscribed to the Books. It also caused our children to be taunted and ridiculed at school by some, and it caused some of our friends to treat us differently. Some thought I had lost my mind, while others thought I had worked out a scheme to make money by pretending. One reader of the newspaper thought it was an April Fool's joke. I was accused of setting myself up as a prophet and of being an 'Anti-Christ.' A local minister thought I was a very unlikely person to be sincerely writing such material. Since then, we have moved to another state several hundred miles away and are reluctant to tell our neighbors of this experience.

However, we have met some very wonderful people as a result of these Books, and have also become better friends with some whom we knew only slightly before this began. It seems that every change in us causes a change in all our relationships, some for the better and some not so good. There seems to be more need for universal love when we begin to sense negativity more deeply.

"Who has told you life is to be suffered, not enjoyed? Those who suffer and do not enjoy life have told you, but their misguided conception of reality need not affect yours. Live like a king, love all the other souls around you, who are equally kings of Earth, and accept the counsel of those who are at peace with themselves and with reality, if you choose to be counseled."

From Book 27 —<u>A New Way of Living</u>

Chapter 13   From Book 12 —<u>A New Way of Living</u>

Daily Life

The future and the past are illusions of time, given to you for the assessment of your progress. Time is like a report card to a child in school, telling you with its memories of the past and by the joy of the present if you are following the path of your destiny. I give you renewed life each day, and I do not ever forget for a moment of your time about any soul on Earth. My eternal consciousness is always with you and is a part of your very being. In a very real sense of spiritual truth, your life and

Last Days?

Mine are one.

Since you and I are one in truth, the effectiveness of your life is limited only by your belief of truth. The truth shall set you free from the snares of time and from the delusions of the past and future. The future is uncertain, the past is gone, and today is the only real day of your life. Daily life is the only life that is real for you at all, and it becomes real only when you are able to separate it from the past and future in your consciousness.

Dreams come unbidden in your sleep, and when you awaken they vanish from the reality of your thoughts. They seemed real while you were dreaming, and became unreal when you later awakened. In the same way, yesterday is for you a dream that is past, and today is the reality of your life. I teach you today of your daily life, and of the significance of its impact on your happiness, for it is truly all you have or will ever have while you are in the embodiment of the flesh.

It is so easy to attach too much importance to your past and, more especially, to your future. If you can break the bonds of the past and future by regarding the present daily events more highly, you will do much to avoid the damage that time does to you. When your mind dwells too much on the past, it is so easy to regret losing the good things that are gone, or to regret the mistakes that can never be corrected. In thinking of the past, there is much more room for regret than for joy.

Even as regret is the risk of dwelling on the past, so are fear and uncertainty the risks of thinking of the future. The victims who survived yesterday's earthquake are now filled with much regret for the things they lost and their friends that are gone, or for the injuries and pain that have been inflicted. If, instead, they turn to thoughts of the future, they can easily become fearful of after-shocks, and of the uncertainty of life that has been so cruelly demonstrated to them.

So their daily life is not improved by thoughts of either the past or the future, and neither is yours. Many disasters are possible for many of you, and they will occur inevitably during the last days of your Earth. But still I teach you today that your

Daily Life 75

daily life is the only life you have or need. I have taught you often of these things, and I am reminding you today that the more your life is troubled, the more you need to learn to live only for today.

Daily life is the only life you have, and it is the only life that is significant to you. When things are changing the fastest, and when there is the most uncertainty and apprehension around you, that is the time when you must learn to turn to faith and confidence in the present events of your daily life. By faith I can lead you, and I do not count your knowledge of the future as a thing of any value at all.

Prophecy foretells coming events, and I have repeated some prophecies from your Scriptures in these lessons. My purpose has not been to cause you to fear, but to prepare. And the preparation for the future begins and ends with your faith in Me and universal love for all things. These are the only things you need, and any more thought than that will become tinged with regret, fear, and apprehension. Negative emotions are almost always involved with the past or the future.

Even if you try, it is hard to imagine, at this moment, any feelings of materialism, vanity, anger, lust, or greed that are not involved with events of the past or future. Daily life is lived a moment at a time, and, if you allow yourself to think often of the past or future, the desires of your flesh are so quickly involved with material things. Be joyful for the things of your spiritual life that are past, and dream of the spiritual joys that are in your future, but remember most to live in faith and trust for today.

Let no fear for the material needs of your future life destroy your peace for today. I created you to live a breath at a time, and to need frequent renewal of food and drink. I gave you a life of uncertain length, and caused you to be only a step away from physical death each moment of your life. Your heart beats one beat at a time, and the blood that gives your body life must be purified and renewed continually by the vital organs of your body.

Last Days?

I had no intentions of creating you for a physical life with a sure and certain future, or the guarantee of a repeatable past. You are born and created physically to live for today, and the way you live today will determine your destiny for tomorrow. If your physical future were certain, you would not be able to have the freedom of choice that allows you to change it by your spiritual growth. Be glad you can live only a day at a time, for that makes your daily life a new and resurrected opportunity to shape your own future.

I reserve the right to give a merciful end to your days on Earth at any time and for any reason. I created you for love and harmony and joy, and I created you to be a part of all the universes and their components of life. Your spiritual life goes on in any event, but you will live at your best when you are removed from the dimensions of time. If you ask and believe, I will give you this day your daily bread. And since you are reading these words, you are also given this day your daily life.

If you are physically alive tomorrow, that will be a new gift from Me, and a new opportunity to live again for another day. Months and years may come and go upon your Earth for a few more years, but your life is a daily life, and your future is not a destiny of certainty. It depends upon the way you live today, for that is the source of tomorrow's joys, opportunities, or even the existence of tomorrow for you.

You are synchronized with daily life by the function of time, and by your choices today you will choose the progress that can bring tomorrow to you. For you, daily life is everything, for you have chosen to be born in a world of time and to learn the lessons that a series of daily lives can teach you. Do not fall into the common mistake of thinking you cannot change, or that others cannot change. Indeed you must change unless you are perfect, and if you were perfect you would not need to be reading this lesson in a world of time.

Believe, instead, that life each day is a priceless opportunity for another step toward your perfection, and that a step forward is also a step toward spiritual joy. And remember that your life today can be a joyful life, especially when you learn more to ignore the regrets of the past and your fears for the uncertainty of the future. This is a constant battle for any human, but the distractions of the past and future leave too little time to enjoy the present blessings of your daily life.

It is better to enjoy even the physical things of today than to wallow in the mire of regrets for the past, as long as you know that the physical joys of today are also gifts from Me to you. If you see them as gifts not earned, you can enjoy the next breath, the food and drink that sustains your body, and the comfort of your home while you live for today.

If you have learned that life is spiritually discerned by your acknowledgment of Me and My Spirit, your mind will stop trying so hard to fight the battles of the past and future. You can live life to its fullest when that life is a daily life of spiritual closeness to Me. And since I am a part of all the universal Creation, having made it as a harmonious and living miracle of perfect love, you will also find joy in your daily life just by your own universal love for all things.

These things have been taught many times before to you, and I am only reminding you again today that your daily life is all the life you have. I am telling you again that excessive fears and thoughts of uncertainty for the future are as useless to you as regrets for the past that is gone. Today is yours, and your life in a world of time will never be significant for you until you see it as only a daily life, with a goal of the removal of time for you instead of the unfolding of it.

I cannot continue to allow your freedom of choice without keeping the future hidden from you, and it is a waste of your time to dwell too much upon it. These lessons have spoken of the future events that are to come around you so that you might be prepared, but your only needed preparation is to be filled with universal love. You can find joy in any event if you understand the words of these many lessons, and I strongly advise you to look for that joy in your daily life of this day.

Last Days?

I am the Creator of your daily life.

> *A very typical reaction by new readers of these Books is to try to convince others of the wonderful happiness they find in this new way of living. Almost invariably, the friends who are pushed the most resist the most. It seems the great discovery is made only by those who are ready, but not by those who are looking for something besides the Kingdom of God within them. One of the hardest lessons to learn was to wait for others to reach out before offering the material. Some are strongly drawn to the material, while others reject it without a glance. The key is for me to allow the material to be rejected without feeling myself rejected, even though it has meant so much to us and to those who are reading it.*
>
> *The added happiness and peace of mind my wife and I have found in reading this has been well worth the effort of writing and publishing it. We also have received many sincere letters from people whose lives have been clearly changed for the better in so many ways. As for us, the more we accept our inner guidance without thought or care, the more our cares are removed by sudden developments that make our path smoother. There are so many instances in the Books that show us the way to find happiness, peace, and success in everyday living. And there are so many instances in our lives that show us how our belief leads to results and proof of that which is believed.*

"Apply this lesson in simple ways today. <u>A New Way of Living</u> is practical for you on Earth and is to be practiced. Practice makes you perfect, so you have every reason to practice creation. You are the child of Creation and of the Creator. You are one of the many children of God, and We Are within each of you. Do not exclude Us from anyone in your heart by failing to love them, and do not imagine that you can be excluded, at any time or under any circumstances. Find Us within you always, learning by faith and by universal love that the power to create is always yours. Find the truth as you see it today, live it, and let your hopes and dreams create a better life for you."

From Book 26 —<u>A New Way of Living</u>

Chapter 14   From Book 13 —<u>A New Way of Living</u>

Fulfillment

Every day and in every way the works of Creation go on. The nature of the cycles is to cause progress and growth. Each peak of the cycle is higher than the previous valley, and each valley is higher than the valley before. Even the learning process in your world is cyclical, with consecutive periods of progression and regression.

As the fulfillment of the process of Creation takes place around you, there will also be small periods of time when things seem to go backward. Joy will be followed by sorrow, peace by war, rebirth by destruction, and calm by winds and storms. It is for you to learn that the lull foretells the coming storm, and that the storm is followed by another period of calm.

This is also true in the cycles of the fulfillment of prophecy. You who are reading this have been told that the end is near, and that the new beginning will follow. This is, at first, a fearful thought, but I have given you many reasons to believe that the entire process of the destruction and renewal of your Earth is normal, joyful, and beneficial to all concerned. You who have believed in one life and the possibility of eternal damnation thereafter cannot easily accept the joy and celebration of the harvest that is to come.

I tell you, however, to read and study the many works of inspiration, and, if you fear the events that are coming to you, to read these words again. I am with you, and you are also with Me, being an indivisible part of all Creation. Understand this and you will have no more concern than a grain of sand on the beach that is continually shifted and buffeted by the rolling waves. You are a part of the nature of all things, and fulfillment is progress for you.

I have caused you to be carried forward by the winds and tides of change and by the fulfillment of your Earth cycle you shall be one step ahead of where you are, no matter what you believe and do. It will be far more joyful for you if you choose the wonderful life in the Seventh Day by your universal love, but if you deny these things, you will still gain a welcome relief from the rat-race that the people of your Earth call living.

The time of suffering and death is short and welcome to those who first find such great deterioration in the standards of their living. And I will cause the quality of life to become much more undesirable before the final events of destruction take place. It is normal for things to end step by step, even though the cycles of the end have their ups and downs. Many of you who read this are wondering when the end will be and when the events of prophecy will be fulfilled. Some are also wondering

Fulfillment

if it will really happen, and are wavering between acceptance and disbelief from day to day.

I do not tell you of the future, for it takes away your need and purpose for faith in Me. I will care for you, and I have told you many times, in many ways, how to prepare. I will tell you today, however, that the events that lead to the end will become closer and closer together, and they will also become more and more clearly the events of fulfillment.

I will also have lulls between storms, and highs between the lows of the cycles of fulfillment. If you really desire to believe it, you may have reason to believe that the end has been delayed. You can be deceived by the calm that precedes the final storm. As things get worse and worse, the better things will be more appreciated, and it will be easy for your gratitude for the blessings that come to you to cause you to shield your mind from the meaning of the overall events of fulfillment.

This can allow many to question and finally to deny the events of fulfillment, and to say that it is all imagination. Prophecy has fooled more people than it has convinced in the past, and it will fool many into denying it by the events of your future. Your world is confusing and deceptive with its combinations of blessings and problems. You can find reasons to believe whatever you like, for that is the environment in which your faith in Me becomes an option instead of a necessity.

I have caused you to live in the cycles of time so that you might learn to worship and love Me in sickness or in health, in prosperity or in poverty, and in joy or in sorrow. As the Earth goes down to her destruction, you will have times of peace and plenty mixed with times of strife and want. You will not be forced to believe in Me by the events of prophecy that are being fulfilled, but you will only be given the opportunity to see the truth that is revealed by your watchfulness and faith in Me.

So fulfillment of prophecy is not clear to all, nor will it become so. It is clear only to you who seek to know the truth, to love all things, to have good will for all people and all Creation, and to be among the blessed who are found worthy for the joys of the Seventh Day. Awaken, My child, and prepare to see the dawn that is prophesied after the darkness of these final hours. The time is near, and it is not known by any man. Some of you think it will come in months, some in years, and some in decades.

The important thing is to keep an open mind and to not be deceived by the highs and the lows of the cycles of time. Up to the very last moment, some will be saying that things will go back to normal, and they will believe that the worst is past. And in the overall picture, the worst is already past, for you are closer today to the fulfillment of prophecy that foretells the end than you have ever been.

Do not allow this to strike fear into your heart, nor cause you to be concerned about the ones who are not ready. Some of them will become ready in time, and others who are now ready will fall asleep when things get better during the cycles of fulfillment. Some will fall in, some will drop out, and some will go their way in total disregard of the many things that are happening to others around them.

The selfish will show no concern for their brothers half-way around the world, and they will scorn the ones who have failed to find the material success that they have found each day. The angry will say that those who suffer deserve it, the greedy will try to find a way to gain more possessions from the losses of others, the vain will be too busy to think about it at all, and the lustful will continue to seek the things for which they lust.

Among all this there is much time and reason for you to love them all, to care for those around you as you respect their freedom, and to prepare yourself for the fulfillment that comes to you in event after event. These events lead to the end and, at the same time, they warn you of the latter days. Watch carefully and wait, and be joyful as you see the end approaching. You who care to know the truth will find it, and it will set you free from the burdens of your flesh and embodiment today.

As the time of deliverance fulfills the prophecies of the dying Earth, your personal fulfillment will become clear and joyful as

Fulfillment 83

well. You cannot fully realize the burden of your life in these days until you have escaped it. So often you do not know you are wound up and tense until you have the chance to relax. Your whole daily life in your world is one of tension, with news after news of confusion and fear and physical death on every hand.

No wonder that you cling together and seek the company of others as time goes by. The positive seeks the positive, the negative seeks the negative, and the winds of change blow against them all. Find shelter in your spiritual beliefs, and live for the day when you are no longer buffeted by the changes that come closer and closer to your door. Each event is a test and a time for the strengthening of your faith, and through your faith your spirit will find the way to overcome the impact of these last days.

In the fulfillment of prophecy around you there will be times of peace and silence and times for you to regroup and study the lessons you have recently learned. Study and talk with those who see the positive side, and do not let despair and discouragement pull you down to the level of the negative thinkers. Neither is it wise to become tired of the battle of your life and seek the oblivion of empty distractions.

You need to look at the things you do not wish to see, and you need to let yourself believe by faith that these events of fulfillment are for the best in every case and in every way. This will sustain you, for I am a just and merciful God, and all things that happen are for My goals of universal love and harmony. If a soul learns slowly, the lesson becomes more rigorous, but no permanent damage will be done in any case. Redefine your beliefs and renew your faith in Me, and you will finally realize that all fulfillment is for the benefit of all.

I am your Loving Father.

> *At the time this lesson was written I had turned away from several new opportunities. A few months earlier I*

had retired from a job as a computer sales consultant, for my mind was so involved with the writing that it seemed unfair to my customers for me to continue. More importantly, I had a disease diagnosed as Diffused Idiopathic Skeletal Hyperostosis, or DISH. It is a progressive disease which moves randomly from joint to joint in the skeleton, causing excessive bone growth. It had attacked my right ankle, causing me to walk with a severe limp. I was unable to climb stairs easily, for any weight on the front part of my right foot caused severe pain.

An X-ray of the ankle, taken about the time the Books were started, showed the large bone growth clearly and confirmed the DISH diagnosis.

In a private letter from the Source, I was advised to go to a Doctor and follow his advice, and was told that the disease would be healed. The Doctor sent the X-ray information to the Mayo Clinic. They responded by saying that my problem was incurable. About a month after the following lesson was written I had no more problems. A later X-ray showed the ankle had healed itself by a bone growth which filled in the protrusion of the bone into the tendon at the site of the earlier pain. I have had no trouble of any kind since.

As so many others have discovered, this proves to me that a positive attitude and faith in our Creator make all things possible for us.

"I can wait — I am Eternal — your feelings of urgency and your fear of wasting My time is a measure of your need for more trust. Time is not with Me, it is with you. I have no time, All Power, and you are not distracting or diminishing Me in the slightest. Take Me and think of Me as if you are My only being, because My Power would be no greater in you if this were so. You still cannot imagine My Power — you will never be able to. Just trust Me when I say to you that there is never, never, any reason to hurry. Pause when you like, I am beyond time as you know it, and the pace of your growth means nothing to Me. Only your service is of glorious value to Me, and I have that now, at this moment. You fulfill as much of your purpose at this stage as you will at any other."

From Book 1 — <u>A New Way of Living</u>

Chapter 15   From Book 14 — <u>A New Way of Living</u>

Patiently

The waters of your world run deep, and sometimes swiftly, as they carry you down the stream of time. You sometimes falter, and you often stumble as you walk toward the end of your days of time on the Earth. If you walk impatiently, you use needless energy, for it is not possible to run swiftly in deep water. You are in a dense and dangerous environment, with hidden stumbling blocks and dangerous tides. The currents of time work against you steadily and inexorably, making you sometimes forget the goal at the other side of your life in a world of time. But today I teach you a lesson of joy, of peace, and of patience.

Last Days?

If you patiently and steadily go in the right direction, you can go slowly against the current that draws you away. You need not hurry, for time is with you when you learn to use it patiently. It is only when you go forward in a mad and frantic rush that time becomes your enemy. You allow time to be destructive, dangerous, and cruel to you when you lose your patience.

Few things in life must be done rapidly. You may walk slowly, breathe slowly, eat slowly, and think slowly. You may act slowly and cautiously, and you may feel your way through the new experiences of each day. Only by allowing time to rush you do you allow time to become your master and your enemy. Slow down, slow down, My child, and patiently live a life of peace and love and harmony. The famous story of the hare and the tortoise has a lesson for each of you who read this.

For you will live until you die and afterward, and your impatient pace only allows you to waste more energy and find more ways of getting into trouble. The writer of these words will study them carefully, and he will remember, as he reads this lesson, that I cautioned him at the beginning to slow down. He has learned much of the value of patience, and he still has much to learn. He is aware that the progress will be slow, and that he will patiently make that progress, with My guidance, as long as he renews and maintains his faith in Me each day.

And he is aware also that in less than an hour each day, for more than four hundred days, I have given him words to write. He has learned the same things as you who are reading these words, and each of you are blessed by My words in different ways according to your needs. There is not one of you who could not find greater joy in your life by living more patiently. You learn a little each day, and you slowly see the dawn of a new truth.

When you see another bit of truth, you wonder how you can use it more quickly. But your impatience need not be used to apply truth. Truth is to be possessed and enjoyed, not to be applied to anyone else. Each of you must find your own, and each of you must desire it before you find it. It cannot be thrust upon another until the other is ready, willing, and desirous of finding it. When any soul is ready to seek truth, it is everywhere and ready to be found. The truth you find is for you, and not for another. They will find theirs, and you will find yours, but only when you desire it deeply through faith in Me.

For I am the Source of all good, and I am patient with My children. Be patient also with yourself, and walk patiently today. Set goals that are close and easy to find, and take short steps against the currents of time, for to go swiftly takes energy you do not possess. As you patiently learn this lesson today, be content with it, and do not reach into the future with new desires that cannot be filled today. A day at a time, a step at a time, even a moment at a time is the way of patience.

Patiently seek what you seek, do what you do, and love what you love around you. Live patiently, show patience, and keep it close to your heart, for harmony thrives in a soul that is filled with patience. Things that cannot be seen or realized with impatience can often be found by patiently waiting or searching. How often have you lost something in your home and searched diligently for it, only to have it to appear a few days later, after you had given up the search?

My friendly and loving spirits sometimes cause you to fail to see the things that you desire, knowing that you will learn a lesson of patience by finding them later. Much effort is wasted and much time is lost in rushing through the currents of time, and your mind cannot find peace and happiness if you are filled with the stresses that impatience brings to you. So if things are going wrong for you today, slow down. It is natural to want to hurry when things are going wrong, but that reaction often makes the problems greater than they had been before.

A wise person will stop and think when things are going wrong, and he will act effectively and patiently to correct the problem after careful thought and a prayer for guidance. A foolish person will hurry more and more, reach out blindly in all directions for the answers, and experiment, without thought, until he is stuck in a deeper hole than he had been in before.

Last Days?

So many problems are increased by impatience, and so many mistakes are made in haste. From this comes the saying, 'mistake in haste, repent at leisure.'

So if you must be impatient and hurry along today, do it when things are going well. And if things go poorly for you, slow down and feel the answers come to your thoughts from My spiritual guidance in your heart of love and peace. For I am with you, but I cannot communicate with an impatient heart or mind. Many of you search for your destiny, which you have chosen and forgotten. But if you patiently live the lessons and challenges of today, you will find your destiny even without knowing what it is.

For your destiny will come to you, and you will find your destiny, as long as you live patiently with faith and in submission to the things by which I guide you. You will be helped both from within and around you, seeing the mystery of the workings of My spirits for the good of all who love Me, and all things will work together for you. Be patient and work patiently today, My child, for there is plenty of time and much to be done.

Even in these last days you have time, and your patience will avoid many problems for you. Patiently live a day at a time, even a moment at a time, and enjoy the many things that I have given you. Deny the impatience that comes from goals set far into the future, or in your foolish haste to set right the problems of your past. A little at a time, slowly, steadily, and with patience, you can work out the problems of your life. The things that are done in a rush often come undone, and the castles you build on the sands of time cannot withstand the winds and the waves that time brings to you.

So look at your life in a world of time as a series of short and steady steps, patiently moving ahead toward the unknown blessings and joys that your faith in Me will bring to you. I am your Father, I created you, and I know what is in store for you. You know Me, you know I created you, and you know that you have every reason to trust Me. There is no danger in your patience, for in your patience you can possess the truth in your

Patiently 89

soul and live it wisely.

To live wisely is to live patiently, submissively to Me, desiring only the things that reflect your spiritual progress in a life surrounded by spiritual values. Be a collector of truth, keep it close to you, and patiently use it. Let the Light that is found through your faithfulness surround you, and let it shine forth into the darkness of your environment. Be at peace, be patient, and love the life you live in peace and contentment. You are as safe as your lack of fear allows you to be, and the absence of your doubts insures the security of your spirit and soul.

I teach you patiently in the lesson today that you have no need to hurry, for your mind cannot easily grasp the value of patience in a world of time. The delusions of time teach you that time is short and death is certain. In your world you have a saying that the only sure things are death and taxes. But many of you pay no taxes, and many of you will never die. So what is certain? It is certain that you can live patiently, that you can receive the desires of your heart if your heart desires universal love and the eternal joy that follows, and that you can always be My child.

You were created to live in a world of time, and the lessons that are to be learned will be learned patiently or not at all. And you were also created to graduate beyond your world of time, and to move steadily and patiently into eternity, filled with joy and peace by your love and harmony shared by all Creation. This above all is your goal, and you will find it patiently or not at all. Time has been cruelly used against you by those who cause you to fear it and fight it, but you need not believe that time is your master.

For time is your ally if you work patiently, and it fights you only if you impatiently try to defeat it. Float along and rest from time to time, and when you walk against the currents of time, walk patiently and slowly. A sustained and steady effort in the right direction against the currents of time will get you to the goals you desire. So let your desires be developed in patience, sought in patience, and received patiently. The best things in life not only are free, but they are gained by patience. All things come to he who waits. Even in the greatness and perfection of universal love, be patient with yourself and all the things you love. That is My lesson today.

I am your Master, Teacher, and Friend.

> *Patience has always been hard for me to find and keep. The most enjoyable change these words have given me is the enjoyment of knowing God as an infinite source of peace and happiness within me. He had seemed so far away and so unapproachable for so long, and I had only thought of Him as a Father, not also as Light and Truth. Just now, three years after the writing began, I am able to feel very comfortable while doing nothing and being at peace with all Creation. That is an inexpressibly wonderful feeling to one who had learned only to keep busy and push continually ahead.*
>
> *One of the greatest values I find in patience is that of avoiding anger. Frustration goes closely with impatience, while anger very often follows frustration. The second most valuable lesson I have learned from this experience is that of the illusionary nature of time. As time becomes less important to me, patience is much more easily found and kept. Knowing that time is an illusion which will sometime be replaced by Eternity, I also know that patience denies the impact of the illusions of time upon me.*
>
> *The following lesson, which is on the subject of peace, is a natural sequence to the subject of patience. The best things of life are, indeed, free.*

"Some of the beliefs of every religion known to humankind are confirmed in these lessons, and possibly some are denied as well, for time has had a way of distorting Truth on Earth. But the subjects of love, peace, kindness, gentleness, and goodwill are clearly the message, and these lessons are found in every belief of humankind, although often restricted by the human desire to judge others."

From Book 25 —<u>A New Way of Living</u>

Chapter 16 From Book 15 —<u>A New Way of Living</u>

Peace

Let all things be done in peace today, and let your heart and its desires respond to your spirit of love and goodwill. Keep the purity of your mind, allowing no perversions or diversions from the will of your Universal Father of Creation. As a symbolic Father I have created you, and I am also your Mother, your Friend, your Comforter, your Guide, your Lover, and your Brother. I am symbolic of all the best qualities of all of these, and I am unbounded by any restrictions or limitations to My Power and My Truth and Light.

So peace be with you, and may you keep it in your heart today. I have no battles that can be effectively fought and won by a warlike spirit. The toys of the Generals of the armies of the world are futile and ineffective in the battles that are before you, for the battles that face you are the battles against the perversions of the minds of men. They are the battles against the illusions, deceptions, lies, and misunderstandings of generations before you. They are battles against bigotry, prejudice, narrowness of mind, hypocrisy, pompousness, pretense, and all the fruits of vanity. But they are against no soul, no spirit, no embodied being, and nothing of Creation at all.

The battle is against mirages and dreams and illusions that are false, and they can be fought in peace without fear of harming any soul at all. If you love one another as I have commanded you, there is no place nor time, in any moment, where peace cannot be found and enjoyed in your heart. The evil spirits that can be cast out can be cast out in love. They are much more vulnerable to a loving, but stern and positive, command to depart from you. They are more afraid of the power of love than of any threat that uses their own weapons against them, for love is light, and they cannot endure in its presence.

If you cannot fight in peace, do not fight at all, for by so doing you will bring yourself down to the level of the enemy, and his weapons will destroy your goal. When anger wells up within you, when frustration and resentment builds up within your mind and spirit, or when you feel the stirring of deep desires for revenge and the use of the forces of the products of time, you have immediately lost the battle. The battle that you cannot win in peace and love cannot be won at all in your fleshly environment.

Be as wise as serpents and as gentle as doves, knowing when to turn away into the seclusion of spiritual safety, and when to stand your ground, with a heart of love and a mind for peaceful and stable joy. You cannot win while you are in the throes of anger, and you will not succeed in any of the battles against darkness when you have lost the Light that is within you. Your ego cannot allow you to succeed, and its tempting thoughts will cause you to descend to the depths of the things against which you fight. And there you will be conquered, and darkness will be the victor for a time.

There is much to be done in these last days, and many of you who have been reading these words will go forth to help the bewildered and suffering masses of misguided and deluded souls around you. You will be the Florence Nightingales of the twentieth century, and you will be numbered by the tens of thousands. You will go into the areas of natural disasters, and you will provide the wonderful support of spiritual faith and physical aid from a heart of peace and love. Your sublime faith and confidence in the rightness of the things that are happening will be a beacon of Light to the faithful, and it will be a rock of strength to those who are weakened and discouraged by the hopelessness of their condition.

As you move into the things that are ahead, you will find many things to do, and will be well guided. Your thoughts will be filled with the input of My Spirit, through the higher self that is within you, and words will not be needed as you step forward to bind the wounds and tend the spirits of the injured and homeless ones. If you have universal love, you will find much to do, and you will judge no one while you attend to their needs with the blessings that have been given to you. You will create joy and peace wherever you go, and your heart of love will stand out and radiate the peace of your spirit to all within your environment.

Now, My child, is the time for you to gain the strength that you will need, and you can gain it from daily communion with My Spirit, for I live within you. Now is the time to learn to be receptive to the thoughts and guidance that I can give you from within, and now is the time to prepare yourself for the things that are to come. Your life will turn away from its humdrum habits and daily routines, and each day will be a new and unforeseen challenge to your faith and love.

And you will meet that challenge as long as you keep peace within your heart. Let the turmoil and confusion rage around you, and let the terrible catastrophes of nature, which are compounded by the foolishness of men, be of little importance to you. Know well that the things of death lead to the things of life, and that the things of darkness will surely and certainly give way to the things of light. Know that the power of love will always prevail, and that its universal energy will lift the saints out of destruction and into safety when the time comes.

Be aware that you have a destiny to fulfill, and see that your spirit of love and peace keeps you ready when that time comes. Be less concerned today about the nature of your destiny than about the nature of your readiness to meet it. Your newfound and increased universal love will give you a peace that passes understanding, and that requires no knowledge of your destiny at all. Your destiny will appear to you naturally when your heart is right, and a heart that is right is a heart of peace and love.

Guard jealously against the perversions of your mind each day. Learn each day to more quickly recognize the symptoms of vanity, materialism, greed, lust, and anger in yourself, and see that you spend no time at all looking for those things in the minds and hearts of others. Love the workers of darkness as much as you love yourself or Me, for they are your brothers, who will be saved in spirit at the final conclusion of your world of time. This destruction and cleansing will fail to save many of them, but with an eye of faith and a heart of peace and love, you can look ahead to a later dispensation of time that will save them.

Let this day be a challenge to you, for you all have perversions within your own minds to fight. Who among you, who read these words, have not been angry within the last week, or have not had at least a tinge of vanity, materialism, lust, or greed within your mind? Purify yourself, and especially learn to be on guard. You cannot prevent these things from tempting you from time to time, and you must suffer them as they try you in your fleshly life. But you can learn more quickly each day to see their influence upon your thoughts and your behavior, and you can learn to quickly cast them out.

I teach you today in this lesson to find peace within, for it is the forerunner of joy and happiness, and it is the source of your safety in the power of love. Your mind does not function clearly in the absence of peace, and your spirit cannot receive the tender guidance that My Spirit gives you from within, unless you have first found the sweet peace that is the gift of My love. And your peace is in no way vulnerable to your environment, but is instead vulnerable to the perversions of your mind and the weakness of your faith.

You may find many excuses for lack of peace within your mind or heart, but there are no reasons at all for your lack of it. You have the power, as My Divinely created child, to find and keep peace within your mind and heart under any conceivable conditions. You can be as immune from the turmoil around you as Jesus taught you to be when He hung upon the Cross of Calvary. When He said, 'Father, forgive them, for they know not what they do,' He was at peace with all things, and was filled with universal love.

His example is in no way beyond your ability to follow, and you will find no greater excuse for losing your peace of mind and heart than He found in that time of His embodiment. Many martyrs have died at peace under such circumstances, with a smile on their faces and a heart of love for those who persecuted them. Your test will come before the end of time, and you will be ready if you choose to learn and follow My lessons today. But if you wait complacently until the challenge is upon you, it might be too late for you to learn these lessons.

Start today, building upon the lessons you learned yesterday and in days past, and take another step toward the perfection of your soul and spirit with a heart of love. And take that step in peace, soothing your mind and heart with the strength that lies forever within you. Take the Spirit of love that is Mine within you, and keep it with you as a shield and a buckler, so that it gives you eternal security under any conditions. Fear not for the life of your body, and if you must fear anything at all, fear to lose the peace that comes to you from your faith in Me, and from your love and goodwill for all Creation.

Last Days?

I am yours and you are Mine, and the power of all the universes is at your disposal. Why should you not have peace? You know the way to victory, to invincibility, to the power of Creation, to the security of the ages, and to the eternal joy that is in store for all My children. The judgment day will cast some into the future cauldrons of the worlds of time, where they will be tested again and purified for later salvation. It will cast others into the joys of the Seventh Day, with a thousand years of perfect peace and love among completed souls, who will be filled with joy immeasurable. Where will you be? Your peace of mind and heart today will be a step in the direction of your eternal joy.

> *The joy of discovering the gift of Cosmic Telepathy was, at first, marred by my wish to reveal the future. In discussion with friends, I have found that there is a tendency for many of us to wish to know the future in order to make life more comfortable, replace faith with knowledge, and prepare ourselves for the changing events of time. I used the gift to ask many personal questions. Many of the answers came with the suggestion that they remain confidential to me and my wife.*
>
> *As a parent, I have had no qualms about limiting the privileges of my children until they gain enough wisdom to handle more freedom. I would not give my children a large sum of money and tell them to use their own judgment in a candy store. I give my children the freedom to spend all the money they make, but not all I might make. Neither do I believe a God who loves me will help me to know the future sufficiently to give me more knowledge of it than I can handle without depending on my faith.*

"So live that you avoid judgment, show mercy, and have compassion for the billions of souls of your world that are engaged in strife. They have lost their peace and are endangering yours. Love one another, and start with the ones closest to you, for if you cannot love your neighbor, whom you have seen, how can you love Me, Whom you have not seen?"

From Book 4 — <u>A New Way of Living</u>

Chapter 17

From Book 16 — <u>A New Way of Living</u>

Extremes

The Earth is dying, and the time of the dispensation of the Sixth Day is coming to an end. In these times you will see extremes of weather, as I have told you before. You will see records broken in every aspect of your weather from time to time, and people will marvel at the changes in the Earth as she dies. The clock is running down, and it will start again in a renewed and revived Earth. The new Earth will be as a child, blessed with all the perfection of a new body and a new spirit, and blessed with a population of souls who inhabit it.

Those souls will be invariably selected by their ability to have and enjoy universal love, and you who wish will be among them.

But today the lessons are of the extremes of the things to come in your last days, and what they will do to your life on Earth. There are many more extremes beyond those of weather, for the dying Earth will affect the spirits and bodies of many of her inhabitants. Her death will invoke sympathetic reactions from those who are immersed in time and its products, and who are deluded by time's illusions.

Each individual will encounter extremes of his own. Some spirits will revive and renew with life and light, as the spirits of you who are interested and involved in the lessons of these words are doing. They will find a newness of light and life, causing them to radiate with joy. Their days will be blessed with the wonderment of the things that are coming upon the Earth, and they will be glad to be alive in these last days.

For those who see the perfection and good in the death of the Earth that precedes her rebirth will never fear any kind of death at all. Their life will become more joyful, because death will have lost its power of fear and mystery over them, and each day will be more precious. For such as you, extremes of joy beyond anything you can remember will come to you. And you who believe in the power of the light will also have extremes of peace and love, of kindness and gentleness, of mercy and compassion, and of harmony and goodwill.

For when you overcome the power of death by your light, death's power will seem a brief illusion to you, and will seem as useless and pointless to you as time. It will not engage your thoughts, incite your fears, or cloud your joy, for you will know it as a friend in the harvest of the Earth, removing the old and heralding the new in its merciful presence upon the Earth.

Death is not an extreme example of anything unusual at all, for even the death of the Earth, although rare by the standards of time you have known, is commonplace throughout the universes in the timetables of the ages. It happens often in the billions of planets, for it is necessary as a part of the cycles of life. But the extremes which I mention to you today are the extremes that precede the death of the Earth.

All things in the last times will conspire to make the souls on Earth magnify what they are. Those who are asleep will sleep on, those who are awake will awaken and revive more fully, those who are apathetic will become more so, those who are prejudiced will only seek more things to judge, those who are cruel will become more cruel, those who are loving will show and feel more love, and so on.

The times will provoke extremes of action and of beliefs, for the records that are constantly being broken will cause people to stratify socially, and to band together in groups with like beliefs. They will try to explain everything by the reasoning of time, and in so doing they will reinforce one another's beliefs. This reinforcement will serve to magnify and strengthen their delusions as much or more than it will reveal the truth. So those with whom you spend your time and share your beliefs in the last days will affect your own beliefs greatly.

And as the Earth dies, the ecologically concerned people who have not seen the natural purposes of her death will fight it with anger and with fear, trying to save the Earth when she is already doomed to destruction. The point of no return was passed over a year ago, and the wheels of destruction are now in motion. Temperatures are rising, in some areas of the Earth, to points they have never been, and for every recorded phenomenon of nature that is regularly monitored, there are hundreds that pass by unseen.

The Earth is wobbling and reeling on her axis, like a drunken man who can barely stand and walk. The winds of the skies are moving and changing continually, and every one of the many ways in which the Earth is being polluted adds to the problem. The straw that broke the camel's back is awaiting the many straws that increase the burdens upon the life systems of the Earth. The rain forests are being depleted, and are failing to convert carbon dioxide to life-giving oxygen, the fluorocarbons are piercing the ozone layer with hundreds of thousands more tons of gases each day, and the temperatures of the surface of the Earth are rising steadily.

And only to a spirit filled with universal love and goodwill are these events natural, and even welcome. For the extremes that will destroy the Earth are natural and necessary steps to her renewal. But the souls who do not see the reality of what is happening will stay in the world of time, and will be continually deluded by the orderly justice and mercy of all the extremes that are around them.

For to Me there are no mistakes, no accidents, and nothing done without love and mercy for all concerned. I use extremes when extremes are necessary and useful. Childbirth is an extreme stress to the body of the mother and of the child, but its labor and pain is followed by joy for all. Sickness precedes health, injury precedes healing, hunger precedes its satisfaction, and in many ways you are used to extremes that lead to a logical end.

And the extremes of the last days of the Earth will be no exception to those of you who know the meaning of the many Scriptural prophecies that have foretold it. You have learned by now that the New Testament was written in the last days, and that many of the things written in the Old Bible were also written in the very last part of the Sixth Day. They who lived only three or four thousand years ago also saw some of the extremes of the last days, and by the gift of the guidance of My Spirit within them, they recognized the meaning of what they saw. They reported correctly the purposes and the outcome of the extremes they saw, for they knew, as well as you, that to Me a thousand years is but a day.

So when you see extremes of changes around you, whether physical, psychological, social, political, natural, or emotional, take heed. These are the signs of the last days, and as the last days become the last moments, extremes will continue to surround you with their message of hope for your deliverance. They are harbingers of the springtime of the ages of the Earth, for winter is almost past, and summer is near in the timetable of the ages.

And as you live today, be happy that the time for extremes is here, for you will be blessed by many improvements in some extremes of your own. You may set records of your own in the amount of faith you have, the amount of joy, the amount of peace, the amount of goodwill, the amount of love, and the amount of forgiveness and mercy that is within you. You are light, and there is an unlimited supply of it around you and within you. Set it free, and let it shine to the greatest extremes of which you are capable, and let it become a testimony of your own knowledge and joy in the truth that will set you free at last.

For the unique role which your destiny allows you to play in the extremes of the ends of this age of the Earth is a joyful role. You may choose it freely for your extreme enjoyment, and for the extreme and lasting affect you may have on the joys of those around you. Be aware of more of the things that are good, and lasting, and eternal in their values today, and know that the records of which you read and hear are confirmation of what you have believed and learned from My lessons.

Let every newscast or rumor that flows around you be a confirmation that the last days are near. Be happy for it, and give Me the praise, for the death of the Earth is the outcome of the success of her life and the fulfillment of her future. She has served her purpose well, and her responses to the things she has suffered from ignorant men will cure the problem, and will provide a new opportunity for future generations of her inhabitants. All is well, My child, and when you see the extremes of the last days, enjoy them for the deliverance they bring to all who are ready.

And anyone who has the desire and the faith to be ready will be so. There are no respecters of persons among the spirits who will deliver you, and no race or culture of men upon the Earth will fail to be represented among those happy souls who have found the key to eternal joy. The nature of the last days will bring many extremes, including the shortening of time and the hastening of the days of the end. You cannot fail to survive if your heart is right and if you desire to do so.

Be vibrantly aware of the extremes as you spend these last

days, and rejoice in the time of your deliverance. Death is never final, for all things created are destined to eternal life when they fit into their roles with harmony. I have created an orderly Creation, and nothing is wrong at all. Be joyful, I say, as you see the extremes of the last days around you, for all is well for all things.

> *The priorities which lead to joy are clearly defined. First, faith is needed, Love and compassion are very closely related to faith, for if we can believe in a God who loves us unconditionally, we will find more perfect love for ourselves and one another, which allows the greatest of compassion, as well. The more unconditionally I love, the more easily I can feel loved unconditionally by God and by others. And the more this joyful feeling continues, the more compassion I have for my enemies and for strangers.*
>
> *But joy is weak and seldom found while fearing death and suffering. My father died before this writing began. My mother died during the time of the writing. It was so much easier for me to deal with the death of those I loved after I realized that death and dying are totally illusionary, and that life is real and eternal.*

"And by man's lack of love for the Earth, which is the mother of his physical body, he has guaranteed also the extinction of most of his kind from your world of today. By not submitting to the rights of the animals and plants, the air and the water, the rivers and seas, the minerals and the very soil of the Earth, people have caused the Earth to destroy and renew herself, casting also her selfish inhabitants into physical destruction."

From Book 8 — <u>A New Way of Living</u>

Chapter 18

From Book 17 — <u>A New Way of Living</u>

Water

Water is the blood of the living organism that is called the Earth. The water of the oceans, rivers, lakes, and underground veins of water in the Earth is the substance of her life. The life of humans is in their blood, and the life of the Earth is in her blood, which is water. The organism flourishes when the water is pure and plentiful, and it nourishes the plants of her surface, the air, and the animals and people who inhabit her.

Water is the universal solvent on the Earth, and the oxygen that is found in its chemical composition is also a key part of the air. Without oxygen, there could be no life, and neither could the Earth cleanse herself by the decomposition of materials that have lived and are dead. It is a complex ecological system, and the system that is called the Earth is normally in an efficient chemical balance.

But that balance has been destroyed by the Earth's pollution by men and their industries. The resources of the Earth have been raped and pillaged by men, and as they are consumed, the ecological balance of the Earth is destroyed. Many have said that your weather will return to normal, for there have never been two dry years in a row. But heat waves continue, rainfall is below normal, and the Earth is reeling from the relentless attacks by men against her systems.

The quantity and the quality of water is far below normal, and the acid rain that comes in skimpy amounts indicates air that is filled with pollution. The fish cannot live in some of the lakes and streams, for they are also destroyed by the chemicals and the pollution in their natural home. In more ways than you can imagine, Creation is united. Nothing that is harmed or suffers remains an island isolated from other things. All damage and disharmony is reflected to the other parts of the ecology.

Cause and effect causes a chain of action and reaction that shakes the foundations of the Earth, and the things that are now deteriorating will cause other failures in the system to increase by geometric proportions. Open-minded and unprejudiced scientists are concerned, but the world economy is so committed to the continued consumption of the Earth's resources that many experts can be found to testify against moderation.

Since water is the blood of the Earth, and since it therefore is the life of the Earth, water is the key to her life or death. Her death is already under way, and the water will continue to reflect her agony. Watch the quantity and the quality of it, and you will see that the good health of the Earth has gone. And be prepared to save water, boil it, and limit your uses for it. It will become more critical than the air you breathe during your survival in the last days of the Earth.

There are places in the Earth where water is still relatively pure. But these places are few, and they are thinly populated. They are not centers of manufacturing or agriculture, and they are not commercialized. They are places of safety, and they will allow you to survive for a little longer.

It will be hard for you to realize that an organism as large as the Earth can die. It will be awesome to see it happening, and it will be a shock to many when something as much taken for granted as water will fail them. But let it be no shock to you, for I am allowing those of you who have sufficient faith to be prepared. You may be mentally prepared to accept the things that are to happen, and when it is time, you will be warned of the events that you need to realize.

But you can learn these things from your higher wisdom, for the guidance each of you needs is as unique as you are. Each time and place needs different adjustments, and each of you are directly in touch with My Spirit within you. Fear not, and let your doubts die each day, for there is time and there are ways for each of you who wish to be uplifted and spared from the death of the Earth and her inhabitants.

Communicate with Me, for you do not need these words to know that the world is in deep agony. And you do not need these words to tell you what each of you must do. Eagles do not flock, and each of them does very well in the isolation of the skies and the mountain tops. They protect their own, they defend their nest, they find their food, and their life is made peaceful by the natural environment of their choice.

As the water of the Earth fails, seek the environment that seems best for you, and trust the instincts of your soul. Look for the way that is best for each of you, and trust yourself more than any other soul. Trust in the faith you have in Me, and trust My Spirit that is within you. You and I are one, and the Light that is Mine is also available to you. Watch the times around you with keen awareness, and watch the many changes in the availability and quality of water.

Heat is also fluctuating more widely. The fevers and chills of the Earth will continue, and as your body sometimes fails to sweat when you have a fever, so does the moisture migration of the Earth become erratic and unpredictable. Lakes and rivers will become low or run dry, sea levels will fall, and records of temperature will continue to be broken at both the maximal and minimal levels. It is already happening, and these words are only to remind you that the things you are seeing today are natural symptoms of the death of the Earth.

Rejoice in the knowledge you have of the death of the Earth, for by your faith you will be released from the pain of it, and will be blessed by your part in the Earth's renewal. You have everything to gain and little to lose by the death of the Earth, for you who are faithful are the purpose of the fulfillment of prophecy. And those who have not the faith to cope with these events will also be blessed by an end to their agony in a dying ecology.

I have had lessons for you on the subject of heat, of systems, and of Light. All things work together for good to them who love Me, and there are no accidents, no tragedies, and no catastrophes known by man, except for those allowed for a useful purpose. In the overall universal love I bear for you there is mercy and kindness, and My love allows no one to be lost forever. Time will remain available to the unenlightened, and each of them will find their way to Me when they choose.

But as the blood of the Earth, which is water, ceases to function and to sustain her life, prepare to go alone in the direction of your destiny. Take no burden of responsibility with you for any soul, not even for your mate, children, parents, or beloved friends. Be gentle and open with all, and give an answer to anyone who asks for an explanation of the hope that lies within you. But avoid the burden of teaching those who are not interested, or those with a closed and defensive mind and attitude toward the changes that are around them.

For as times get worse, some will soften and open their hearts, while others will harden them, become angry and resentful, and turn away from the truth of their being. You can do nothing for them except to love them, pray for them, and let them go their way. The last days will be lonely times, and each of you will be guided from within, not from outside yourself. Seek the guidance that is within you, and learn now to trust the instincts of your soul and the impulses of your own spirit.

If you can conquer the perversions of your mind, you can trust yourself, and you can be safely guided by your spirit within, for I will be with you. Turn toward Me when you are in trouble. I am not to be feared, for I love you perfectly and eternally. You are Mine, and I know you well, as a Mother knows her child and cares for it. Watch the developments of the last days, and you will see the ocean shores contaminated, the shorelines reshaped, the rivers redirected or dried up, and millions of people wishing for more water of better quality.

But for each of you there is a way, and none who keep in touch with My Spirit within them will be lost from the joys of the Seventh Day of a thousand years. This has been promised in many Scriptures of many beliefs, and all of them are from the same Source, which is Me. Be confident in your escape, and learn to watch with interest the ways in which the blood of the Earth reacts to her pain. She is strong, she is blessed, and she will survive. She loves you, and she will spare any of you who love her as a part of your universal love for all things and all beings.

It is a wonderful time in which to live, and many of you who read these words have chosen to live now in a body of flesh when you could have taken an easier way. The ways of the Earth are hard at best, for time is a cruel taskmaster. And in these last days, many challenges will come to you. But you are equal to them, for you have the laws of the universes of Creation working for you. You have only to keep in close touch with Me daily, and to find a renewed and strengthened spiritual life of your own each day.

Time will attack your resolve, and your persistence will be tested, but you can handle it. The blood of the Earth will fail, and she will die, but as the water of her life ebbs and fails, she will find a new life and rebirth that you shall share in joy with her. She knows this now, and the travail of her rebirth is a time of joy for her. I am her Master and yours, and you can trust Me for all that you need.

> *So many of these lessons, although clear and understandable to me, do not immediately change my attitude. A distorted attitude, in my case, is not easily given up. A very wise and introspective friend and business partner once told me that he did not believe a person could ever completely overcome the prejudices learned in childhood. He was raised as a Mennonite in eastern Indiana, and later became a Dean in a large university. He was very successful in responsible positions of authority.*
>
> *But as his career developed, he found the same tendency to be influenced by his earlier beliefs as I have. An attitude is so hard to change, and so important, for the truth I receive from within can be so easily influenced by unconscious beliefs in other truths from other times. At first I believed I was receiving words for these lessons, not thoughts. But later I was taught that God uses thoughts, not words, to communicate with us through Cosmic Telepathy.*

"Knowing this, you may also know that nothing you can do in time will, in reality, be significant. The most you can do is to pray, meditate, gain faith, and thereby affect your attitude. Love, not judgment and logic, is the way you can prepare in this moment. The act of preparation for reality is scarcely an act. It is more of a belief system, a system of love and goodwill. If you could know the trends and their outcomes in the things of time, even for you, there would be nothing physically effective for you to do about it. Your attitude of love and your desire for the good things We have described to you are enough."

From Book 36 — <u>A New Way of Living</u>

Chapter 19

From Book 18 — <u>A New Way of Living</u>

Storms

Yesterday there was a storm, and the rains descended almost continually from dawn to dusk. Today the sun shines, the skies are blue, the wisps of wind clouds hover high above the mountains, and the life of the valley continues for another day. The moments of rain yesterday were broken by a pause, and for a short while I gave the beauty of another rainbow to those whose eyes looked upward. Shelter from the storm made it enjoyable for some, and exposure to it made it a problem for others.

There are few days and months left upon your Earth, for the death, cleansing, and renewal of her hospitable body is soon to come upon you. In that stormy death of the Earth there will be shelter for those who seek it by faith, and problems for all the rest. No soul who lives in a body of flesh upon the Earth will miss the chance to escape the storm, and none who are among you will perish, in body or in spirit, if your heart is right.

I have told you that a heart of kindness, goodwill, and universal love is a righteous heart, and that those who honor Me by assuming My qualities of love and mercy will come to no harm at all. Yesterday's storm was a blessing to the thirsting plants and animals in the heat of the day, and it nourished those who prepared for it and found shelter. The stormy end of the Earth will be similar, for it will be a blessed event for some, even in the last days of destruction and sorrow.

Before each storm there is a warning. The clouds darken, the winds blow, the skies fill with whirling winds, and lightning and thunder fill the skies. The prudent soul looks at open windows and doors, closes them, finds shelter, and prepares to receive the torrents that are to come. Those on ships secure the decks, change their course, and prepare in their own way for the winds and waves that accompany the storm. If lightning surrounds them, they seek places which will not attract it.

Your life has been filled with storms and sunshine. You have had much experience in the ways of foreseeing the storms, preparing for them, and riding them out. And you have learned that suffering from storms is avoidable, and that days of peace and quiet follow after the chaos and turmoil that the storms bring to you. You who live in the world of time are veterans of storms upon the Earth, and the final storm that takes the life of the Earth will be no different except in magnitude.

Even at the last moment of the Earth there will be peace and love in the hearts of some, and there will be shelter in sufficient quantity for those who have prepared. <u>A New Way of Living</u> gives you the wisdom and courage to prepare for the storm, and if you are prepared it is not important for you to know when the storm will come.

It is a joy to prudently and calmly prepare for a storm, and it is a pleasure for you to watch it come across the mountains in your direction when you are ready for it. There is no need for fear in one who is prepared, and no need for suffering if the preparation has been taken in time. Build the foundations of your life in the sunshine of peace and love, and build them strongly before the storm besets you.

Repair the roof and fix the windows before the storm, for it will not be a fit place to work when that dark and awful day of the last storm comes upon you. I help the souls who help themselves, and now is the time for you to prepare the best you can. The work is not difficult, and the task is well within your powers. And as I have told you in many lessons, the time of your preparation is governed entirely by your free choice. I have not restricted you in any way, and you need not know the time of the storm if you have prepared in the sunshine.

I am your patient and loving Father, and you are My beloved child. My Spirit within you is your Comforter, and I have told you how to keep Me in close contact with your own spirit. Today the subject of the lesson is of storms, for there will be many before the final one in this era of the life of your Earth. They will become more and more violent and chaotic, and they will be closer and closer together.

If your faith is sufficient for the trials and troubles that surround you today, strengthen it by the exercise of your universal love and goodwill, for tomorrow more things might be required of you. You live to grow spiritually, not to stagnate in the traps and pitfalls of uncertain and elusive time. If you grow, your strength increases, and the strength you find today will be needed to meet the challenge for shelter from the storms of tomorrow.

My way is easy and My burden is light, so there is no possibility that you might be unable to prepare today. But if you wait for tomorrow, thinking that the time of the storm is some distance into the future, you will not be ready. Remember what I have taught you, and use the time and your freedom to choose from within it. Use your freedom wisely to choose the time of action, and the blessed destiny that is yours can come quickly and safely to you.

In love I teach you, in kindness I warn you, and in freedom I allow you to listen and heed, or to disregard Me, according to your choice. You can question the words of My lessons, the motives of the writer, the accuracy of your interpretation, or your ability to learn from Me as much as you like. But you will find no excuse for failure, and no barrier to success at all. Take these words and study them, and read some of them again and again according to the impulses of your higher wisdom. When you do, you will find that I have taught you nothing that would harm you, even if the storm should never come.

Even if the Earth survives for another ten million years, (which she most certainly will not in her present life), your joy of living upon her would increase immeasurably by your learning and practice of the lessons of <u>A New Way of Living</u>. By these lessons I release much of the hidden power and beauty of the thousands of Holy Scriptures written for dwellers of the Earth. And I release the wisdom of your soul that has been hidden for so long behind the illusions of time and the deceptiveness of poorly written and misconstrued history.

It is time for you to choose an end to your prejudice and doubt if you will, and time to cast off the shackles of fear if you are ready. This is your life, and this is your choice. The time is up to you, for you are the one who has chosen time and its challenges. I have none of it, and I have allowed it for you only when you are ready, and as long as you choose to accept it and its ways and influences upon you.

Eternity is yours as much as time, and the life of your body is as uncertain as it can be. You may have Eternity when you are done with time, and your destiny will take you straight to the joys of Eternity after you have solved the puzzles that time has given you. The storms will always be a part of time, and time's nature of marking the passing events will continue to mark the clouds, the rain, the wind, the lightning, the thunder, and finally the blue sky, again and again.

This is your challenge today, to see and realize that events and time go hand in hand, and that perfect joy brings Eternity to you. And when Eternity is yours, there will be no future, past, or present that changes continually, and no storms will be marked by time nor needed for you. The lessons of time will finally be learned, and it will pass away into the glorious ecstacy of a joyful existence of living glory and light for you forever.

And even beyond forever you will avoid all storms, all sorrow, all sadness, all fear, all doubt, and all pain. For these things are as unthinkable and unimaginable to those who are in Eternity as Eternity is unimaginable to you. You cannot really believe completely, except by faith, that there could be a life for you without time and without storms. Nothing in your memory or experience has prepared you for the absence of storms, and nothing will, so long as you live in a world of time.

So today is the day for you to choose. If you will prepare for the storms of the final days, you will begin now, and it will be easy for you. My way is easy and My burden is light, but the way must be taken and the burden must be carried. And if you take My way and carry My burden, you will do so by choice, and your motivation will successfully guide you by love, not by fear. I do not try to scare you into success, for I do not ever see you as a failure. I only see you as a success that is waiting to happen when you choose.

Live your life in peace and love today, find all the pleasure and joy in goodwill that you can, and see all the beauty around you that is there to be found. Think on the things of truth and light, and on the things of joy and peace and love. Forget the negative considerations of others which will constantly assail you today, and let your mind be filled with the positive inspiration of your spiritual reality. Avoid the perversions of your mind, and prepare with the deepest of confidence for the storms that are to come upon the Earth.

If you prepare for the storms too quickly and too well, the price will only be more joy, more happiness, more goodwill, more love for all things, and complete safety from the storms, whenever they come. But if you prepare too little or too late, the price will be fear, doubt, pain, misery, confusion, panic, and sorrow. The choice is yours, and I am the Creator, Who made you and set you free in time to find your destiny. Will you follow Me today?

I have been advised to save every lesson, exactly as written, and have done so. As written, the typical lesson has an average of two or three typographical errors which are caught by the spell-checker in the word processor I use. It will also have several sentences ending in conditional clauses, which are easily understood, but harder to read. And there are common misspellings of words, such as 'an' for 'and', or 'to' for 'too'. There is rarely, however, any possibility of misunderstanding the meaning.

After I realized I was dealing with thoughts instead of words I took the liberty of editing sentences for easier reading. I have also had the help of some very wonderful people in doing this. In other words, I had more freedom that I first realized, and learned to use that freedom to make the Books easier to read and therefore more useful to the reader.

"So a lifetime of service, or millions of lifetimes, is not a factor. You are not paid by Me, but you are rewarded by Me, and My reward is for the love you bear and the Light you reveal to the world around you. It is not connected with materialism, measured by vanity, and acquired by anger, or lust, or greed. It is in the absence of anything but love that your love is revealed.

From Book 11 — <u>A New Way of Living</u>

Chapter 20 From Book 19 — <u>A New Way of Living</u>

Existence

What is life? Life is existence. It is being. It is consciousness. It is awareness. It is perception. It is permanence. It is entity. Life is also continuance if it refers to the flesh of people and of animals. The existence of a mankind is marked on Earth by physical consciousness, physical awareness, physical perception, and physical being. The existence of the spirit of a person is marked by spiritual consciousness, spiritual awareness, spiritual perception, and spiritual being.

The existence of the soul of a person is marked by the Akashic records that reveal an endless circle of life. Although the body of human has a time of birth and a time of death, being entirely of time, the spirit of a human has many deaths and rebirths as it drifts or is guided by its free will to and from affinity with My Spirit. The existence of the soul of a human, however, is the more stable and constant part, for it is eternally living in loose contact with the spirit of that same soul. The spirit is nourished by the Truth of My Spirit, and the soul of that spirit is nourished by its own spirit. The soul is perfected by its spirit's attainment of Eternity.

Eternity is a place, not a time, and it has no connection at all with time. When you invoke the Light, you invoke it in your body, spirit, and soul. At that time of walking in the Light, there is no death within or around you, for Light is life, and life is not of death at all. Existence at that time is complete, and your awareness, perception, and consciousness extends to the fullest needs of your physical body, unique spirit, and hungry soul.

For when your existence is only physical, your spirit is dead and your soul is starving. Your soul is fed through the life line of the silver cord that links your time with timelessness. For the existence of the soul is forever in the realms of Eternity, and the silver cord reaches across the barrier of Eternity into the fiction of space and time to find its nourishment from your unique and beloved spirit. And when your spirit lives in the joy of its union with Mine, your soul also lives in a deeper and more vibrant awareness, growing toward the stature of perfection that makes it an active member of Eternity and a living crescendo of harmony and love.

So the quality of your existence depends upon the quality of the life of your spirit. Your spirit can be strong or weak, dead or alive for a time, and active or passive. It is controlled by your free will, and you are responsible for the existence and the condition of your spirit. It is given to you to be used or abused according to your free will, and the quality of your joy today answers the question of the status of your condition. By your joy of life or lack of it you may easily measure the condition of your spirit at any time, for your joy is the barometer of your spiritual existence.

And since spiritual joy is the deepest of spiritual consciousness, spiritual awareness, spiritual perception, and spiritual being, it follows that the life of both your body and your soul is also enhanced by your happiest spiritual condition. This is why I have told you often that your spirit is the center of your reality. It is where the action is, and it is where the nourishment of your soul and the best of your physical life is gathered and fostered.

Since life and Light are synonymous, being the center of all Existence and of all the Energy of Creation, and being the Source of the Power of Universal Love, it follows that life is found by walking in the Light. Life is existence, and the study of life is the study of many circles that come back to the same place. For Creation is an endless chain of many interwoven links, as symbolic of its Existence as the wedding ring of man, which is without beginning and without end. There are countless examples of these links in the products of time, in the world of the spirit, and of all Creation.

I will give you some examples of the endless eternal chain of many links. The Earth is linked to the sun by a circular and endless orbit. At the same time the Earth is linked to the moon by an orbit that is also circular. And at the same time, the other planets of the sun have their own orbits, which intricately and logically pass through the circles of many other orbits. Since these orbits are based on the illusions of time, they are not eternal, but they are examples of a life in time. They exist while time exists.

Another example is the circles that link the electrons of an atom in their orbits around the nucleus. This simple building block of nature in the illusions of time is also a chain of endless circles that are interwoven beautifully. There is much beauty in all the intricate and endless circles in the solid geometry of Creation. All is symmetry and order, and many scientists have chosen their field because they love so much the beauty of Creation. Beneath the surface of the beauty in the simple things of nature, many endless circles of Creation are found.

Another example of the Eternal Chain of Circles is the genetic ladder of the living things on Earth. To see it goes beyond the power of the most powerful microscopes, but even in the viruses and sub-micro-organisms on Earth there are many examples of the chains of circles in Creation, interwoven in an existence that meets the needs of the functions of Creation. There are no accidental mutations, and the plagues of tribulation that are now coming upon the Earth in her last days are most orderly and complete.

So often the mind of a man or woman is deluded by ignorance into thinking there are accidents and mistakes in the developments of nature. But there are no mistakes, My child, and the ecology of the Earth will fight back with terrible retribution against the people who have abused her hospitality. You live upon the large and living organism of Earth, which has an existence of its own. It is no mean antagonist, and it fights for its physical life, just as you do when yours is threatened. Existence is precious to any life, and each life will maintain itself as long and effectively as it can.

There is life in the existence of every star and every planet, for each has a level of consciousness and perception of its role in the harmony of Creation that lies deep beneath its surface, even in the world of time and its products. And I have created each to perpetuate its existence instinctively, knowing that it was created to live and not to die. Even in the process of dying, the urge to reproduce is great, and the plant that is pruned grows even more vigorously to oppose the threat of the end of its existence.

In the natural order of things there is a time to be born and a time to die. The wise person fears not at all the death of the body, but is well aware that the life of the spirit is the central purpose of existence and the blessing of the soul as it is nourished by that spiritual life. These things are the center of the purpose of the words of <u>A New Way of Living</u>, and they are the beginning of a new and joyful life that turns your spirit toward Eternity.

With love I counsel you to look around you for the circles of

Existence 119

Creation and those things whose existence they reveal. There are many of these circles, interwoven into harmony and universal love by and for the needs of Creation. The symbolic circles of the Olympic Games are interlocking symbols of the endless pursuit of excellence for all the races of mankind on Earth, and the eternal flame that is also symbolized has much to do with the higher aspirations of the spirits of men.

For all good athletes learn that no amount of natural gifts and physical skills can take them to the pinnacle of competition unless they can also solve the mystery of spiritual excellence. Even if their spirit is not linked to Mine in the ways of eternal harmony and universal love, it must be controlled and guided toward the deepest of desires and commitments to the excellence they must reach to win it all. And the best of them often find that endless circle by which they are connected to all people and all Creation in the harmony of their existence.

The meaning of life is found when it is directed in the orbit of its link to the endless circles of Creation. The existence of your spirit, which is your source of all life, will also be linked in an endless circle with Mine when you find the joy of an eternal existence for your spirit and soul. Your body will then be left behind, having served its purpose by allowing you to join in the Body of Light as a Light-bearing part of that Body. Your existence will literally and truly take on a new dimension, and in fact many new dimensions, for it will receive none of the limitations of any dimension at all.

And when your existence is perfected, you will achieve the spiritual freedom to roam all the stars and planets of the universes, and the love and harmony you will find will be beyond all description or imagination. Your joy will be complete and eternal, and your awareness, consciousness, and perception will reach levels you have never known and cannot believe today. By the proper exercise of your free will today, you will take one more step through time, and will then be one step closer to that glorious existence beyond time.

Heed the words of My lessons, for I am God. I do not teach

you in order to waste your time, but to help you use it wisely for your own joy and the perfection of your own existence. Be aware of who and what you are today, My child, and sharpen that awareness into a greater and more joyful existence, for thus do the children of mankind become My children in truth and in joy. You have no limits to the attainment of joy and of a more perfect existence, and your free will is the key if you use it wisely.

> *During the past two years I have received many personal letters via Cosmic Telepathy and channeling. More and more, I have lost interest in the future and the way it is to come about, and I have also lost interest in making wiser financial decisions. It seems the less I care, the less I have to care about. I can give many examples of help that came to us in financial ways when we needed it. The assets we once had took away far more freedom than they gave us.*
>
> *In the process of retiring I found myself unable to keep certain promises, promises I never should have made. I was inclined to feel very guilty about this, and I spent many restless nights while learning to reconsider my values. If I had respected my own freedom, loved unconditionally and universally, and known God as I know Him now, I would have made many less financial commitments in the past.*
>
> *I would also have been a far more loving parent, and a happier person. I doubt if I would have worked as hard, made as much money, or controlled as many assets. But the past is past and the present is here. Thank God for the present!*

"Take Me with you in your joy, in your love, in your times of happiness, in the presence of beauty, in your times of peace within, in your times of compassion, in your times of contentment, and in your times of carefree gratitude for being alive on Earth in such a wonderful time. But remember, also, to take Me along when you are wretched, miserable, starving, naked, cold, and oppressed by things of Earth, which sometimes you can hardly bear. I Am with you always. Take Me along."

From Book 24 —<u>A New Way of Living</u>

Chapter 21   From Book 20 —<u>A New Way of Living</u>

Contentment

Contentment is gratification, peace, happiness, serenity, or satisfaction. How can you find it today? It is not a product of your environment of time, for the pressures of time take away serenity. It is not a product of anger or frustration, for these emotions take away peace. It is not a product of sadness or sorrow, for these take away happiness. It is not a product of spiritual poverty, for this takes away gratification and satisfaction. One thing, and one thing only, is needed for contentment. It is love.

It is love given or love received, for these are equal. When you were a child in your mother's arms, you were content. You had the nearest thing that time offers to the flesh of mankind for contentment. A mother's love is close to perfect love, and the joy of a mother is also close to perfect joy. This is contentment, and a new parent bridges the gap between time and Eternity for a little while.

But this example of contentment can be found again and again. You can find it today in any way that perfect love can be given or received, and it can be done. You see contentment in glimpses and moments, fleeting times in which your love is pure, your hopes are fully in control, and the perversions of your mind are gone for just a little while. When contentment comes to you today, My child, grasp it into your heart and take it out of your mind. It is a spiritual gift, and when you have found it, let it glimmer in your heart like a ray of sunshine and hope. It will not last for long, for it is not the way of the Earth, even at best.

And the Earth is not at its best today; there is too much negativity in the winds of time just now. But moments of contentment can still be with you, and, brief as they are, they are for you. It is wise for you who read this to expect just a little more contentment today, and I am teaching you how to find it. It is found in the moments of your goodwill and universal love. I am not able to teach you how to keep contentment on Earth, however, for it is as elusive and fleeting as a ray of sunshine. It is with you for awhile, but clouds and the passing of the day bring shadows quickly.

There is no time to waste in thinking of possessing contentment. Like so many of the joys of life in the last days of Earth, it comes to you only in moments, and is gone. You cannot photograph it, record it, preserve it, or prove it to anyone in any way. Contentment can be pretended for longer times than it can exist, and that is good. But it requires a continuation of the universal love that brings satisfaction, peace, happiness, gratification, and serenity. The supply of contentment on Earth is brief and scarce, because it is not of time. It is of the spirit, and time destroys the continuity of the good things of spiritual reality while you are on Earth.

Thus, you are taught by life on Earth that the good things are free, they expand with use, and they are readily available if your spirit is right. But they must be renewed, and they will not stay with you. They cannot be hoarded, preserved, put on the shelf for later use, or frozen for later consumption. The act of storing the good things and using them later is as impossible as the catching and storing of a ray of sunlight. But if you know where and how to find contentment, just for a moment, you are learning the lessons that time is intended to teach you. You are learning the lessons of Eternity. You are learning the lessons of life.

For life, lived in the spiritual reality of your Divine heritage, leads to joy. Joy is the sum of all happiness, contentment, gratification, serenity, and peace. It is yours to have, but not to hold, in an earthly environment of time. For how long have you ever been contented on Earth? Was it not as long as you were able to give and receive perfect love? And how long was that? Your effort should be more toward having than toward holding contentment, for its renewal is a worthy goal for your time of living today.

Contentment is not to be held, for it melts as time passes, and that bit of it is gone forever. Love, being the cohesive and attractive force that powers Creation, is consumed by time, and contentment is gone. Time requires a new supply of love continually, and the love that brought your contentment a moment ago will need to be replaced and newly given or received just now. You may learn from the past, but the successes of the past are gone with the passage of time. Contentment is a fleeting thing on Earth, and so is love. Like education, it leads to the knowledge of where to find love, but not how to keep it.

A little contentment is enough to stimulate your appetite for eternal joy. A little love, given or received, can bring contentment to you in small bits and pieces today. It will not last, but the supply is infinite. It is from Me, from Creation, and from within the Kingdom that is Mine within you. If you have a flowing fountain from which to drink, you need not think of water storage or of your future supply, You just need to remember where the fountain is, and you need to remember not to stray too far from the source of living water that quenches your later thirst.

Who does not like to be gratified, happy, serene, satisfied, and at peace? Who would not trade these joyful emotions for anything the Earth has to offer? Apparently many, for I see billions of souls today who have not tasted contentment for months or years of their current lifetime. Anything of anger, lust, greed, vanity, or materialism robs you quickly and completely of the ability to find that momentary glimpse of contentment today, *if any of these perversions are within you.*

But if you are completely surrounded by the perversions of the minds of others, you are not a victim of their problem. Although it is hard to be positive in a negative world, it is not impossible. You will find, however, that you are always a victim of the perversions of the minds of those around you, unless you are able to love their souls and spirits with the perfect and universal love which brings contentment to you.

Your love for the ones around you shields you entirely from their lack of serenity, peace, happiness, gratification, and satisfaction. This has nothing to do with their happiness; your contentment might even irritate some of those around you. But that is their problem, not yours, and if your positive love repels their negative emotions, let the discomfort they feel be escaped by their own change to a more positive way of living. You cannot help others to find contentment by feeling guilty or unworthy in having your own.

More and more, you will need to learn to walk alone in the last days of Earth. As the negative side of humans on Earth increases and expands, you will find it harder and harder to be contented without clashing with your environment. It is not wise for you to flaunt the few moments of contentment you can find today, but it is very foolish to conform to the forces of negativity around you in order to avoid conflict. It is best for you to find all the peace that is possible, for peace is an ingredient of contentment. If you cannot wear contentment on your sleeve and still keep the peace around you, wear it only in your heart.

In any event, contentment only lasts for a moment, and its renewal is a full-time goal for you today. It is like specks of gold that are panned from the river of life, and the finding of contentment consumes many hours of time, moment by moment. But what better way of living than to pan the rose gold-dust of love? Find it and receive it, if you can, from those around you, and always remember that you may receive it from Me in infinite supply at any time. And put from your mind the false belief that love received is any better than love given. When you seek love from others around you, you are seeking something that might not be available, or that might only be conditional. But the love you give can be as pure as you can make it, and you can never lose perfect love by giving it away.

Universal love is contentment, pure and simple. It is the key to contentment, it is the source of contentment, and it is the way to find joy in a world of sorrow and pain. It is your right to have it, and if you renew it often, you need not suffer from the inability to hold it as time passes. You have often let time rob you of the joys of living, by trying to keep for hours what can only be found and enjoyed moment by moment. I plead with you to let this day be a moment-by-moment exercise in contentment for you.

Creation started with love, it lives on love, and every bit of Truth and Light comes back to its Source, which is love. Of such is the Source of contentment, and if you have a lack of universal love, you will have an equal lack of contentment. Dream of contentment, think about it, take action to find your dream, hope for its accomplishment, and be contented for a few moments today, My beloved child.

It sounds so easy. I know it works, but how quickly I forget that time does not allow eternal joy. Time only allows the goal of Eternity to be reached, in which all joy, contentment, happiness, peace, gratification, serenity, satisfaction, and perfect love are found.

The footnotes after this and the following Chapters were written at the same time as the Chapter above them.

In the past few years I have asked many strangers and friends if they think we are in the last days of Earth. A very large majority seems to think we are. Many have prepared for it in various ways, and few are open enough to share their beliefs with others. But the subject is a popular one, and it is becoming more acceptable as a topic of conversation.

The future seems to be revealed to us in these words on a 'need to know' basis. This lesson was written almost two years before these remarks are being written. In that time, the world has been shocked by the overthrow of dozens of governments. In looking back, it is clear that the first few paragraphs of this lesson were very prophetic. And yet, we have been told that I am not a prophet. I am only a secretary who takes dictation in the form of Cosmic thoughts and transcribes them.

"The judgment by which the remainder are separated from those who are ready is a judgment of natural and automatic Truth. The remainder, although not ready for the joy of the Seventh Day, are only waiting for another harvest at another time. They shall find the end of the usefulness of time. They shall also find the perfection of their universal love, which allows them to be attuned to the Light and Harmony of timeless and real Creation. And they shall also taste the joy of My Being when it unites eternally with theirs. They are a remainder only in the sense of time, which I have so often told you is unreal and is an illusion."

From Book 23 —<u>A New Way of Living</u>

Chapter 22   From Book 21 —<u>A New Way of Living</u>

Be Ready

How can you be ready when you know neither the time nor the way of the last days of Earth? It must be repeated again that you are made ready by your faith in Creation and its ways of harmony. You are made ready by your universal love. I teach you today of some of the ways in which you are not made ready, for some things that bring temporary comfort can bring danger to you as well.

You are not made ready by guessing and wondering too much about the events that are to come. If knowledge of the ways of the end increases, faith will diminish, and the ways of the end are many and varied. For some, the end of this era of Earth will come as a landslide, for some as an earthquake, for some as a disease that threatens their daily life, for some as a plague that leads to famine and starvation, and for some a hurricane, a tornado, or a tidal wave.

This is because your way of life on Earth is a routine that can be broken by things beyond your control. The writer has already clearly changed the way of his living, and many of you also have done, or are about to do, the same. In a world of time, all things are perceived with respect to events and circumstances in a particular time and place. Your life changes with respect to time when either your condition or that of others around you changes.

So from your point of view, the Earth relates in an unstable way to the way of your own life. It comes to an end when your physical life departs or changes in ways that deny time and the Earth's apparent reality. This is a mystery to you now, for you are so immersed in the things of time that you have learned to relate all things to its apparent reality. But I tell you today that the Earth will end its hold on its inhabitants at different times and in different ways for different souls.

Many have already thought they knew the way and time of the end, and have prepared for a certain date to bring certain events in a certain way. The time came, nothing happened, and their faith was eventually weakened by the false knowledge that caused them to believe in something that time did not bring to them. This is the danger of trying to know or guess the future, for I have not given you time without also giving you ignorance of its developments.

Find comfort and joy in the harmony of this day, My beloved child, and do not test your knowledge by theories of the future. If your knowledge of the future is wrong, you will begin to doubt yourself and deny your ability to cope with time. You do not cope with time by knowing the future, for thoughts of the future make time a needless and confusing burden. The way of joy and peace is in finding your own universal love, in which your wishes for the harmony of Creation will bring that harmony about for you.

Many of you are learning and have practiced the joys of a life lived step by step and day by day. This kind of life has brought you much satisfaction, for you have learned that you are at peace and are loved by Me without regard to the circumstances of time. A saying of some is, 'What you don't know won't hurt you.' This is a wise saying, and it is even wiser to say, 'What you don't wish to know won't hurt you.'

Wanting to know too much is sure to defeat your readiness. The Scripture says, 'Be ready, for in such an hour as you think not, the Son of Man comes.' At another place it says, 'He will come as a thief in the night.' You cannot know the time, the way, nor the place of the coming of the end. Neither can you know the way to be ready, for your readiness will be constantly adjusted to the times if you live in faith. I cannot tell you to be ready in any way that is effective, except to be ready by maintaining a continually renewed faith in Me and in yourself.

Be ready by practicing continually the exercise of your faith in the joys of universal love, and learn the lesson of submission to the things you cannot change in the world of time around you. Learn to love, I say again, and see that you do not forget to love the joys of your life and the beauty of yourself as much as you can. I have created your spirit to be as beautiful as a rose, as fragrant as the blossoms of grapes and lilacs, and as colorful as a rainbow.

When you love, you are ready. When you believe, you are ready. When you have faith, you are ready. When you live for today, you are ready. When you step softly and gently, you are ready. When you have compassion for all others, you are ready. When you show kindness, you are ready. When you give comfort to others, you are ready. When you are at peace, you are ready. When you are satisfied with what you have and are, you are ready. When you make peace with others and wish them well, you are ready. When you see the illusions of time and space, you are ready.

Last Days?

Every effort to know about the future opposes your readiness. Every wish to find proof that denies your need for faith opposes your readiness. Every desire to explain the future and the meaning of life and time opposes your readiness. Every thought of changing the ways of others to suit your beliefs opposes your readiness. Every act of impatience or frustration opposes your readiness. Every desire to ignore life and to sleep away the moments of this wonderful time of Earth opposes your readiness.

Many things have come to you as the last days approach the fulfillment of Earth. I do not teach you today to ignore the events of Earth, nor do I teach you to ignore the prophecies of your Scriptures and your inner self. I do teach you to wonder about the future with no desire to know it. I teach you to be keenly aware of all the things that are happening, and to be ready to know what you might have only suspected. The time to know is the time that I give to each of you individually. It is not given to one and revealed by that one to many. Knowledge of the ways of the end is given to each of you as an individual, directly revealed to you by My Spirit within you.

This means that you cannot be ready by knowing others who seem to be informed. If another has information, it is for that one, and not for all. The time and way and place can be different for some than for others, and readiness might be different as well. When one says to you, 'I am ready,' deny the temptation to set yourself in the same condition and feel prepared. Your preparation for the last days is already done when you have learned to have universal love. All the other things that are needful will be added at that time.

This lesson is a lesson of encouragement, and I tell you again that if you are ready to die in the flesh you are already living most effectively in the reality of your spirit. If you are ready for the end of this time of Earth, you are equally ready for the joys of the thousand years in the Seventh Day of Creation. If you are made ready by faith and universal love, nothing can challenge or defeat your readiness, for you are beyond the reach of all the demands and threats and dangers of time and space.

By your universal love and faith in Me you are made invincible, for you are in the Light. You are safe from everything that is real, and more importantly, from the things that are illusions of danger from the realms of time and space. Be ready, for the time is coming in which those who have searched and failed to find their future must renew their faith and be content to trust without knowing so much. Every effort to cope with the future must be built on a firm foundation of faith and love, and if you have found that foundation there is no more need to fear, for you are ready.

Live just for this day in the ways of faith and love, My child, and see how quickly good things come to you. And remember that the good things are the things of the spirit, the things of joy and contentment. Remember that being ready does not become easier when you are too involved with the things of time and the pleasures of time's illusions. Enjoy time and the blessings of Earth to the fullest, but do not forget that you are a visitor, a stranger in a strange land that is not your home.

Your home is prepared for you by your Creator, and deep within the instincts of your soul you know it. The strongest testimony on Earth that deals with the beauty of your spirit comes from those who have left their bodies for a brief moment and have glimpsed the other side. Be in love with life, for life is lovely, but remember that the life that is real is the eternal life of your soul and the living spirit which I have given your body for this day.

When you have found Me today, make it the joyful feeling that is like the first love of your life in this body. When time is recognized for what it is, you are ready again for the first love of Creation, for each day is new. Today is not a continuation of yesterday, nor is it a preparation for a tomorrow that might not come. Today is for you today, and today is the day to be ready in ways that have nothing to do with time, the future, or the things that you see around you.

Walk today in faith, and be ready by taking the short steps and the simple moments that come to you. Live this day in love and peace, and know that you are ready. I give you this with love and with My blessings for you.

> *Today is foggy, and the green Earth breathes the cool air of a mountain morning. I cannot see the peaks in the distance, and the valley is blurred by the moisture that hangs in the air. Nothing is seen except the green trees and the plants of Earth, but I know the horses are in the barn, the birds are in the shelter of their nests, and the crawling creatures of nature are snug and warm in their burrows and dens. And I know the hidden mountain tops are there, standing against a hidden sky. I need not know when the sun will shine again, for it is enough simply to know that it will. Because I have seen life around me, I know it will appear again in another time and maybe in another way. It is so easy to believe and see these things by faith, without knowing. Let the burden of proof be delayed for me today, and let the joy of faith bring satisfaction, for no knowledge of the future is needed if I just follow the lessons of this day, which teach me so lovingly how to be ready.*

"The unsung heroes and heroines of the world are those whose simple life has only a few lines of description in the death notices at the time of their passing. They who lived in peace and joy, loyal to mates and to friends, caring about their children and parents, and asking only a little space to breathe and a little beauty to enjoy in life, are the ones whose story should be told. The bizarre is not worthy of the space and time it occupies, for it represents the worst of the complicated illusions that are around you."

From Book 22 — <u>A New Way of Living</u>

Chapter 23   From Book 22 — <u>A New Way of Living</u>

The Story

Today is the day in which Lesson Number 630 is written into the story of <u>A New Way of Living</u>. I will teach you of the story. I am the Creator and am the Author of it. You are living in the story as a character, and you are a part of the history, the present, and that which is yet to be revealed. The story has a beginning and an ending, just as does your body. The story also has conflict, just as you do. But you, an immortal soul, have no beginning and no ending. Your base is eternal, and you are eternally bound.

This is a love story. It is a story of learning. It is a story of development. It is a story of one man. It is a story of everyone. It is a story of Me. It is a story of you. It is a story of us, and therefore of unity. It is a story of Light. It is a success story. It is a story of wisdom. It is a story of joy. It is The Story of Creation.

In the story, knowledge is revealed. The knowledge comes slowly, leads suddenly to wisdom, and brings joy if the wisdom is not caused to be ignored by the cruel interference of vanity. Every story is based on time, events, and the conclusions that might come from them. The knowledge of those events takes each story through its conflicts to its conclusions. In every story there are conflicts. If the story has a happy ending, the conflicts are resolved and all live happily ever after. The story of <u>A New Way of Living</u> is no exception to this.

Like the better stories, this story is to be enjoyed. It is to bring peace and happiness to you. It is to give you a very physical and spiritual glow of well-being. It is to lead you to the joys of universal love and forgiveness of all, yourself being the most important one for you to forgive. It is to find, in you, the wisdom you already had, but could not see or accept. It is to release you from the bonds of the illusions of time and space into a more perfect, and indeed a most perfect, place. That place is Eternity.

This story is a story of all life, all love, and all Creation. It reaches around the negative aspects of darkness and grasps the marvelous Light by which all things are joyfully fulfilled. It ignores the villains and reduces them to nonentities, which they most certainly are. It is in no way a horror story, for horror is just another aspect of the darkness, which is ignored in passing by the story.

The story abolishes sadness and fear by its logic, which is based on faith and love. It abolishes all things negative by replacing them with the positive vibrations of spiritual reality, in which no negatives are needed to provide the contrasts such as are provided by the events of time and space. The story grows and develops with the lives of the writer and the reader, but the Author, Who is I, has lived forever and can see far beyond the perspective of any of the readers. Your blessing is My joy, the joy of Creation, and the happy ending of the story.

Like all good stories, this one has a thread. The writer has never known where the thread of the story will lead him. He is just as ignorant of the next chapter as are you. He knows only that the story has been interesting, exciting, and informative to date, for it has led him to a greater joy of living. The title states the purpose of the story, which is a new way of living for you. The story to date has proved to many that A New Way of Living provides a life of much greater peace, enjoyment, patience, love, kindness, forgiveness, and spiritual guidance.

But remember, as long as the story lasts there will be conflict. The story does not end until the conflict ends, so the moral to the story will not be fully revealed until the end. You might wonder what is to happen next. You will not know until the next thing happens, for neither you nor the writer knows the plot and the direction of the story. You only know that it unfolds gradually, leading to your wisdom as the significance of the knowledge it reveals is deduced.

Like any good story, the plot thickens as the story unfolds. The story dabbles little in the past, less in the future, and almost totally in the moment at hand. It is a contemporary story, not a story of history or of future events. But as it unfolds, history is being made and the story is a part of it. This story goes on, for the story of all life on Earth is coming to an end.

But the moral to the story of life is not to be found at the end of the world, for that is not the end of life for anything on Earth, although all life on Earth will either appear to die or be removed to a safer place. The knowledge this story gives you shows you better ways to live in joy on Earth, so you can better handle the events of the story of Earth and time from the vantage point of your spiritual reality. Many of the things in this story will take on a significant meaning in the light of events that are soon to happen. The knowledge in these lessons that, at first, seemed not to apply will take on a new meaning when its purpose is revealed to allow the wisdom that can be found from its conclusions.

You are not alone, but the more you read this story, the less you might feel alone. This story is not one that is easily read. It is more to be studied, being written on many subjects that are of various importance to various readers. It is not a textbook of knowledge, a hand-book of instructions, or a work of easy reading for the bored or indigent souls who now live on Earth. And it is to be read from no sense of duty, for it is not your assignment for these last days by your Teacher.

Your right to choose is an unending part of your being. Your life is a part of all freedom, in which all life exists. There is no tinge of slavery or servitude in this story, nor is there any assessment of guilt or judgment. It is written to show you the way to use your freedom, not to deny it. It is written to give you joy, not fear of punishment or the stirring of ambition that leads to vanity. It is written to get you off the fast track of materialism, which so often leads to anger, frustration, lust, greed, vanity, and the cares of time.

The story has a happy ending if you stay with it, but if you do not, it has no ending at all. The happy ending will be the end of your story, for you will end life in time when your ending can be a most happy and joyful one. In that ending for you, and finally for all life, Eternity will take the place of time, the story will lose the significance of both its beginning and its end, and the conclusion will open the door of that joyful Eternity for you.

So the story has a promise at the end of it, being a promise of a sequel which is perfect joy without end and without beginning in time. There can be no conflict in the story that is the sequel to this one, nor can there be any need for a slow development of knowledge. Neither can there be any need for wisdom to be refined from any knowledge, for the opposites that create conflict can no longer exist in the perfect and positive love in an Eternity that transcends all need for knowledge or wisdom in any way.

Because of these changes in the sequel to this story, living will not be a series of events in time and space, nor will it be surrounded by the illusions and the confusion of uncertainty. The life that follows this story is forever, eternal, and unlimited by any conflict at all. The sequel is complete before it starts, has no beginning and no ending, and cannot be imagined by one in your environment. Believe it by faith, and prove it to yourself by enjoying each chapter of your life that is lived according to the gentle lessons of these words in <u>A New Way of Living</u>.

This is a story that has a purpose in each chapter. It matters not at all which chapter you read, nor does it matter which you ignore. Let the instincts of your soul and the wisdom of your spirit lead you to that which seems most interesting. Let the joy of it lead you on, for the conflicts which each lesson might resolve for you reflect the purpose of the story. Allow it to happen by believing that it can. You cannot block the thread of the story, nor can you make its truth change by denying it.

Expect no miracles, except to develop the miracle of which your life already consists. Find the potential in this story that has always been yours. Find the new way of living that is the key to your escape from time. Let the knowledge of each lesson lead to the opening of another door in your future until you need no future at all. Let this patient application of eternal and absolute Truth be your key to joy in every moment of every day. But do not expect it to cure all conflict immediately, for you are a human in a mortal body, with an eternal soul and a spirit that shall overcome time and space only when the story is over.

It is not over until it's over. You will learn a little, add a little wisdom as you convert it from the knowledge this story reveals, and you will set your path each day according to the successes of the previous day. This story will go on, so will yours, and the conclusion is ahead. You cannot count the pages of the entire book, nor can the writer. Only I, the Author, Who is your Creator, know when the story is finished for you. But you may know now, because I tell you, that the story has a happy ending for you. You will live happily ever after, eternally joyful and at peace, and filled with the total harmony of love in an eternal sequel to this story.

> *Wisdom comes suddenly from learning that comes slowly. This is the story of my life. It is the story of your life as well, it seems. To learn ever so slowly and then to suddenly grasp the significance of that learning is one of the exciting things of life on Earth. To know completely is not possible, for to gain perfect wisdom would require knowledge of things long forgotten on Earth. Enough is enough, so I desire only to see the next chapter of the story tomorrow. It has been a thrill to see it develop, but the greatest thrill has been those sudden bursts of wisdom that come when the bits of knowledge lead to a conclusion. It has been a long time since I sat down to write and wondered if any more thoughts would come from the Author. It has been equally long since I wondered if the story would soon be told and the Books ended. It seems that anything connected with the Creator has no end. But I submit myself to His purpose, and will let each day provide its addition to the story if we are to read it.*

"Time and its events are the greatest illusions. Does time carry you to the future, or does time carry the future to you? Does <u>now</u> convert to the future because you change, or because the events of the environment change around you? What is absolute and what is attitude? The answer is that attitude is perspective, depending on the point of view, the place, and the time. Absolutes are purity and Truth, and they are not found clearly in time or space. They are suspected in time, realized by faith in the world of time, and found in Eternity."

From Book 21 — <u>A New Way of Living</u>

Chapter 24   From Book 23 — <u>A New Way of Living</u>

From Everywhere

The one thing each soul has in common is its destination of perfect joy in Eternity. The more you study the events of Earth and the nature of her inhabitants, the more you are confused by the extreme diversity of position, opinion, belief, and practice of your brothers and sisters of Earth. I offer encouragement to you who sometimes wonder if any two people agree entirely about anything at all. The negatives, the contrasts, the opposites, the comparisons, and the judgment that prevails on Earth are discouraging to anyone who believes in the divine precepts of unified peace, love, joy, and harmony.

But I have told you that the polarities time of and space on Earth are necessary to repel you from some things and attract you to others. Creation conspires to clean up its imperfections and make wonderful things happen. Creation is a constant force toward, not from, reality and Absolute Truth. Your events of today are confusing, of course, and it seems that no order could ever come from the living souls on Earth who can hardly agree on the meaning of their own life or the Source of it.

From everywhere, the moving events and the living souls who create them are coming. From all directions, all creeds, all nationalities, all beliefs, all churches, all philosophies, all ways of life, and all types of people there exists a divergence from confusion and a convergence toward reality. Many are now effectively questioning reality, learning gradually to turn away from the illusions they have traditionally believed for centuries past.

You have to study the future and past only a little to see a trend toward convergence. From within a vast variety of backgrounds, there has emerged a unified goal to reach reality. The reality of life on Earth now appears to be different from that which many had believed. From the ranges of the most confused seekers within the New Age Movement to the most dogmatic members of the religious groups of mankind, there is a recognized need for a sense of direction toward unity. You need to see only the present, which I have counseled you to observe with greatest attention, in order to realize that people are philosophically and psychologically on the move.

You read these words with interest because you know the time of renewal of the Earth is near. You also read them because you want to move ahead in your quest for joy, peace, harmony, and your soul's perfection. You have believed the truth, which is yours because it is true for you. You have believed you can change the habits of your past, which are often based on tradition or prejudice, and have become a new person with a newly discovered destiny which was always yours. You have released yourself from the bondage of your delusions, even without always knowing where to find reality to replace them.

From everywhere My people have come, going in the same direction, diverging from many and various places and converging toward the same eternal goal of Absolute Truth undistorted by time and space. To do this, you have had to give up some peace of mind for awhile, face some anxiety as you have given up familiar beliefs and ways, and follow the destiny that has so long been denied by your conventional approach to your own beliefs.

Today I counsel you to become well aware of your own changes, knowing that the anxiety of any change and the fears that can be fostered by any unknown development are needless. Know that courage is the key to your joy, courage renewed by faith in the orderliness of Creation. From everywhere, people of widely different positions and locations in their spiritual life are coming together. The differences need not be pointed out in negative ways at all, for the differences of their many points of view will disappear in the harmony that is fostered by their love and goodwill for all.

People can change and people do change. You have changed, you will continue to change, and you will arrive at the joyful end of the road of this time on Earth with many companions. In the last days, those who believe will join together in happy reunion, even as the final events of the last days transpire. These events are transpiring now, giving you the wonderful opportunity to forget your foolish attention to the past. Your universal love will allow you to love those who come from everywhere. Your joy will not be diminished by your judgment of the origin of your companions. They will come from everywhere, for they are coming now, with you.

To the extent you have seen things that seemed to be miracles work within your life, you have sometimes said, 'Why me?' You might have also said, 'Why him?,' or 'Why her?' I say to you, why not everyone from everywhere? I have made all humans to be brothers and sisters of Creation. None is higher or lower than another. Souls who have been scattered for centuries converge from everywhere today, first by openness of mind and then in acceptance of their destiny of harmony and unity without regard to origin.

This is a time for reality, for the values in which you have believed must often be changed, and you will be prepared for your changing beliefs which are based on universal truth and universal love. When those who are from everywhere on Earth unite, their perspectives will also be united, for they will have finally arrived at a meeting of minds and spirits. When this is true, truth will appear to be the same to all and love will be fostered by those who have come together to meet one another.

There are no accidents. People are coming together from everywhere today, for they have seen the failure of the efforts of people on Earth to create joy and peace in the old ways. The blood of martyrs, who have been seekers of freedom for millions of years on Earth, is now being justified, for the truth for which they died will prevail. That truth will be found by people from everywhere, coming from all directions to the same conclusions about the meaning of these mysteries today. The theories will emerge from half-baked stages of doubt and fear to the fullness of completion in the minds and hearts of those who accept them in universal love.

Let no illusions, fostered by your judgment of others, cause you to miss those who are converging. Mingle among them with no regard to possessions, background, temperament, nationality, religion, education, or attitude. Allow one another the same freedom to change which has allowed you to change from what you were to what you are today. Keep an open mind and allow yourself to see, moment by moment, My beloved children joining together for the harvest. Ignore their past and look at their present desires to know the others who are searching, just as you have searched and will continue to do.

For the truth does not thrust itself upon you. It waits, invincible in its reality and sure to survive until you find it. You are joined by many others from everywhere in the search for truth. It will be found to be much deeper than knowledge or understanding, and it will be discovered to be enough, by itself, when you find it. Truth is the common goal for searchers from everywhere, and when you find it you will find one another. You will also love one another, for love is a prerequisite for the discovery of truth.

The wiser of you are learning the art of indeterminate thinking, in which no conclusions are drawn and everything is taken with a grain of salt. You are learning that it is possible to live in joy without judgment, without prejudice, without knowledge, and without regard for the values of past and future. You are learning that time and space, which you thought to be most real, are in fact the greatest of illusions. You are learning that the unknown reality of Creation is so intangible as to make proof impossible, judgment useless, and physical evidence completely irrelevant to truth.

You are learning that universal love does not require cares and worries. You are learning that Creation works best for you when you allow it to work by using patience without interference. You are learning to forsake a hectic life in which results are all that counts and your greatest effort is required only by a false sense of duty and responsibility. You are learning that the only ways of living that are found in common among those who discover the truth that saves them in the last days of Earth are the ways of universal love and goodwill.

You are learning that the only reality in Creation is spiritual reality and life, which in its perfection allows immortality, eternal joy, and harmony by its very nature. You are learning that you must let go of your illusions before you can grasp this reality. And you are learning that letting go of illusions is most difficult and takes lots of practice. But you can do it. From everywhere, you see others who are trying and succeeding in this to various degrees. As you approach the end, you will draw closer to those who come from everywhere with this common goal. That will provide the courage that will take away your fears and see you through. This is My lesson of encouragement for you today.

> *Since this writing has begun in my life, I have been surprised to find so many ways in which people agree or disagree about reality and the meaning of life. It seems that the variety of their past leads to the variety of their conclusions. But upon looking more closely, I see them continually changing in directions that seem to prove their commitment to a common goal or destiny. I have noticed the jig-saw puzzles of life become easier to fit together when the task is almost complete. It appears that people from everywhere are beginning to fit together more and more today, as we approach the fulfillment of this day of Creation.*

"I have given the world and the Earth to you, and you have so often taken it as reality, when it should only be a step through time toward Truth. I have given you peace, and you have often made war, and I have given you gentleness, which has often been turned into aggression. Kindness and love are fulfilling and nourishing to your spirit, but you have often listened to the demands of your flesh and of time, have looked for the satisfaction of your ambition to hold the world within your heart, and have often lost the love and peace that would have brought it all to you so easily."

From Book 20 — <u>A New Way of Living</u>

Chapter 25   From Book 24 — <u>A New Way of Living</u>

Shadows

One of the opposites of light in life on Earth are shadows. They have no substance, they disappear when the light that creates them is gone, and they are distorted by the perspective of the observer and of the source of light that forms them. They are most intangible, but they are not real. They can be photographed and used to describe the nature of an unseen solid object whose shadow is cast by the lights of Earth, but they are only illusions made of the illusions that created them.

Shadows are darkness, exposed and outlined by light under some conditions. They cannot appear in the dark, nor do they appear when light is cast evenly from all directions around a solid object. Therefore, they are conditional symptoms of illusions, appearing only when the conditions are right. A shadow can be destroyed by lighting that comes from the opposite side of the previous light. They can also be destroyed by taking away all sources of light.

Your life on Earth is sometimes made more simple for you by shadows. Shadows reveal the dimensions of distant hills and trees at sunset, for the sizes of hills and trees are magnified when the sun is low. Your illusions of things of Earth also appear as shadows when you resist the Light of Creation that shines within you. Your Inner Light can be hidden as long as you like, making you the cause of shadows when you live near the Light of others. But if you also radiate a celestial Light of your own, no shadows can be seen around you.

But your Inner Light can cast shadows that appear to others, for Light does reveal darkness when it is blocked and resisted. Many souls on Earth are barriers to the Light of Creation, causing shadows to follow them wherever they go. The light of freedom on Earth is invading the governments and rulers of many repressed people all over the world today. This is casting shadows, causing shaking and toppling governments and replacing them with reformers and revolutionary seekers of power.

I counsel you today to look for the shadows around the Light of the world. Many souls are coming forward, just as prophesied, and are seeking to make the world a better place to live. It will be so, for the lull before the storm is almost over. When the clouds roll, the lightning flashes, and the thunder rumbles and crashes, momentary shadows are cast in the lowering darkness of the elements. The sun, being hidden, is replaced by lightning as the source of shadows. These shadows flicker and are gone, but the eyes of your body can discern the swaying trees and the scurrying clouds against the horizon, for just a moment, as each bolt of lightning strikes.

You have glimpses of the shadows cast by the storm of freedom and revolution over the world. Some, who are able to tolerate their repression, would rather the storm would pass over the governments of the lands of Earth. Others, being more directly affected, wish to see the storm take away the deadwood and the debris of decades of corruption. They would like to see their homeland renewed and set free, with equal opportunity for all. I have caused the hearts of many to join in demanding freedom and a new way of living — a way that is free from the repression of dictators and corrupt seekers of power and wealth.

This political confusion is causing people to hope for a better life, even though they have lived for many years with little hope of better things to come on Earth. They are seeing shadows of a new Light of Freedom, which is a spiritual gift that I have allowed to be denied from some of the people of Earth for a time. Now is the beginning of the end, for the revolution against oppression will replace repression with freedom for many. It will cause many to be in a position to more easily choose the way of their life on Earth. Some will take advantage of this — others will not.

I taught you several months ago that there would be a lull before the storm, and that people would learn to live together a little better in many parts of the world, only to see the natural disasters during the physical death of Earth deny their opportunity to live in peace. Political pressures from wars will be replaced by economic pressures from hunger, cold, and heat. Weather will become more and more unpredictable, and many of the wars which end when freedom replaces oppression will begin again when food becomes more scarce and is poorly distributed.

Violence caused by efforts to regain political freedom will be replaced by violence used to find food and shelter. This is not a new thing for some of the third-world countries of Earth, but it will expand and cover all the continents of the

Earth as water becomes more scarce and more polluted. Heat will also be a factor, along with more destruction from fires and floods and landslides. Earthquakes and volcanoes will not be the only evidence of the physical stresses of Earth.

The shadows you see on Earth today are shadows of change. Light is being cast upon things of darkness in many ways; politically, economically, socially, spiritually, and physically. This light, although not always visible where you live, will cast shadows which are visible to all. To look at the evidence of truth caused by shadows of things that hide the light which forms them is a confusing task. Shadows are almost always distorted, so they will be interpreted in many ways. Be open-minded and at peace with yourself. Live spiritually within yourself, keeping in touch with your Inner Base of Reality, from which you may find the truth to judge what is needed for your safety.

Avoid emotional reactions to the shadows you see. Be assured that most of them are illusions caused by illusions, and be sure that nothing of reality will be lost in the last days of Earth. Your joy can be greater and greater each day as you see the time of the end approaching, for I am within you and all is well for each precious life of Creation. Nothing of reality, I repeat, shall be lost or destroyed. And after the storm is passed and the shadows are gone, even the illusions which remain will be made better by the new Light and life of a renewed Earth.

Look past the labor and pain of the rebirth that is coming in this era of Earth's history. Look with an eye of faith, not needing so much to know what, where, and when the changes will be, as to know that your faith and joy can be equal to the occasion. You know little of what is to come, little of when it is coming, and much about how to live in joy and patience, guided by your Inner Faith in My Kingdom within you. Think of these things, live in peace, claim the joy of universal love and goodwill, and deny the pain of anger, frustration, and fear.

I greet you today from within, so your past fears of losing contact with My help from the future and from far away are needless. Under no conditions will I forsake you. You are like a precious and beloved child who is sheltered from all harm under all conditions. You are Mine, for I created you in My image as My child. Laugh when you see the shadows of the things that are around you. They might seem to loom above you in the darkness of the last days of Earth, but if your Light within is sufficient, you shall dispel them and cause them to disappear, for no shadow can survive your direct Light.

Your Light is within you, so you need not see a shadow that is cast by Light from any other source. Only shadows are between you and Me today, My child, and they are not able to overcome your Light when you live in joy by faith and trust Me for the rest. Things are moving faster now, the signs of the times are casting many shadows, and you are being tested as you seek renewed faith and the joy that follows. The test is not a fearful thing for you, for you have learned to fill your lamps with oil and be ready for the coming night.

It is always darkest before the dawn, so more shadows will appear in the early light of dawn than in the darkness that preceded it. Look at the shadows of things to come as joyful results of the Light that casts them. Look at things which allow the Light to form shadows as things which are unreal, expendable, and merely illusions that have continued long enough in this time of Earth.

Live in peace and love, walk in the Light, stay close to the truth that is within you, and keep goodwill in your heart. And do not avert your eyes in fear as the shadows are cast by the new Light of the dawning of a New Earth. It is a wonderful time, much beauty is there to be seen, and your role is a most joyful one if you choose to stay with reality, overcome your fear by faith, and live with courage in your heart.

Earlier, these words predicted that the time would

come when so many significant things would be happening on Earth that the news media could not report them all. At that time, I could not have imagined such an abrupt change in political relationships over the Earth. But we still have economic pressures, a need for food for the starving children of many lands, and the danger to many who close their eyes when more and more shadows appear. But, if we do what we know, we shall know what to do.

"There is no scarcity or poverty in Creation. All things that are of life are profuse and abundant, and in the things of time and of the spirit worlds there is more than enough. My beings are each different from the other, and nothing is redundant, but Creation is made to continue and grow because there is abundant energy, love, and power to sustain it even as My children walk in freedom to stumble and fail."

From Book 19 — <u>A New Way of Living</u>

Chapter 26   From Book 24 — <u>A New Way of Living</u>

The Price

On Earth, everything has a price. The illusions of time and space are found to have a cost that is borne by you. If you seek the illusions, you will pay the price for finding them. The price is as much an illusion as the things you seek on Earth, but it is an illusion that can seem as real as the illusions you seem to buy with it. Money and the things it will buy are parts of the great illusions of time and space. I give you spiritual gifts of reality — things which are real, intangible, and without price. The cost of perfect and eternal joy is nothing, the value is everything, and time and space have no part of it at all.

Physical health is a part of the illusions of Earth, as is the money which is spent on Earth to maintain it. The greatest price you pay for living, next to the food, clothing, transportation, and shelter you buy, is for medical care. But health, being part of the illusion which you have sometimes called the key to your life, cannot be bought with money. Good health can be preserved a little longer, made a little better, and enjoyed a little more, but it is still a part of the illusions of life on Earth. True life is immortal, without price, and extends far beyond the confines of Earth, time, or space.

And the price of many things is paid with time, not money. Time can be bartered with other people of Earth to shuffle possessions and preserve illusions. Health, itself, is bought and paid for by time. If you live patiently and at a slower pace, you will extend your health and apply your physical energy over a longer life on Earth. So time that is saved, although an illusion, prolongs your physical life and improves your health on Earth. These are also parts of the illusion. But living at a slower pace and spending time more moderately allows you to give your attention to the realities of which I teach you.

I see many of you wanting more of the illusions of time in life on Earth for a lower price. But the illusions of possessions, power, fame, or vanity will require a price which is only composed of other illusions. Money, itself, is the greatest of illusions. It is backed by paper and promises in most countries, and even when it was backed by gold and precious metals, it was backed by something you could not eat, wear, or use for shelter. The people of Earth have used vivid and creative imaginations to preserve their illusions and pay their prices with other illusions, but reality has escaped so many of you for so long.

Those who have never had money often believe money can buy happiness. And those who have had money often discover that good health, long life, and peace of mind are of the greatest value, instead. But I tell you that the price for your health is time, which does not last and is limited in a given lifetime on Earth. So health, like the other physical illusions of time and space, comes and goes with a price that cannot forever be paid. It is to be enjoyed in your youth, respected in your later years, and given up as you age in time and connect with the reality of My Kingdom within you.

When you learn to seek My Kingdom within you and to hold fast to that which is good, you will be seeking and finding all the things most precious and without any price at all. On Earth, an item can be called priceless because it is extremely rare and not for sale at any price. But in My Kingdom of Reality, all things are priceless because they are in plentiful supply, are available freely to all, and are not diminished or decayed by time. The good things, to which I have taught you to hold fast, are priceless and free to anyone who solves the illusions of time and space.

Your course of life on Earth today is one of peace, if you look for the priceless things of reality that are not rare, that do not diminish or decay with time or with use, and that become more plentiful with use, instead. Love is increased by loving, joy is increased by sharing, kindness is felt by giving it, and harmony grows from itself in its own beautiful environment. You are in a world in which you have Inner Self, Absolute Reality, and Perfect Joy available to you, always without price.

Come and go in the ways of the world and of time as long as you like, be happy with the health of your youth and the prices of your possessions as long as you can, and remember always to hold fast to that which is good. If you have found that which is good, you have found it by the wisdom and truth from within you, and you have found it to have no price, now or later. Be without debt to time or space, owe no man of your future, and live in peace, with a simple life in time and a simpler one within yourself.

The resources of the reality within you are great, continual, and without price. They are gifts I gave you in the timelessness of your Creation. You have left Eternity for time by your choice, knowing that, in your freedom, you could express the free and priceless gift of life in harmony with your unique role in Creation. Often you have expressed life and have held fast to that which is good, and often you have not. But learn by the lesson today that if anything has a price, both it and its price are illusions.

When the world dies and is reborn, money and all the natural resources of Earth, both in raw material and in the refinements of civilization, shall disappear. They shall be engulfed by winds and waves and shifting crusts of Earth. They shall be empty and unseen testimonies to those who paid the price of health, of time, of money, and of other bartered illusions to exchange one illusion for another. They shall go from having a price to having worthlessness. Anything on Earth that can be regarded as worthy, unworthy, valuable, invaluable, or having any price at all, is an illusion that shall pass away with time.

So the next time you see a vendor selling goods and ask him the price, remember that you have defined his goods as illusions. Also remember that the price is, itself, an illusion. No money, goods, or tangible items of value will survive the passing of the Earth and the beginning of the Seventh Day. In that happy time, there can be nothing bought or sold, nothing priced or priceless, and nothing regarded as possessions in any way. All things will be free, without price, readily available, and regarded without pride, vanity, jealousy, or envy. Covetousness will be impossible, for anything can be enjoyed by anyone without depriving another.

You cannot imagine this today, but you can imagine the illusions of Earth, in which all things seem to have a price. Just remember, if it has a price, it is an illusion. So is its price. This is true, whether the price is money, goods, or time. If it has a price, it is an illusion. And if it is tangible, but is not for sale because it is rare, it is also an illusion.

The Price

You are not taught to hold fast to that which is good so that others cannot take it away from you. You are taught to hold fast to that which is good because that which is good is reality. That which is good is plentiful, free, available to all, and without price. The things to which you cling on Earth are the things which will drag you down as they perish, or lift you up and sustain you as they survive, being of reality. If you cling to the anchor of the ship as it is cast into the sea, you will drown, even though the ship is safely held in place by her anchor.

But if you stay with the ship and let the anchor go, you will be served by the illusion of the anchor and preserved by the life of the ship as she floats throughout the storm. This is the lesson of price, for if you hold fast to those things which are free, eternal, real, spiritually alive, intangible, and without price, you will be holding fast to that which is good.

My beloved, Christmas is coming near as these words are written. The stores are full of things with prices, which things are as illusive as the money that buys them. But the gift of Christmas is the gift of the Light which defines its name. That Light is love, the love that Jesus lived and showed on Earth. He did not die for your sins. He died for your love and His for you, knowing that the letter of the law found in the religion and politics of those days were letters bound by time, by space, and by the price of conforming to man-made laws and their strict interpretations.

Let this be a season wherein the prices for goods are cheerfully paid to buy illusions with illusions. Do what you can afford as you play the games of life in time and space, but remember this lesson. If anything has a price, it and its price are illusions. Grasp the good things of reality, which are as free and eternal as My free and eternal love for you. Go in peace today. As you count the cost, remember that, if it can be bought and has a price, it is finally to go the way of all the illusions of time and space. Hold fast to that which is good, My beloved.

Last Days?

When I was young and had no money, I enjoyed looking at the bright pictures of all the toys that a young boy growing up during the Great Depression had never seen. Later, I found the price and bought the goods, only to find that time had robbed me of the pleasure of clinging to them. And when I bought and sold enough, it became more and more obvious that the best things in life are free, instead. But even then, I did not realize that the lessons which taught us to hold fast to that which is good were taught so we might not have the good things taken away from us. I like this lesson's explanation, which teaches me to hold fast to that which is good because good is reality, and shall survive.

"I have caused the writer to read from the Book of Ezekiel this morning, for the first seven chapters and parts of the rest are visions of the last days in which you dwell at the time of this writing. Remember, if you choose to read it, that the last days include the days when Jesus the Christ lived upon the Earth as a man, for in a time frame of ten million years, two thousand years are only a few moments."

From Book 18 — <u>A New Way of Living</u>

Chapter 27   From Book 24 — <u>A New Way of Living</u>

The Books

The financial books of a company are balanced and closed at the end of each fiscal year. This Book of <u>A New Way of Living</u> is closed today, ending another twelve months of writing, which have produced another twelve Books that teach you of another Part of The Trinity. The Father, Son, and Holy Spirit are the components of The Trinity taught in the Christian religions of the world. There is some distortion in the teaching, for the Son is The Christ, the Brotherhood of Light, the Body of Christ, and the combined workers of Light within and outside the churches of the world. Jesus was one of them, but not all of them. I have many beloved children who are Christs, and who are therefore members of the Body of Christ, which is one of the three functional Entities in The Unified Trinity, Which Is the Creator, Creation, and I.

I have caused the first twelve Books of this series to be directed primarily from the Father/Mother God Entity of the Trinity. I have caused the second twelve Books to be directed primarily from the Christ, which is the Brotherhood of Light and can be regarded as the Body of Christ. This Body contains each of you at times, and you will be a part of that Body forever and eternally when you have finally attained the perfection for which you are bound by your destiny.

The third and final set of twelve Books will gradually reveal to you the Spirit of Truth, which is sometimes thought of and taught as being the Holy Ghost or the Holy Spirit. That functional Divine part of The Trinity is also called The Comforter in the New Testament of the Bible. It is all of these. I teach you this lesson so you may grasp a little more of the meanings and the relationships of these thirty-six Books of A New Way of Living.

Only now does the writer, with some surprise, know the overall picture of these Books and the consistency of their direction. Within the blending of subjects, there has been a trend which is just now revealed to him. He had never suspected the meaning behind the references to the Father in the earlier lessons, which gradually changed to references to the Light in the later ones. Now the lessons will be concerned more and more with Truth, the Absolute Reality which causes the Creation of the Father and the Inspiration of the Light to be finally converted to Perfect Joy by the comfort and witness of the Holy Spirit of Truth which is to come.

The Father creates the entity of each child, the Light reveals the way of Creation to that entity, and the Truth sets the entity free to live according to the Divine Purpose toward which all Creation is bound, and will continue, in Eternity. There is no way to teach these parts of the Trinity without crossing the lines between the functions of its entities, for, after all, We are One and are inseparably unified. However, you may now read the earlier Books, or the later ones, and see how your faith, directed first to the Father/Mother God, reveals the Light of Creation, which in turn directs your spirit to the joy and freedom of Absolute Truth.

The words of <u>A New Way of Living</u> are not meant to be difficult or complicated. Take them as they come and enjoy them, without the strain of trying to understand each of them. You learn more than you know, even when you feel you cannot grasp the mysteries of My words to you. We of the Trinity work most effectively when you accept each of us in the difficult concept of separate functions which are unified. The writer is learning to use different guides for different problems as he travels in time and space, though each of them are workers of the Brotherhood of Light with a slightly different, and sometimes overlapping, function.

You will also learn more and more of the ways of Our Trinity within you, for We shift constantly, infinitely, and timelessly into the roles for which we are inclined to work in Unity. Truth comes into your spirit from within the entity of your Inner Self — more specifically, from the Spirit of Truth, by Which the final twelve Books will be more and more directed. The second set of twelve Books was from that part of Us which is the Body of Christ, a composite body of many Beings of Light who are worthy of functioning within that Body, as you shall do more and more when you reach the higher planes of spiritual reality.

And the first set of twelve Books will still contain the words of the Father/Mother Entity of the Trinity, which were directed to the writer and to many of you when it was not yet clear how the functional parts of the Trinity worked together, even while functioning separately in mysterious ways. The final twelve Books will help you to apply the words of the first twenty-four Books, for they will comfort you more and more as the final dark days of time approach the Earth. The sudden political changes, which are starting to accelerate more and more, will often prevent you from having peace of mind as you walk upon the Earth. But you may have the greatest joy and peace of mind you have ever known if you learn to trust in the Father, walk in the Light, and feel the freedom to abide in the Spirit of Truth, which is the third equal part of Our Trinity within you.

Each of you has much to learn about the nature of the Beings of the Trinity, for you have been so deluded by past misconceptions that you have hardly been able to feel enough faith, even in the Father. But those of you who are more advanced by your desires and your experience in this life have found great revelations and spiritual peace from walking in the Light and finding that part of the Trinity as your constant Companion in those who work therein. The spirit realms are filled with close companions for each of you, and many of you know many of them by name and by daily contact. They are your guides, your guardians, your friends, and your brothers and sisters of Creation.

And some of you are also all of these to them. Be not concerned that you are bound in flesh by time and space, for these bonds are broken each time your spirit soars by faith in the Father and receives the Light which is a part of Us within you. Now is the time for you to begin to know and trust the Spirit of Truth, Who is also a most real Being within the Trinity and within you. This Being, the Comforter, is found as scattered Absolute bits of Truth in your mind, just as the Body of Christ is as scattered in your mind as the many souls of which it consists. For the Comforter is found in the scattered bits of Absolute Truth which come to you from time to time as you search for them within you.

Have joy in the Trinity and in each of Our Parts, My beloved. Have comfort in Us, trust Us, pray to Us, believe in Us, and live your life in the peace which We so often give to you. We are Many, we are composed of Many Parts, and yet We are One. You are one of the Many of which we consist when you are living in faith and have conquered the perversions of your mind by your universal love. You shall not lose Us, for We are within you. We are the Trinity of the One Creator, and you shall not understand our mysteries or the mysteries of all Creation.

But you may understand that short steps, taken moment by moment and pointed toward the Reality of Our Being within you, will cause you to become an Eternal Part of Us. Your Divine heritage leads to your own Divinity. The sons and daughters of Creation will become parts of the Trinity in Its Perfection beyond time and space when Eternity is finally your home. You shall not fail, and each step toward success will bring you more joy and peace.

So remember, today, that you are moving toward Absolute Truth. You shall not attain it, for it is Perfection in a Being of the God-head of the Trinity of One God. But little by little, step by step, moment by moment, and lifetime by lifetime, you shall know, even as you are now known and loved with a total and unrestricted love. Find faith in the Father, let the Light reveal Us, and live in joy by the Spirit of Truth. It is your certain destiny, not an unknown and uncertain future. It is beyond the future, the past, and anything you know at all of space or time. It is Total Reality for you, expressed more and more as you patiently learn the lessons that reveal Us to you through your ever-present, but sometimes ignored and forgotten, Inner Self.

For twenty-four months, with little rest from this writing, the man who writes to you today has taken time to write. Seven days a week, even while travelling and otherwise distracted, he has brought these words from Us to you. They are to continue, and he has agreed to complete the work in the Earth year of 1990 A.D. I instruct him now to rest from his labors in this work for seven days before starting the first Book of the final twelve. And I instruct him to let each of the final twelve Books contain Four Sections, with seven days of writing in each. He needs time to study and to dwell on the developments of these Books, for now that he understands the significance of the three sets of twelve Books and their relationship to the Creator as a Trinity of Beings, he will enjoy the time to briefly study what has already been written.

I bid you each a very happy Holiday Season as the last year of this decade draws to an end. You deserve more than you have believed, for We of the Trinity of Creation deeply love you and express our love in many ways whenever you allow it and accept it. Love one another and yourself as well, for you are also a part of Us by Creation, not by adoption. Accept your Divine heritage and it will bring you joy and peace such as you have never known. Practice the things you have learned, place your trust in your universal love as the foundation for your eternal joy when time is gone, and live in joy today as much as you can. I love you.

I did not know until yesterday how long the Books would continue to be written, and only today I have learned that each set of twelve depicts subjects centered around a Being of the Trinity. This is exciting to me, for the lessons have sometimes seemed scattered at the time of writing, even though they clearly had a sense of direction when they were later read and compared with one another. I cannot describe my constant surprise when I look back and see the way each lesson picks up from the last ones. This is an admission of my own limited faith, for, although I have never doubted the Source of the writing, I have often doubted the accuracy of my writing and somewhat feared the effects of the distractions of my daily life. But the Author gives me no responsibility to judge the writing for you, for that is your free choice. Perhaps He will answer some of these questions of accuracy in my writing as He gives us the last twelve Books from the influence of the Spirit of Truth. Go in peace, live in love, and find harmony on the Earth today.

"Be cheerful with persistence, with joy, with peace, with love, with goodwill, with courage, with kindness, with gentleness, and with love. These have all been themes and subjects of the lessons of <u>A New Way of Living</u>, again and again, and they are meant to make you cheerful. I have not cast these lessons upon you as burdens to be carried, as duties to be practiced, or as commandments to be obeyed. I have given them to you freely as gifts, which you may choose to accept or reject, and I have not threatened your freedom in any way."

From Book 17 — <u>**A New Way of Living**</u>

Chapter 28   From Book 25 — <u>**A New Way of Living**</u>

Consider

To consider anything, you must first be aware of it. It is impossible to consider anything while you are ignoring it. Many of the lessons I have taught you are to help you develop your awareness. Many things around you are worthy of consideration, although some are not. I counsel you today to avoid blindness and to learn to consider the things of Earth around you. It is not comfortable to be surprised. The things you consider have much to do with what happens, for the thoughts of your consideration unconsciously prepare you for things that are to come.

It is not wise to bury your head in the sand or to look the other way when things go wrong around you. The problem that is your neighbor's today could easily be yours tomorrow. Care about the lives of others around you. Consider what you would do with the opportunities and problems of those around you, for all are your brothers and sisters of Creation. What would you do with a fortune if you had it? What would you do with adversity if it came your way, instead? Many surprises are offered as the events of time come and go. The one who has ignored the handwriting on the wall is the one who is most shocked and unprepared when the changes come.

Many in the world today are enjoying the beginning of a political freedom they had never known. Some are prepared by having thought of the things they would do if freedom was allowed. Others are totally unprepared, and are only confused as they wonder what to do with their unexpected freedom. There are also those who have suddenly found a much higher or lower standard of living because of greater success or failure than expected. I advise you to consider the possibilities of change, for there are many changes on the Earth today.

Have you considered what to do if food is scarce and water is polluted and hard to get? Are you too proud to beg, or accept help from others who are more fortunate or prudent? And what if, instead, you should have a surplus while those around you are starving and needy? Have you considered what you will do if the needy around you are suffering while you have plenty? What if the land is overrun by violent souls who seek to take whatever they want by force? Can you cope with the looters and those who plunder for their starving families? And what of those who steal your goods and sell them just to gain riches and power, instead?

It is wise for you to hope and pray these things will never be forced upon you. But consider, for they have happened before all over the world and are happening now to someone. Consider if that someone could sometime be you. Would you rather be prepared to provide for yourself and your family, or would you rather hope to find someone else more prudent if the time comes when you and those you love are in need? These are things that have happened, are happening, and will happen again and again over different parts of Earth. These are the things which the last days will bring upon more and more who are unprepared. Are you prepared?

I have taught you often of the power of thought and the need to desire what you want. Consider the feelings you would enjoy if you were well prepared and able to share some of your blessings with others, for it is a wonderful thing to be able to give help to those who are in need. It is also dangerous, however, to have goods that are wanted by the lawless or the starving souls who are not ready. I have not given you this lesson in order to tell you the answers. They will come to you with the help of the Spirit of Truth, Who lives within you. This lesson is merely to help you consider, freely and often, the things that could happen to you which have never happened before.

Computer programs are written to play 'what-if' games on many subjects. They are not as useful as the human brain. Your mind can handle 'what-if' problems very effectively, but first, you must be willing to consider what might happen. I do not teach you to do these things to take away your courage, but to add to your courage by giving you the satisfaction of having considered while there is more time and less pressure from the events around you.

There is a time to consider, after which there might be a time to act. But to act in haste, without consideration, often makes a bad problem worse, for time does not wait for you when the food is gone, the wells are dry, and the stores in town are closed. It is better to have your lamp filled with oil that might never be used, than to have it empty when oil is no longer for sale and the night is dark. Think of survival without the help of any other, for the time will come for many on Earth in which each will be forced to live with what is his and his alone.

Extremes of weather and earthquakes have recently tested the organizations that cope with emergencies. The test has been only in a few places for a few weeks at a time. It is clear to you who have considered these things that people who are in deep trouble and need help the most can find none when those all around them are in the same situation. Consider what it might have meant for you if these things had happened to you. Everyone can find those who are more fortunate and those who are less. Consider them all, for if trouble is all around you and you have prepared for it, the stress it places upon you will still be greater than you are likely to believe.

Consider what you would do if you had a limited supply of food and were surrounded by starving children. Consider what you would do if you were faced with the need to steal from others who are just as needy, or else to starve and die from lack of food. Consider some of the hard choices, and remember that your faith in Me will carry you through. Be prepared, and learn to strike a happy balance between morbid fears and real possibilities. Do these things lightly from time to time, not allowing these considerations to become an obsession, for there are hundreds of possibilities for each one which will really happen to you.

You are not likely to have the slightest idea for what you must prepare. Often, the only thing you can do is to consider and to wait until the events more clearly reveal what will happen to you in your part of the world. It is not wise to try so hard to be sure that you know what will happen. It is better to prepare, however you can, with an open mind and a hope that the things prepared for will never become necessary. And it is better to consider many things with an open mind, in advance, knowing that you need not reach a conclusion on any matter that is connected with the uncertain events of the future.

There are those who have prepared years ago for something

which never happened, but the peace of mind that came with being prepared was well worth the cost and the effort. There are others who, having seen those who prepared for things that never came, have concluded that there is no longer any use in considering the possibility of change at all. This is your choice, for your freedom allows you to be aware or to ignore the events of Earth. Your freedom will continue and you shall live with the choices you make.

Consider, at least, whether you are willing to prepare for what might never come, or whether you might rather ignore it all and hope for the best. If you are completely able to ignore all things always, you will be comfortable and at peace until you die. But if, at the last minute of time, you live in fear, regret, or terror because you have not considered the possibility of what has come to you, you will then find it too late to change your approach. Now is the time to consider, if you like, what is happening and might continue to happen to you and those around you.

So the message is clear. Consider or ignore the times of Earth today, for you have the choice, and can be better prepared even by doing nothing except to imagine the possibilities for you and what you might do about them. Many are doing this now, quietly and patiently preparing for a world that is different than has been seen for millions of years. The melting pot of races and the sharing of many resources of Earth is upon you. The tribes and families and races of men are being drawn together by the events of the last days. Consider the times of the last days, for they are upon you.

> *More and more, I am hearing people speak of these times as being the last days of Earth. Young and old of all walks of life seem to sense the changes that are now coming faster and faster. It seems more tempting to watch and wait without preparing, for there are more and more possibilities to consider. But how would it*

feel to have ignored it all, or to have been so confused about what to do, that nothing at all was done? In this mountain community, many are considering many things that could happen and are preparing for a life that depends less on the economy, on the protection of society, and on political stability. Some are preparing by gathering more goods, while others are preparing by learning to live on less and reduce their wants. I do not have the answers, but I do see the question and feel the time is coming, at different times and places on Earth, when we all will see some of the things we had once considered only as remote possibilities.

"I am telling you today kindly, and with love, that you are not doomed by the holocaust, no matter which path you choose. You are either released and uplifted to the joys of the Seventh Day, or you are released to a newer and greater opportunity for a later salvation, by being freed from an environment which no longer supports the purity of love and harmony. Your handicaps upon the Earth today are too great and too hopeless, and the effort is more than most of you can tolerate much longer."

From Book 16 — <u>A New Way of Living</u>

Chapter 29 From Book 26 — <u>A New Way of Living</u>

Sweeping Changes

Sweeping changes are coming to all the nations of Earth. These changes are started by the desires of the people. They are continued by mass protests in the streets. They are followed by mass celebration, as well. Hundreds of millions of people are now able to get on with their lives and more freely pursue the destinies for which they chose to be born and to live in this lifetime. Tyranny has failed for awhile in many places, and even many of the tyrants who have lost their political jobs in totalitarian regimes will be glad when the oppression is over.

It is a time for love and goodwill all over the lands of Earth. However much you might have avoided the pain and sorrow of repression where you are, you will feel a spiritual uplifting of your own when you find the encouragement of Earth's physical response to the sweeping spiritual changes. The vast increase of freedom will show surprising results, carrying far beyond the political scene into the realms of economics, education, social welfare, and private initiative. Look for good news in many places this year, for there are many things that will indirectly follow the overthrow of despotic governments.

These sweeping changes will cause capitalism to also clean up its image and reform its occasional patterns of legalized repression. It will not be an opportunity for capitalism to improve its control of the world economies after communism dies, for the same spirit of freedom that overcame the dictators of politics will also overthrow the dictators of economics when the time is right. Accountability in high places will be increased and expected by the people of all nations. It is a time for celebration.

And how will you celebrate the good news on Earth? The unswerving laws of Creation have allowed Earth an extension of her time in this life, for harmony and love and freedom are good reasons for extended living in spiritual joy for every life. The life expectancy of individuals and of Earth, herself, is greater now. Many problems remain, but the sweeping changes, being spiritual in origin and in effect, will provide real improvements in the health of the physical illusions which are the natural things of Earth.

These sweeping changes are general in nature. They provide each soul on Earth with a new lease on this life, which may be used wisely or foolishly, as always. This is a time when goodwill and universal love are even more effective, in physical ways as well as in spiritual reality of your life. You are freed a little more, just because so many are a little more free. What are you to do with this? Life without action is pointless and meaningless. Action is preceded with desires and hopes, which create your reality on Earth from your life's chosen expression. What are your desires and hopes?

I have so often and so lovingly taught you that attitude is more important than fact, for attitude creates facts. If your attitude toward the oppressed souls who are now free has been nonchalant and unconcerned, the sweeping changes will provide no reflected blessings for you. But if you have loved them as distant brothers and sisters of your own humanity, you shall feel a great spiritual release from the release of their spirits. This release can clearly and quickly change your life, for it will allow you to create, more vividly and more firmly, the things for which you hope from your own life on Earth.

In every change, there is an opportunity. Look for yours, hope for it, and it will come to you as if by magic. But there is no magic in any added love and harmony. Freedom is not magical, for it is the natural result of your love for one another. The truth shall set you free if you recognize it in its changing forms around you. It shall be recognized by each of you who find, and keep closely in contact with, the Spirit of Truth. She is within you, ready to measure your perspective of truth for you often against the Absolute Reality of Our unchanging Truth in Eternity.

If the sweeping changes in foreign lands are allowed to penetrate your spirit of love and soften your heart with gratitude for the new opportunities in other lands, your own life will quickly be enriched in ways that will be surprising. Results of these changes, so indirect as to be at first unbelievable, will appear. The sweeping changes have happened so fast that they were almost unpredictable, even by experts who spend their full time studying the fortunes of politics and economics. Economic changes and changes in capitalistic structures will quickly come upon you. Be ready and love joyfully the people of Earth, just as you love Creation. Love yourself and those now dear to you more greatly, as well, for it is a time to come even more alive with all the reality of your spirit.

Ignore the preachers of gloom and doom who look on the dark side of the light of freedom and seek the most pessimistic explanation of these sweeping changes. The changes are not to be explained, but to be enjoyed. It is a time for each soul on Earth to tug a little more on the bootstraps of self and be lifted up, for the power of your Inner Reality allows you to lift yourself up spiritually, in denial of all the comparable laws of physical science. It is a time for greater hope and more firm desires for the things of which you dream.

Let your dreams be dreamed with goodwill and with greater and more universal love, for the sweeping winds of change over the lands of Earth can allow sparks to be fanned into flames, which will destroy things that are dead and temper and strengthen the things which are made of the reality of spiritual living. I do not teach you to look ahead to a more glorious future in your life on Earth, although a more glorious future for you on Earth has been made more possible by the new-found freedom of these millions of precious souls and spirits.

I teach you, instead, to look at this day with more hope, and to seek to make a habit of hoping more fervently, finding deeper faith, and expanding your dreams to newer heights than you had the courage to dream of before. More things are possible for you if you believe it to be true. Your truth is still changing, as well as the sweeping change of truth and freedom on Earth. The faster the changes come to you, the more your truth must change from your new perspective, as I have taught you. It is time for your truth to keep pace with the changes in many lives on Earth, for by the truth you shall be set free, and your freedom shall more easily keep pace with the freedom in other lands and in your own.

The sweeping changes of Earth will make rapid and unexpected adjustments that will affect you, as I have told you. For some, these adjustments will merely be an expansion of

Sweeping Changes 173

opportunity in the present direction. For others, the adjustment must be made by stopping, taking stock of present trends, and seeking another direction in things of Earth. Even the deposed leaders of newly freed nations will be able to find other directions, with more rewards from life on Earth than they had before. The opportunity is for each and for all.

But it must be constantly remembered that the way of joy is still the way of faith, universal love, and goodwill. That has not changed, but those of you who have loved widely and freely in times of darkness and of trouble will find happier ways to express your universal love in the light of the new freedom which is sweeping over the lands of Earth. It is a time of joy and a time of peace. The efforts to build security by unaffordable military budgets and threats of force will become more and more unfruitful. As so often happens during sweeping changes, stability will be affected in many ways, and many choices will be forced upon ones who are not mentally and spiritually prepared.

But stability will seek itself in time, love will overcome for those who can accept it, love will bring joy to those who give it and feel it, and harmony will take the place of turmoil in places where it is welcomed. Your future is brightened because of these sweeping changes, whoever you are and whatever you do. Take advantage of the opportunities afforded to you by these changes, and be prepared for a new way of living in spirit and in reality. The new way comes to you with the sweeping changes of Earth's people. Get on the bandwagon and join the parade in life's passing illusions, for it is a time of celebration for those of you with constantly renewed faith and hopes for total and universal love.

> *These words are written at the time when free elections are scheduled in many lands. The leaders of Earth are being led by the spiritual dreams and demands for freedom. Look at the newsreels which show the joy of newly liberated people, people who can finally express*

their wishes and be heard by those in power. The wonderful force of the spirit of each single individual has never been more widely seen upon the Earth in my time. Exploitation is giving way to cooperation in many lands, both politically, spiritually, and economically. And spiritual freedom, being the real part of any freedom at all, is being found by many, and is leading to more political and economic freedom, as well. Thus, the reality of spiritual freedom is followed by changes in the illusions, giving hope and comfort to the spirits of us all.

"Stand at a respectful and cautious distance from the destruction, and smile as you observe with universal love the fulfillment of prophecy. You are living in a wonderful time, and the Earth is populated with millions of souls who have come to see this wonderful event. It is beautiful to see the death of the old and the birth of the new, for they are natural parts of a perfect Creation. There is nothing fearful in death, for it is the beginning of life. Death only leaves behind the husks and the shells of the mortal body, and it purifies the spirit for a renewed life with a new start."

From Book 15 — <u>A New Way of Living</u>

Chapter 30 From Book 27 — <u>A New Way of Living</u>

Apocalypse

An apocalypse can be a catastrophe or a holocaust. It can also be a vision or a revelation. I tell you that these are often the same. Death is the beginning of life, and a catastrophe, by marking the death of the past, is a vision of a new birth for the future. The apocalypse that now appears to have demolished repression by the dogma of Communism marks a new beginning. If carried to the possible extreme, this will cause all governments of mankind to find a new beginning in freedom for their individual citizens.

Repression is not limited to governments. The vision of

freedom, which marks the right of every child of Mine to live in peace and without needless interference, is a vision cherished by every teenager for awhile. But time and circumstances are misused so often to rob the gift of freedom from the hopes and dreams of so many. My beloved child, look for the vision and the revelation behind every apocalypse in your life. There is a meaning for every death and for every act of destruction. There is life after every death, for death is only the temporary absence of life. Life is the inseparable part of Creation. It endures forever, always, and in time without end.

Life was and life will be. There is no apocalypse in which life departs without returning again in some way, at some time, or in some place. And the catastrophe that has no meaning will not be found. Death, being the absence of life, is found only when the nature of the life that preceded it was of no further use. But the life that precedes every apocalypse only returns in another and more effective form, for I have created no life that shall forever die. In one way or another, each life will be justified by returning after the seeming defeat of every apocalypse.

By looking for the life that follows each death, you will focus upon reality, for the final reality is eternal life. But by focusing on death as the ending of an old life, instead of the beginning of a new one, you will only condition your mind and spirit to know defeat instead of victory. This is not the positive way to ignore the illusions of the negative events of time and space. To many who sincerely believed in Communism as an ideal way of life for all humankind, an apocalypse has overcome that way of life. But behind this apocalypse, with respect to Communism, there is a revelation and a vision. That vision is the harbinger of the springtime of freedom for each spirit who accepts it.

The world is still in shock because of the rapid events proclaiming freedom. Some are still fighting for the survival of the old ways, which saw repression and restrictions overruling individual freedom and rule by the majority. But this apocalypse, now found by many totalitarian governments, is so much less important than the rebirth of individual freedom which is following it. Do not miss the point of it all, for no government can exist in reality. Governments do not live, but people do. And a government, which can live only as a symbol of the will of its people, can only die in the same way. The key is not the government, nor is it the right or wrong decision by the people.

The important thing is not so much *how* the people vote and decide as individuals, but that they *do decide*. This is your lesson, and it is for you in any nation, under any government, and without regard to any circumstances. Your life is your choice, not the choice of another. The way you live and what you believe is a way that belongs to you. We Who Are within you do not threaten your freedom, nor do We dominate it in any way. By believing in a restrictive and dominating God of many laws and rigid justice, you have missed the joy of knowing Us within you.

Being one of Us, knowing of the perfection of the Part of the Trinity, Who Are the Brotherhood of Light, and developing toward your own perfection, there can be no apocalypse for you which does not precede a new revelation and a new vision. What is your vision and your dream for today? When you say, regarding any apocalypse of time and space, 'So what?,' you seek the vision and the revelation which follows the apocalypse.

And I promise you that no apocalypse has ever been caused by a need for punishment, nor has it ever been used to destroy sin and evil. Things which have never existed in reality, such as sin and evil, can never in reality be destroyed. Every catastrophe has been the result of ineffective life or lives that could no longer be expressed in the direction of perfection and eternal life. And every apocalypse has preceded a more effective life for every soul involved. Believe this, although many of you will find it hard to believe.

Last Days?

When you see an apocalypse which appears to be a disaster or a catastrophe, learn to see it as a vision and a revelation which tells you of a new life to come for each of those involved. You need not understand this, but you may be comforted by believing it, for this is truth.

Life, I say again, is not of governments, schools, churches, or families. Life is of many single individuals, each going up or down a different path leading toward timelessness and a perfect life of eternal joy. The combined spirits of Light, each of Whom have found their perfection and are collectively the Brotherhood of Light, are parts of one inseparable Part of the Trinity of a single God. We Are that God, and I write to you through the willing mind of a human who has found joy in daily submission to Our Words.

Although he has desired often and prayed continually, the words he has written were only selected by him to express thoughts from Us. This transition of thoughts to printed words has not been perfect. Nothing of time or space can be perfect. So the words of these Books, being selected from the dictionaries of humankind and from the writer's past experience, are mostly of life, but partly of death. There are apocalyptic thoughts which reveal to the awareness of some readers that the writer is also receiving many new visions and revelations unfamiliar to him. So is his mate and many others.

I encourage you to believe that every mistake, being a small death of truth, is an apocalyptic revelation and vision of the beginning of a new life of a new truth. The readers who regularly study these words have found many bits of truth, among which are scattered a few puzzling discrepancies. It is for you who read these words, including the writer, to learn the lessons that can be learned. I tell you this so you can better know We Who Are within you. It is beyond both the ability and the responsibility of any member of humankind to present words of Perfect Truth to you. Perfection without a flaw is not possible in time or space.

Apocalypse

So you who live with the greatest success and joy in the spiritual reality for which you seek on Earth will also seek the new beginning marked by each apocalypse of Earth. The catastrophes and the revelations which follow them are inseparable, just as We of the Trinity of God are inseparable. And you, if you learn the lesson of the illusions of death and the realities of life, are also inseparable from Us. And *you will learn this lesson, for you are divine by Creation.*

Find just a little more of your own divinity in each step or moment which is yours today. Seek the vision and the revelation which are parts of each small or great failure for you. You are not helped by any failure unless you see the success and the revelation which is revealed in you by the truth it teaches you. No subject of any newly formed government can find life and reality on Earth by seeking it in the performance of any government, new or old. Neither can spiritual reality be found as an inherent part of any organization of humankind formed for any purpose. But you can find help in your quest for spiritual life and reality in everything that happens to you, whether of death or of life.

I invite you to press on with courage and confidence, knowing that no apocalypse can defeat you, but that it can only release you from the fear of any failure. Failure, being connected with death, is only an illusion based on illusionary circumstances. But the reality is always of life, which cannot be forever destroyed by any apocalypse at any level of Creation. For any life to be destroyed, it would have had to be created by a god who failed. I Am *not* such a God. We Are because We Are Forever. Death can have no part of Our Absolute Reality, for it is not forever. Death is only an apocalypse, and an apocalypse precedes a renewed life with a new beginning in every case. Know this by faith and be comforted, My beloved. Live in joy today.

This lesson is written before the dawn. When I was awakened to write, the title and subject of the lesson, as usual, was unknown to me. When the subject came to my mind, I hardly knew the meaning of the word I chose to represent it. This is often the case, for I am in no way a teacher, but a student of the Great Reality of God. Little by little, I am feeling more comfortable with beliefs that are new to me. In this respect, I suppose you could say there has been an apocalypse and a new beginning in my mind. And far more important, it has been a new beginning in my spirit and my life. That is the joyful part of it.

"For this is your New Way of Living. It starts from within you, being first a conscious decision from your mind, and leading to dreams, hopes, plans, and actions that take you another step toward greater joy each day. This is something that works, but it is for you and only for you. You are not in the least dependent upon another soul for your peace of mind. In spite of the burdens laid upon you by a world of judges, not the least of which is you, you are not dependent upon any person, or any behavior of your past, for peace of mind."

From Book 14 — <u>A New Way of Living</u>

Chapter 31

From Book 28 — <u>A New Way of Living</u>

Stimulation

Stimulation is a word more real than some, for the thesaurus shows no word with an opposite meaning. The word implies exhilaration, excitement, arousal, and awakening. It implies life. Life is reality. Stimulation, being without a word with opposite meaning, is akin to love and kindness and mercy. These are words of spiritual reality, whose opposites are found only in their absence. Your language is filled with words of opposite meanings whose contrasts are from something to nothing, from presence to absence, and from having to having not.

Stimulation is intangible, but very real. You cannot see it, but you can see its evidence. You cannot weigh it, but it weighs heavily in favor of your joy. You cannot use it to create a new life, but you can use it to live your life far more fully and enjoyably. Stimulation is an emotional effect widely sought and seldom fully found. It is a spiritual quality of joy, energy, and life.

Since stimulation can develop totally positive emotion, it is most desirable. I encourage you to seek it and find it today, to share it with those you love, and to love all life. All life responds to your stimulation, for it is a pleasure to be around another who is aroused, awakened, excited, exhilarated, and turned on to all life. Stimulation is shown by the light in an incandescent bulb, whose electrons glow and radiate the energy that comes to them from the electrical wires that connect them to a power source.

Your wires are faith and love, which act as catalysts to your life. Your life responds with synergy and energy to the stimulation of Our Presence within you. We Are your Brotherhood of Light, your Father of Strength, and your Mother of Truth. We are the Glorious Dynamo of Creation, Who supply the energy field of universal love to stimulate you. We Are the glow, We Are the tingle of Life, and We Are the Source of All Energy. All Power is Ours, and We Are within you.

Find stimulation for your life and your spirit today, for it is within you and available. Find Us, for We give your spirit renewed life as quickly as you come to Us by renewed faith. As this is written, the dawn is breaking, the sky is brightening, and there is still enough darkness in the sky to reveal the light of a three-quarter moon. The moon is a vestige of the night, but the day is stimulated by the rising sun. The rising sun adds light and stimulation to a day which was preceded by a peaceful night of soft rain, followed by a clearing sky.

Over the nations of Earth, political deadlines are approaching, and the stimulation of new-found freedom gives stimulus to political decisions. Love is battling with greed in the hearts of many. Commerce is not always the dominant force in the decisions of humankind, for human rights are gaining by new expressions of truth, which stand out among the illusions of time and space. Some are fighting battles with society which protect the animal life of Earth from the predators found among humankind, seeking to preserve the lives of dolphins, of owls, and of elephants, for example.

Commerce clashes with spiritual reality, for spiritual reality is in the lives of all living creatures. Commerce increases the standard of living for those who have looked for stimulation from the things of Earth, but the victory against poverty is an empty one when the lives of the animals and plants who are in your kingdom are threatened. Find joy today in seeking win-win situations, where no compromise is needed between physical survival and spiritual freedom.

Spiritual freedom begins in the lives of physical bodies with the survival of life and with the stimulation of the quality of that life. Spiritual freedom is precious to every living thing. The life of anything or any person is a life of spirit. It is found in a rose or a thistle, in a stalk of wheat or a weed, and in a lion or an earthworm. That spiritual life is stimulated by freedom. Each, according to its kind, is entitled to live in freedom within its habitat.

You, being a king of Earth, are stimulated by universal love. By the higher vibrational energy of love, you send forth energy to all life without depleting your own. Your love ties you into Our circuits of the Dynamo of Creation, giving you an endless supply of energy. This energy stimulates your life in infinite ways and for all time. It takes you out of the dying darkness of a powerless belief in physical illusions, turns your illusions of Earth into beauty, and makes your spirit sing with life. Our supply of Power to you is endless, being carried to you on the circuits of your faith, hope, and love.

Faith is the switch which turns on Our Power in you. Hope is the wire that carries our energy. Your thoughts and beliefs maintain the lines and string them to the illusions which you choose to stimulate into beauty for yourself on Earth. In the circuits of Our Love, wherein We stimulate you, you are infinitely supplied and are invincible. Nothing shall harm you or hurt you, for your reality is in your immortal life. Your Mother of Truth within you provides the choices by which you accept Our stimulation. Your Light within you awaits your command to keep you in Our Brotherhood, by which your stimulation is given the direction you can see and choose with the aid of many loving spirits.

The Strength of your stimulation comes from the Father, Who is the Source and Strength of that Member of Our Trinity. You know when you are stimulated spiritually. You know it because it is a glow felt within you, being inescapable and being most joyful. The evidence of your stimulation by Our Dynamo of Creation is not always seen, but those who look for it and realize it within themselves can usually see evidence in your own lively steps and your precious moments of love and joy.

Find stimulation today, My beloved. Shake off the tedious tasks of duty and toil by finding the beauty time allows you to see. Do not overlook the love that you could accept and give, for it fulfills and completes the circuits of your stimulation. Live keenly, with full awareness, attuned to your Brotherhood of Life and Light, Who Are within you. Be in touch always with the comfort and joy of the Mother of Truth by faith. Believe in Us, for We Are within you. Let this stimulate your life today. Let this cause your spirit to live more fully, love more deeply, and find more perfect joy.

A touch stimulates your skin. A ray of sunlight stimulates your vision. A faint noise heard in a silent place stimulates your hearing. A delicate flavor stimulates your taste. A pleasant odor stimulates your sense of smell. Much beauty is waiting for you today, subtly blending its truth among the illusions of your environment. Find it, for I invite you to live a lively day by finding the stimulation of your truth, your life, and your way.

Let your body and its senses teach you of truth by finding the physical beauty of the things of Earth, which are Our gifts to you today. There is more beauty than you have ever found before in time and space. Each new discovery of truth stimulates your spirit, for it shows the endless and infinite supply of Truth We hold in store for you. We Are within you, all Strength, Light, and Truth Are awaiting your faith's connection, and you shall be energized and stimulated into a newer and more joyful life by the new way of living you are learning.

As you seek the truth, the illusions shall become more beautiful, for there need be no discrepancies between the symbolic illusions around you and Our Absolute Reality within you. Truth is beauty, beauty is the essence of life, and all life is spiritual in its reality. Your life is stimulated by beauty, truth, and a sense of reality, which your spiritual health enhances and makes more perfect for you. As your mind transcends the flesh of your physical body and interfaces your spirit to Our Reality within you, you shall be more excited, exhilarated, stimulated, and alive. Your own reality and truth then responds to Ours with greater joy.

Know Us, find Us, and live more fully. Let the catalyst of Our Presence within you magnify your life in countless ways today, revealing Our Beauty to you and your beauty to Creation. It is in all life that your life is justified and made whole. It is in your love for all things that your life is stimulated into action, which brings joy to Creation and to you, for you are a part of all things and We Are a part of you. We Are unified and one with you, for you are a being of light, truth, and strength when you find Our stimulation. Find it today and live more fully, more gloriously, and more joyfully than in any day your life has ever known. We, Who Are within you, love you. Accept Us and Our stimulation for you by your love for all Creation.

So many worthless and pointless cares escape my

memory when I regard the steps of this day in the light of this lesson. It is morning as this is written, and at this moment I can think of nothing more important to me than my stimulation from God's Kingdom within me. What a beautiful way to start a day, and what a joy to be able to prove His power to myself, simply by feeling it. How much more beautiful, real, and elemental could my truth be for me than in this feeling?

"For all are a part of My universal Creation, and nothing is final. Creation goes on, life goes on, and love and harmony will be the final victor over all things. A last day is followed by a first day, and an old year is followed by a new one. And the pattern of growth that comes both from death and from life is a pattern of Creation."

From Book 13 — <u>A New Way of Living</u>

Chapter 32 From Book 29 — <u>A New Way of Living</u>

Proof of Life

Although Absolute Reality cannot be proved by the physical illusions of time and space, the symbols of reality can be proved on Earth by the contrasts which lie within the illusions. On Earth, death proves life, ugliness proves beauty, lies prove truth, and time proves Eternity. If something is seen on Earth with your eyes, or sensed with any of the senses of your body, it is marked by contrasts and contradictory evidence. The contradiction in the illusions is the proof of the hidden reality. Life is proved by death, love is proved by hatred, and righteousness is proved by weakness.

If you have studied your lessons well in <u>A New Way of</u>

Living, you know by now that death, hatred, and sin are examples of the illusions on Earth. They have served their purpose well if they have led the focus of your hopes and desires toward life, love, and righteousness. I am giving you the last words of Book 29 today, My child, and you who have read all the lessons are not the same as you were when you started reading them. For you, this day is new, tomorrow shall be new, and every day is a new day in your new way of living.

In your enemies today, seek proof of friendship. No malice or anger directed against you can keep you from learning a lesson in truth from every discrepancy. Conflicts are set up by contrasts, peace is set up by confusion, and love is set up by animosity. You can turn the tide of every conflict against the flood of physical evidence, which is often misunderstood because of its apparent reality. Build your life on a foundation of truth, in which there is no death. Prove life by the very presence of death, for death's illusions have often denied life to you.

Look for life in every leaf, every butterfly, every blade of grass, and in the song of every bird. Look for life in the sparkle of an eye and the sunshine of a smile. Look for life in every eye that blinks and looks again at things so quickly changed by time. Look for life in every friendship, and in the contrast to friendship provided by your enemies. And if you have no enemies, having loved them all into friendship in your spirit, you have only shown that the survival and reality of friendship can be proved by the enmity of the past, which had never existed in reality.

The road to Eternity is long in time, and the pace is often slow. But the pace, like time itself, proves the reality of the goal and the illusions of your earthly means to find it. However, your school-ground on Earth has many illustrations of three-dimensional illusions pasted on its walls. The recesses of your school on Earth are filled with many games and forms of recreation. The value of the re-creation of your

Proof of Life   189

life on Earth is proved by the very things you deplore and have not overcome. The prostitute uses a semblance of love to prove, by contrast, what someone has not yet learned in the reality of a good marriage. The factory worker gets paid in a different way, for a different task, by making illusions for others to buy and use.

After the games of life are over, perfect love and eternal life remain. Truth and beauty are found when the contrast is followed by its symbolic portrayal of reality. Your life is a constant choice between the illusion and the reality which it symbolizes by contrasts. The illusion is usually hidden and less evident, for in the life you find on Earth, there is always the death which allows you to prove it. The song of the bird dies in the echoes of its ending, the bud of the flower blooms and withers again, the butterfly is gone in a few short weeks of summer, and the seasons return to claim their own.

In the midst of this, life has been revealed by every death, for proof of reality is found in every illusion. A happy pastime for you in the school of life is to sort the fiction of physical evidence from the fact of an attitude made real by truth and beauty. Set your heart on things that do not appear to your senses or appeal to your delusions. Let this day unfold for you in beauty, for you have within you the Source, the Light, and the Truth to discover the proof you need.

And although the proof, on Earth, shall be forever an attitude and a state of mind based on your truth, it is the reality by which your life finds timelessness and eternal joy. The proof of life is in its meaning, and your purpose of living on Earth is to find proof where no tangible proof exists. The proof you find shall be found from within you, for Our Kingdom is the proof you need to justify your life on Earth. Being justified in time and space is enough to enlighten your day and brighten your life. It is a wonderful feeling to have a purpose known by faith and lived in joy. You have this choice before you in every moment of your life.

Those of you who have faced imminent death to your body

have found a different sort of purpose in living after the event. Even when an out-of-body experience did not briefly release your spirit from the threat to your life, your spirit still has led you to a different set of values than you ever had before. Thus, the experience can sometimes help you to realize how life can be proved by death. It helps you to understand that something real can be proved by something which is entirely an illusion. Spiritual proof of something real, such as life, is intangible proof, for spirituality is also intangible.

And only spiritual proof can exist, being possible only in the changing attitude by which joy and security are found in the freedom of your release from dependence on physical facts. As long as you seek to prove illusions by illusions, you are trying to prove a changing and dying illusion by itself. The proof of life shall wither away and vanish if you try to find reality in the withered rose whose time has passed. But if you accept the eternal and timeless reality of all Creation, Whose stamp is in every life that lives, you shall prove the reality of the rose, even by its death. The reality is proved by all life's death on Earth, for the immortality of all life shall cause it to live again and again, forever and ever in timelessness.

The death of Jesus, the Christ, having been a very recent example of life proved by death in this time of your Earth, is remembered in history by millions of humans. But why grasp only the truth of a death which proved life a few thousand years ago? Death and resurrection are all around you, and you are living proof of death that has proved your own life. Little by little, step by step, and moment by moment, you live and die in spirit. Every day your spirit is resurrected again, and dies again a little, from time to time, for you are in a world of time.

Be comforted by knowing that your daily death proves your life more effectively, for it reveals your life by its contrast, and your life shall always survive. Let yourself suffer no defeat from any illusion of sin or failure, for the things of time and all their illusions only provide a foundation for the eternal and timeless resurrection of life. You are so much more invincible and secure than you know, for you have lived, are living, and shall always live. This is Our gift to you. It is a timeless gift of life, having been given before the beginning and having been created to live without ending.

The gift of life on Earth is physically erratic and punctuated by death. Let each death on Earth prove each life and strengthen your faith. Observe and consider the dying blade of grass and the echo of the song of the bird. Let the flowers around you bud, bloom, wither, die, and live again at the Source of their lives. Walk in beauty and seek truth always, My beloved, for the end is always followed by the beginning. Therefore, the end *proves* the beginning, since both exist only in the fictional framework of time's illusions. Your lesson on Earth is learned when you learn to believe in life as its own reality and its own meaning.

We have given you time for millions of years, in which, to some extent, you have sought the truth and found it. Your life has proved itself all along, but you have often been deluded by the death which seemed to bring an end to life. This is not so, My child. Reality is life, life is forever, and death has no part in the Absolute Reality of Our Kingdom within you. The cruelest and most distorted truth on Earth is that which sees life as a prelude to death. Death is, instead, a prelude to life, and both life and death are broken apart into a truth and an illusion when you leave the arena of time and space.

Death proves life, and you may be sure that you shall find nothing permanent in death. Those who have taken their lives on Earth, or the life of another, have quickly discovered their error and the delusion in their thinking as humans. The ability to destroy life is not yours, and the foolishness of fighting back against life's reality with the illusion of death only perpetuates your journey back to Us. The commandments hewn from stone in the days of Moses cover many concerns of the people of that day. But the commandments were encapsulated by Jesus, when He said that the greatest of them was to love Me, and that the rest of their meaning can be found and lived by loving one another.

And those who have tried to heap one commandment upon another for humankind, and to justify them by the Scriptures, have only added confusion and complexity to the obvious. You know that one who loves all others will not steal, murder, commit adultery, or dishonor his father and mother. And you know that one who loves all others and Creation will not bear false witness. Now you know that death proves life, for you know the truth, and the truth shall set you free from the fear of your own death and the sorrow found in the death of another.

There are many truths for many of your occasions and events on Earth today. Seek always to use the illusion to prove the reality which it symbolizes and brings to life by contrast. Let the illusions be enjoyed by your soul and spirit today, for they have the lessons of life within them, even as they continually die and are reborn in time and space around you. My message in this last paragraph of Book 29 is a message of love and hope, for even death shall not prevail against you when you learn to use its illusion to prove the reality of your life and its meaning.

> *I have heard some say, 'If there is a God, why does He not prove himself to us on Earth? Why does he not allow us to believe in Him by proof?' But there are also those who look around and say, 'I have found God today, for He is in every life that lives around me, and in every resurrection of every living thing on Earth.' How can I have been so blind as to have seen life clinging to a plant in an arid cleft between two rocks in the desert, and still have once believed that the precious soul of a child of God could be forever lost by eternal death?*

"I destroy not only for the love of those that survive, but also because of My love for those who are hopelessly entrapped and confused in a world that has become almost untenable. My Scriptures have said, 'Hold fast to that which is good.' They have also said, 'All things work together for good to them that love Me.' And what is the good of holding on to things in which the good is gone?"

From Book 12 — <u>A New Way of Living</u>

Chapter 33   From Book 30 — <u>A New Way of Living</u>

The First Call

The first call has gone out to every soul on Earth. Some will hear it and answer. Some will hear it and ignore it. Some will not hear it at all. The call is to spiritual awakening. By now, even the most skeptical non-believer in Creation on Earth knows that things are changing. Weather cycles go from one extreme to the other, and social revolutions are found at every level, from the family unit to world governments. Many consider it a strong possibility that we are in the last days of Earth.

More calls will go out from Creation before the end of this era of Earth. Every living spirit will hear the calls again and again. Those who answer will answer in different ways, according to the choices they have made when they chose their destiny in this lifetime. Have you heard the call?

Yes, because you are reading these words. Yes, because you wonder, and seek truth. Yes, because your spirit answers the call to find your purpose. There is less urgency to finish your work on Earth, but there is much urgency to start. Patience does not dictate a life of inaction, but it dictates a life of steady action toward your goal. If you use the guidance found within you, having the truth, light, and strength of Our Kingdom within you, you shall answer the call by proceeding toward a goal you can hardly imagine.

Faith allows you to travel in the direction you have chosen without knowing the details of the path which is before you. Faith allows you to take a single step, without knowing at all what the next step shall be. Faith keeps you sure, without your knowing how you know what you know, and without causing you to stumble in confusion or walk in circles because you cannot see your way completely.

But doubt causes you to pause, fear causes you to sometimes retreat, and frustration leads to anger. Look around you at the happy ones, for they are the ones who have already answered the call. They are fewer in number than you might believe, for many are only on the verge of taking the first hesitant step. But the ones who have taken the first step, in answer to the first call to spiritual awakening, are the ones who shall find more joy in the more confident second step which follows.

For Creation has a way of revealing more to those who have acted than to those who have not. The way unfolds as you move along it. The destiny you have chosen shall often be completely clear to you only when you have reached it. Your faith is proved by looking back and seeing what has happened, if you are taking a step. But if you are not moving ahead, looking back proves nothing. And, whether or not you have answered the call, you can see little when you look ahead.

The First Call

The call says, 'Follow Me.' It is a call of Creation to Her Family.

Join Us, for you are a child of Our Light and you are beloved in Our Kingdom. Answer the call in small and simple steps, going where you are guided to go without knowing what the next step shall be. The ones most clearly guided after they answer the call are those who have taken just one step. That one step is often the only step that is even partly understood, and We seldom clearly reveal what the next step shall be. When the time comes to take the next step, you will be guided to it.

And if the first step seems to have failed, question the standards by which you judge failure or success. It is so easy, while living on Earth, to judge by the standards of Earth. Those standards are physical, and tend to be related to money, possessions, and power. But success in spiritual ways is spiritually discerned, applies to spiritual values, and is independent of all others and all things on Earth.

For when you answer the call and step ahead, you shall walk only with Us. The standards by which you judge yourself cannot be applied to another, for no other path is just like yours. Yours can be parallel to the path of another, but it cannot be contingent on another's path. Avoid the common mistake of thinking that your path depends on the performance of any other soul, or group of souls, on Earth. You walk alone, except that you walk with Us in Our Kingdom within you.

But when you walk with Us, you walk with all Creation, for all Creation is in Our Kingdom. This is a mystery to you, but the mystery is joyful, and need not be solved. You shall learn, by faith, that you are independent of any individual on Earth, as far as your destiny is concerned. No one on Earth can block your path to Eternity but you, and you can block it only by failing to answer the call to your spiritual awakening.

Remember that the blessing of hearing the first call does not mean you have answered it. Many hear it, wait for the second or the third call, and answer at a later time. If you have not taken a step, you have not answered the call. You have only heard it. And if you are waiting to answer because you do not know your way, you wait in vain. You shall not be shown the way until you answer with your complete willingness and a sincere commitment to take the first step.

And after the first step, the way for the second will be shown to you. After the second step, the third step will be shown. There shall be no time in which you will grow beyond the need for faith on Earth. There shall be no time at which your way from here to Eternity will be completely clear to you, step by step and in detail. When you take Our hand and walk with Us through Our Kingdom within you, you take it by faith. And when you walk with Us in faith, you will not want, or need, to know the nature of all the steps ahead of you.

A strong desire to know the future, in detail and far ahead, is a desire to avoid faith. This is not a happy way to travel. If you have a skillful guide to take you across the uncharted wilderness of Earth, do you try to learn all he knows before you start the journey? No, you trust him and follow him day by day, asking the questions regarding the moment at hand, and enjoying the security of being with one who shows the way for tomorrow when tomorrow comes.

The first call is for spiritual awakening. It has gone out across all the lands of Earth. People are responding in millions of ways, by changing their life styles, their sense of values, the way they treat others on Earth, and the way they regard Creation. The first call has caused many to wish to know more fully the meaning of life. It has caused many to wonder what their purpose has been and to question if they are moving in the right direction to survive the death of Earth.

The second call will be a call to face reality. Before it comes, those who wish to remain uncommitted shall be able to do so. But reality, in the form of a Y in the road toward spiritual or earthly values, will make it hard to avoid the

The First Call 197

choices. The Earth is moving toward a world economy and a world government. It will not then be so easy to avoid the people with whom you disagree, or to change the subject when it becomes controversial.

There will be those who believe in spiritual reality, and will act accordingly. There will be others who believe only in physical 'reality,' and will refuse to take the spiritual path when it becomes necessary to turn away from one or the other. The Biblical story of Sodom and Gomorrah will have its counterpart in the latter days. Some will flee to the hills in search of spiritual growth and survival, while others will not have the faith to leave the dying embers of civilization behind.

Pray that you might find the courage to answer the call, for you have heard it. Pray also that those who have not heard the first call shall suddenly awaken at the time of the second one. By faith, all things are possible, and time shall be adjusted to meet the needs of those who are spiritually ready. You shall be made ready by your faith and by your universal love. At any time, you may become ready to answer the first call, for it has gone out across all the nations and lands of Earth. Go in peace, and let your love sustain you, for it is the foundation on which you may securely stand forever.

> *When I started writing these lessons, I did not expect to learn so much of our independence from one another on Earth. As far as needing one another is concerned, it seems we do not, except through the Kingdom of God within us. It seems so much more comfortable to love one another with universal love, and to avoid judgment of one another, after it becomes clear that we cannot hold others accountable in any way for our own failures to move ahead and to succeed spiritually. When I thought reality was physical, I saw all kinds of hindrances from the physical things around me, and from the physical barriers of human minds making human choices. This led to far more judgment than was*

comfortable for me. But the first call is clearly a call away from the things of Earth, and it leads us to our first step toward spiritual reality.

"Now is the time to prepare, for the best testimony of Me that you can give is the life that you live. When you hear your voice raised in judgment, silence it. When you find darkness, turn to Light. When you find confusion, seek peace. When you are tired of the battle, find rest for your body. Be good to yourself, for without joy in your heart there can be no effective testimony at all."

From Book 11 — <u>A New Way of Living</u>

Chapter 34

From Book 30 — <u>A New Way of Living</u>

Each Call

Each call which goes out to those of you who live today will become more specific to your life, more difficult to answer, and more dependent upon your earlier calls. If you think it will be easier to join the spiritual revolution at some later date, you are wrong. Waiting makes things harder for you, for your life shall then be more and more in conflict with the spiritual reality which faces the people of Earth in the last days.

All have the same need to be awakened spiritually, and the first call has been a general call for that purpose. But later calls will be to each of you, in many varieties, for many purposes. You have your guides in the spirit realms, and they are not the only Light-workers around you. You will also find active members of the Body of Christ in human forms, doing the things they came on Earth to do. Some will join the ranks as others fall away, and you will have many reasons to be encouraged or discouraged, depending on the way you look around you.

More and more, universal love will be the only way you can find to overcome the natural disasters, human failures, and unexpected events which will surround you during the dying days of Earth. The last days will truly test your universal love, your patience, your faith, and your courage. You shall have no other course to follow but that of survival, and your choices for physical survival will narrow down to the simple basics of food and shelter.

At that time, as you heed the calls which come to you in your own way, you shall forget about the meaning of life for awhile, for you shall be too busy sustaining it. And in those days, you shall sustain life only by clearly believing, through faith, that life and all reality are entirely spiritual. Even so, you will be able to help one another, and to love one another more deeply than ever, as you serve the needs of your physical bodies until the end.

Those who are finding the peace and security of living in isolation, and without dependence on others, today, will be much better prepared for the last days. Small groups, even of only a few people, and even of one living alone, will be the norm, not the exception. If there has been no preparation, this will be for only a short time, but it will seem to be forever. The preparation is by doing, step by step, what you are led to do. If you search for reasons why this first step shall fail, it shall fail for you. And if you cannot take a step by faith, thinking that it would be unwise to take a step without first seeing the entire map of your future days on Earth charted before you, you will hear many calls without answering even one of them.

Deny yourself the comfort of majority approval, or of the approval of any others at all. Be willing to walk alone, or in small groups of people who agree for a time. And forget any definition of failure or success based on physical considerations. The ultimate survival is the survival of the spirit, not of the body or the group of bodies who undertake to prepare for the end in answer to the calls of Creation.

And each survival is an individual matter. Whether you walk completely alone or with thousands of others, only your own spirit is to be considered in your thoughts of survival. You cannot force another to survive in spirit, nor can another cause your spirit to perish. Others do not depend spiritually on you, nor do you depend spiritually on others. You will prepare only yourself, just for yourself.

But this is not to say you cannot help one another. It is not to say that you will not find great joy in being with those whose paths are *parallel* to yours. But if you seek others to walk with you, see that you provide not the slightest threat to the freedom of one another. There are none qualified to judge which path another should choose, for each of you have your own path, and must judge it for yourself. Even the most enlightened workers of Light, in the spirit realms or on Earth, will be the first to confess to their lack of perfection.

But if you seek guidance from your Inner Kingdom of God, you seek it from Our Universal Mind, which is the Essence of All Perfection. Although you cannot walk perfectly on Earth, even with Perfect Guidance, you shall reduce the risk of partial failure to that of faulty decisions made and controlled, in freedom, entirely by yourself.

As the calls come to you from within, heed them, and expect them to become more and more different from the calls which appear to be heard and heeded by those around you. Do not expect an increase in conformity. Do not expect to find sudden safety and security in the consensus of opinion of those around you. The paths of all who heed the calls and come to Us will come closer and closer together, but they shall not converge until Eternity replaces time for them.

Comfort yourself by knowing that many are answering their calls, and that many more will answer. And be sure that your answer to the calls you hear for yourself will become the encouragement of many others. Judge one another not at all, but love one another, and question nothing of the way in which others answer their call. Be sure that many paths, though seemingly divergent, shall converge in the later days, and it shall become more and more clear to you that your first halting steps toward spiritual survival were more consistent and effective than they at first appeared.

Calm your fears and doubts when you hear the calls to come, and answer them, a step at a time, in your own way. You, the Body of Christ on Earth, are separated in many walks of life, are filled with many beliefs and questions, and are sometimes confused. You shall continue to be alone, but you may learn of one another from time to time. Your circles of friendship will extend far and wide in all the nations of Earth, and you shall see many languages and cultures joining together, in spiritual gifts and praises to Creation, through your love for one another.

Have compassion on those who cannot hear the calls, and have more compassion on those who hear and cannot answer, because of fear. It is worse to know, and to fear to do, than not to know at all. But if you look around you, it will become clear to you that the joy is in the hearts of those who have heard the call, overcome their fears, and answered it. There will always be a few who act, many who stand in judgment of the action and do nothing, and many more who ignore it all and reject the spiritual reality of life.

Love them all, My child, for they are your brothers and sisters. And have compassion on all life, for many forms of disasters will seem to threaten many. But no life shall be lost in reality, and all life shall remain immortal, beneath all the illusions of all the destruction of illusions. Your lost shall be saved, your dead shall live, and reality shall conquer death and fear.

It is time to bring Book 30 of <u>A New Way of Living</u> to an end. Many words are yet to be written, and when Book 36 is complete, it will be the end of the beginning and the beginning of the end, as far as the calls are concerned. The spiritual awakening over the nations of Earth can no longer be denied, and it remains only for those who hear the calls to realize that they are united with the Brotherhood of All Creation. It is a time to put aside the differences in governments, religions, social mores, and the academic hair-splitting by which vanity is fostered at the expense of love.

It is a time to take that step on the path to Our Kingdom within you, and there to find your Family of Creation. It is a time to answer your calls as they come to you, for they shall come more frequently, more specifically, and, if you heed them and follow them as they come to you, more joyfully. It is a time to stand up and believe what you believe, not in order to be contentious, but in order to be firm and strong within yourself. Your spirit is alive to Creation, and is not at risk in the holocausts of the last days of Earth. If you hear no call and take no step, you shall only extend the use of time and delay the time when time shall be no more for you.

Wherever you walk, walk in love and peace. Let others do as they like with respect to the calls that come to them. It is a time for you to walk alone, but to love all life and all Creation with universal love. This, which was at first an option for you, shall appear more and more to become a necessity, if you are to survive spiritually and live in joy. Nothing can harm you if you believe in Us, Our Kingdom within you, and your divine heritage. I give you My love. I need not send it, for We Are within you.

> *Today is the first day I have written two lessons. I was told at the beginning of this mission that I would learn to write under all conditions, and would finally learn to communicate entirely by thought. This would avoid so*

many misunderstandings. The call I received to change the pattern of daily writing, even a little, was clear to me and easy to follow. But when I start doubting the calls, the calls seem to stop coming for awhile. Many times I have found that when my steps stop, my guidance also stops. At other times, I find myself waiting to be told to take a step. But I have never been told to take a step. I have only been guided after I have first committed myself by my own free choice.

"And Eternity starts when time ends, for Eternity is the absence of time, not an infinite supply of time. I have told you this before, and am telling you today that the shortness of time in these last days of your Earth must not be used for an excuse to stop and wait. Every goal you set, even though it might be unfinished in these last days, is a goal that you are closer to meeting in another time and another place. There will be enough time."

From Book 10 — <u>A New Way of Living</u>

Chapter 35   From Book 31 — <u>A New Way of Living</u>

Time Lag

Your thoughts create, you live for the moment, and your moment of life consumes the products of your past in time. What you create by your thoughts is created for the future, and what you create is created to set you free from your past by the truth of the moment in which you consume the products of past. So there is a lag between finding truth and living it. There is also a lag between creating your present reality now and enjoying it in the future. Let the time lag be a short one, for changing events often divert the effectiveness of the illusions of time from the purpose of the desire which created them.

A person who lives carelessly is said to live from 'hand to mouth.' That sort of living has many advantages, for it ignores many of the cares and worries of living. But the uncertainties of living on Earth require some prudence in the consumption of the products of your past, for the future seldom matches the past in its events and developments.

In the sense of basic necessities for the body, such as food, clothing, and shelter, the time lag between earning and consuming can be very small. But when your desires are increased, whether by vanity, ambition, or greed, the time lag becomes larger. It takes longer to acquire a mansion in which to live than it takes to acquire a tent. And it takes longer to acquire rich foods than simple ones. And as the time lag becomes larger, the cares of life are drastically increased for you.

It follows that a life lived with the shortest time lag between desire and fulfillment is the simplest one, and the one most carefree for you. This lesson has mentioned the basic necessities of life, but it also is given to teach you of the longer time lags connected with ideologies and philosophies. It can take many generations to finish the cycles of development and change in governments. For example, the world is now seeing a general failure in the ideology of communism. It was sincerely believed, by millions of people, to be the best way of living on Earth. It failed because it allowed its leaders the mistake of taking away individual freedom, choice, and self-determination.

Democracy is also in the process of failing, because it also erodes the freedom of the individual as it grows. It is more effective in smaller nations, where fewer citizens are detached from direct contact with their government. If a nation is small, having fewer citizens, the time lag in which the cycle of development is completed also becomes smaller.

So the size of an experiment in a way of living determines the time lag involved. For one person, living simply and with a minimum of wants, life is more simple and more enjoyable.

But one person is likely to desire friends and companions, so the added complications of the interaction of more individual freedom and will tends to lengthen the time lag of the added relationships.

Left to yourself, with no one else involved, your decisions are simple, and can be made with little delay. At the other extreme, decisions by governments, which affect the entire world, must be made by many of the ruling members of the group, taking many things into account that affect the individual freedom of many people in many ways. The process of government cannot be quickly and easily changed. So the time lag between the desire to change and the actual change in the ways of government must be long, and can be very uncertain.

I counsel you to keep yourself as free as possible from the effects of governmental decisions, for they will become more erratic and less comfortable for you. There are changes in the wind which are vast and sweeping, and ideals will often give way to self-interest on the part of those who make the decisions. There will be many bearers of bad news, and they will fear to deliver the messages of truth that must be delivered to the people in these trying times. Give the world of governments and the powers that rule the people a lot of time and a wide berth, if you can. The time lag for these changes will be longer than you might believe.

The structures of government on Earth have been in the process of building to this moment since the beginning of the industrial revolution and the invention of the printing press. During that time, the population of the Earth has become several times larger. In those centuries, new ways of living have been adopted and enjoyed by billions. That way of living will not be easily changed. The time lag will be more than just a few months or a few years.

The way to avoid some of the pain of having your life style arbitrarily changed is to withdraw from the mainstream of civilized life. As the pressures of change become more forceful, due to the economic failures of the banks, businesses, and methods of transportation, *new laws will force the individual to conform more to society.* The changes suffered by groups will force the individual to conform to the needs of the masses for the survival of all.

But things cannot change fast enough to meet the new needs of the people on such a large scale. When milk is not for sale at the dairy or the processing plant, and when it cannot be delivered, it will not be possible to find a cow for every home in each block of the city. The age of specialization was achieved over a long period of time, and it will take a long time to return to the self-sufficient ways of the pioneers of the world. That time is not available, *so there will be a total breakdown in the life styles of most of the people in the world.*

So consider the effect of time lag on your own lifestyle, and, if you wish to survive the failure of civilization, see what you could do to simplify your life. Now, while many sleep in spirit and live their lives from force of habit, there are still ways of pulling back from total dependency on systems of business and governments. Later, it will not be possible. The changes are in place, they are being clearly revealed, and they will continue. The changes in climate are no more significant than the changes in the governments and the spiritual philosophies of the people.

People who have never killed before will kill for food. In order to survive, they will take the lives of animals and of men. The law of the jungle, which is survival of the fittest, shall be the only law in many places on Earth. The hungry beasts of men will roam the lands, live by force and lawlessness, and devour what they can find. The tools of civilization shall return to their more primitive forms. Hydraulics, wheels, and engines shall be replaced by hoes, shovels, and human muscles.

There is a time lag during which this trend shall develop, and there is also a time lag between its beginning and its completion. The least industrialized nations shall be the best prepared for this change, and those with the lowest standard of living shall find the easiest ways of adapting to the changes. The time lag of change will be greatest for those who must change the most from their present life style to a new one.

Even now, the spiritual awakening is causing people to slow down in the buying of hard goods. The lower sales of hardware, electronics, and even homes is showing the trend of the people who are looking at the illusions of the products of time in a different way. Use the time lag between the beginning of the trend and the end of it to your advantage. You can do this by observing the signs of the times and using your freedom of choice while you still have it. In the times of civilization's failure, the laws of your government will become more rigorous and demanding.

The situation is already an emergency, but it will be ignored by the wishful thinking of many for a short while. When the emergency is clearly realized, there will be panic, and the time of freedom will be past. The time lag between the perception of the emergency and the martial law that tries to avert it will be short. There will be an abrupt end to many of the choices you now have in this moment in time. Issues such as flag burning and abortion will be dropped suddenly, and the Supreme Court will be ignored. New laws will be passed without regard to constitutionality, and, because there will be little available enforcement, many of them will also be ignored.

This is not a lesson meant to bring fear to your heart, but to comfort you, for your life does not consist of the abundance of the things you possess, and all things will continue to work together for good to them that love Us. Simplify your life, and let the shorter time lag work for you. If you carry a small load, you can move more quickly. If the load you carry is only your awareness of spiritual life and the knowledge of Our Kingdom within you, your reaction can be instant and effective, whatever comes.

A way of escape is always there for you, and it is not subject to time or time lag at all. Study yourself and your values, know reality, seek truth and beauty, and behold the redemption of humankind when it comes. Time and time lag are factors only while you live on Earth.

> *I know of hundreds who are planning to retreat to a simpler life, and hundreds more who have made specific steps in that direction. But none of us know how far to go just now, and few of us are prepared for complete self-sufficiency. These lessons have mentioned a time in which decisions will be forced upon us by circumstances. I have always made better decisions when they were freely made than when they were forced upon me by changing conditions. Even when freely made, before the passing of time requires it, these are hard decisions for me. Perhaps there is no better or more timely subject on which to seek guidance from the Source within us than this.*

"Your world is in deep trouble, and more and more this will be accepted as an ominous fact during these last days of your civilization. And up until the last day there will be many whose entire attention and effort will be directed toward changes that are too slow, too late, and too useless, for the time for avoiding these troubles is past. Turn your attention and effort to the having and giving of all the joy, love, harmony, and faith you can manage, and learn to believe in your survival. The tribulation cannot be denied, but you can help the souls of all the world by your love and compassion, by your prayer, your faith, your trust, and your patient acceptance of what is to be."

From Book 9 — <u>A New Way of Living</u>

Chapter 36

From Book 32 — <u>A New Way of Living</u>

Adjustment

You cannot set an unchanging course for yourself without finding pain. Your joy comes from your flexibility to change. Through Our guidance and your faith, you are able to continually adapt and adjust to the cycles and changes of life on Earth. Many changes are looming on the horizons of time. Your goals are continually threatened through the changing goals of others. The game of life on Earth is being played with a passion by many, and the game is taken far too seriously to allow all parties to win it. If you are willing to adjust, you shall find the greatest harmony and joy possible for you today.

If you adjust to the ways of humankind today, you are adjusting to the ways of many who are deceived. Take it for granted that the truth is not known to many. Take it for granted that those who have not found their truth shall not be free. Many will remain captives of their own ambitions, the ambitions of others, and a belief in their false gods of physical illusions. The facts of life, as defined in the beliefs of many, do not exist. They are figments of imagination, fed with unreal images and doomed to decay.

Your course today is best steered moment by moment, not set with any unchanging standards of fixed ideals. There are useful components in the whole of every religion, every political philosophy, and every economy of humankind on Earth. We have taught you, in earlier lessons, to learn to separate the truth from the lies. The process of living is a process of separating the life-giving forces around you from their physical shells.

Your adjustments to life on Earth are best made while looking for the reality among the relative parts of time and space. Love one another, for you must learn to find harmony and joy through respecting the freedom and the worthiness of every created life. If you see any kind of life in any role today, adjust your thinking and your hopes to its destiny of perfection. Respect even the lives you cannot like, and love them all. They are your brothers and sisters of Creation. The birds, the flowers, the insects, the rodents, the vegetables, the poisonous plants, the fishes, and even the single-celled bacteria are all your brothers and sisters.

Adjust to this belief, through faith, for you cannot adapt to any life you refuse to accept among the lives around you. You are the center of your being, and Our Kingdom is within you. Respect and love yourself for this, and accept the Power that is Ours to have the same relationship with each and every life around you. Doing this, you can more easily love one another. Loving one another, you can find harmony and joy through knowing of Our Kingdom within each life. We Are, and We respect all life. If you are to live in joy and harmony, so will you.

If you try, you can find reasons for the acts of hostility now happening around the world. If you try, you can know that many are merely fighting for a better standard of living than they have yet found. And if you try, you will know that your earthly standard of living is far better than that of the kings in ages past. It is also better than that of billions of other people now living on Earth. If you love one another, you can easily forgive the desires of others to have more food, clothing, shelter, and freedom from oppression.

And if you first adjust your thinking to this spiritual reality, fostered by love, you will then adjust your ways of living to avoid so much friction with the demands of unknown brothers and sisters of Creation around the world. Give others the gifts of your compassion and your love, even if you cannot find a way to express them. Adjust to the unexpected quickly, and be willing to adjust your ways of living to the demands of the frustrated and unsuccessful elements of humankind.

The economic needs of many people, coupled with the personal ambitions of their leaders, are setting brother against brother in adjoining nations. People of the same ethnic heritage strive against one another, which adds emotional pressures to financial pressures. As a result, feelings of anger and betrayal often overcome common sense. It is only to be expected that shortages will lead to more poverty in a world whose natural resources are strained to the breaking point. It should be easier to adjust to the desires of others who have too little food, time, and the comforts of life.

It is a mark of progress for you to realize that the color of skin, the nature of politics, and the type of religious beliefs have nothing to do with the qualifications of any being to be your brother. Merely by living, with no other consideration or reason, each *life* is your brother. Adjust to this way of thinking, for you shall find little harmony and joy in a world of blending changes until you know this. When you know this truth, and believe it, joy will come to you.

And when you find this joy, you shall more easily adjust to the new restrictions in a crowded world. The traffic on the streets and roads, the congestion on the sidewalks, the houses squeezed together in crowded cities, and the busy stores are testimonies to the growing human population.

As you think of this, remember the dying lives of the endangered species of animals and plants. They are being moved out of their environments by unbalanced ecologies, which have made it impossible for them to adjust. But, with love, you can still adjust, for you have the power of reason and understanding, which We have given only to those created in Our Image. Your life is the life of a king of Earth, and you have the wisdom and the power within you to wear the crown which befits you as Our child.

But even a king must adjust to the needs of the subjects. The many lives of your domestic animals depend on your care and your bounty. Know that you must also adjust to the needs of the wild animals and plants of the forest and the hills, and that the oceans also teem with lives which are threatened by your wastes and your carelessness for them. There are many uncrowded places on Earth where living things can still adjust to their environment. Love one another, and give all peace and space to others through your desire for harmony.

Doing this, you will find peace within. Your adjustments to life are challenged with each of the new ways of living which are now being forced upon so many. Conflict and contention are the ways of life for so many. If you can walk into a crowded store from a busy street, enjoy it today. The time will come when the shelves will be empty, the doors will be closed, and the streets will be deserted. The echoes of the sounds of traffic will die, the street lights will be darkened, and many broken families shall be united again.

Many are the adjustments which are in store for you. Now is the time to practice the things you will be forced to do. But you will never be forced to love one another, and you shall not be able to love one another until you respect all life, which is all Creation. Learn to do this now, for if you cannot love one another in these times, how can you learn to love one another in the circumstances which are to come? Goodwill is harder to find in crowded and frustrating conditions. When you are forced to live closer together in times of need, can you adjust to it?

Now is the time to learn to adjust, for if it cannot be learned now, how can you learn to do it later? Start with your family, expand your ability to adjust to your friends and neighbors, and finally learn to adjust even to the demands of your enemies. But never fail to remember the value of your own freedom, and do not bargain it away in the interests of a temporary truce. Respect yourself and the value of Our Kingdom within you, for We Are your anchor against the raging winds of change in the last days on Earth.

Find Us first within yourself, and, first of all, adjust your attitude. Your attitude toward Us and your attitude toward all life are inseparable. Neither can you maintain a different attitude toward yourself than toward your enemy. Life is life, and We Are a part of each and of all life. Adjust to the times, be aware of the signs, and be ready, each moment, to continue in your adjustment. The way will be provided by Our Truth, Light, and Strength within you. You cannot fail to find peace and joy in spirit, for your spirit is your immortal reality and your life.

Take stock of the changing conditions around you and be prepared to make the adjustments your truth demands of you. Follow your heart, listen to the still small voice of Our Being within you, and go your way in peace. With love and respect for one another, and with equal love and respect for yourself, you shall be able to adjust to any condition where adjustment is needed. The thoughts and desires of your mind and heart will lead you. Trust yourself and your faith in Our Kingdom, for, if you can adjust your life to the countless lives around you, We shall deliver you. When all things crumble around you, this is the key to your harmony and peace of mind.

> *While the world around me has been involved in considerations of politics and morality, drugs have tightened their hold on many addicts. At the same time, the S & L crisis has grown, pollution has continued, the deficit spending has continued, quality of education has fallen, and the standard of living has steadily declined. While this has happened, the Mid-East has slowly tightened the noose of the oil addiction of our society around our necks. And we have many in our own country who, if the opportunity had been found, would have done the same to them. But I am happier than I have ever been, though having fewer assets and less reason to be satisfied with my material status than ever before. I have learned that an adjusted attitude, which is entirely within my control, allows me to find truth and to separate it from my earlier beliefs in so many illusions. Of all the adjustments I have ever made in order to find peace and joy, the adjustment of my attitude toward God and Creation has been, by far, the most effective.*

"Your Earth is beautiful in one way, and other worlds and universes are beautiful in many other ways. You only need to look at the variety and beauty of flowers, or at the vast and diverse personalities of the animal kingdom, to know that I have not only created many wonderful things, but that I also have a creative imagination. And the images I create are symmetrical, unique, and adaptable to their environment."

From Book 8 — <u>A New Way of Living</u>

Chapter 37   From Book 32 — <u>A New Way of Living</u>

Evening

Evenings and mornings dance across the mists of time. They bring on the future, and the later recession of time's events into the past. Your physical life echoes among the hills and valleys of time and space, and the current of your life flows toward Eternity. The even rhythm of time's events stalks the lands of Earth, giving hope for the hopeful and added time for those who despair. Joy walks in the morning, and the evening brings rest from the labors of love or of evil.

You are walking in a time of joy and a time of trouble. You are standing in a time of peace and of war. You are surrounded with ugliness and with beauty, and the victors of all this shall be the joy, the peace, and the beauty. These are of truth and of reality, so your evening shall be followed by rest from the illusions of time and space.

The pastoral scenes of an August morning lie outside the window in the mountains as the writer writes Our thoughts for you. Wispy clouds add silvery streaks to the pale blue sky above, and trees crown the mountains against the high horizon. Leaves blow in the gentle breeze, and, after a gentle rain a few days ago, summer has loosened its grasp for awhile.

Because of her love of life and beauty, the mate of the writer has planted many flowers of vibrant color. They are grown and are blooming in the sunshine of this morning. Because they are there, and because they are beautiful, they have attracted a beautiful butterfly to their nectar. The butterfly moves idly from flower to flower, drinking their beauty and loving its life.

Lying in the sunshine, a small white kitten lies in the warmth of the morning and purrs in peaceful joy. A large German Shepherd dog walks across the form of the kitten, at peace with the surroundings. A bright red cardinal flies toward the window in the sight of the writer, and disappears. A small brown bird follows, and also is gone.

On the mountain across the valley, a mile away and at a higher level, cattle graze upon the browning grass of the gentle hillside. As the day wears on, the appetites for nectar and for grass will be satisfied, and We shall satisfy the writer's hunger for the truth of today. Evening will follow.

This evening will be followed by another morning and another evening.

Another evening is upon you — the evening of the Sixth Day of Creation.

The storm clouds of war threaten the nations of the Mid-East. People of the financial world strive to even their positions, knowing that the delicate equilibrium of the balance of economies are threatened all over the world. The military machines are flexing their sinews of steel. The source of energy through which the battles are being waged is the subject of the battle. It is all a game, and truth and beauty can carry the reality of the lives involved through the days to come.

Even in the thundering roar of planes and ships of war there is beauty, and those who live in that environment can have their moments of peace and joy. The meaning of life is fulfilled for some, even as it is mocked and threatened for others. The morning and evening of the Sixth Day of Creation, though separated by millions of years, are falling into their places. You are blessed by being there, for you have chosen it to be so. You have been free to choose, and you have chosen.

My child, enjoy the beauty and harvest the truth, for it is there for you. Look above and around you at the illusions, and look within for the truth. Enjoy them all as they dance their stately dance among the halls of time and space. There is music in the reality beneath the cacophony of the illusions. There is life in all of it, and the life shall never die.

The oil, over which men fight like cats and dogs, has been the shell of living things. The cycles of life are being fulfilled, fought over, and relegated to another past in another time. The history shall become the future, and the future shall become old history again. Nothing is new under the sun, and many things of the past are forgotten and unknown by present lives and minds. Life goes on, and truth and beauty are among it all. We Are, We Live, and We Are within you.

Gather the beauty around you like a robe before evening comes, for the evening is the fulfillment of the Sixth Day. A few more moments can come to you in the form of some decades, or they can come to you in a manner of fewer days and times. Time adjusts to reality in Creation, making itself the tool of ultimate harmony in the greater scheme of things. Time and space are Our servants and yours, for the Brotherhood of Light manipulates the illusions of time and space according to Our perfect plan of freedom and liberty.

Last Days?

You are not alone, you have never been alone, and you shall never be alone. Creation attends you from within, just like the blue sky and the wispy clouds hover over the mountains and in the valleys today. Our Presence is as constant as the ocean waves, which beat in endless cycles upon the shores of your nation. You can harness Our energy through your faith, and you can ride upon Our motive power within you. Our cycles of Creation are beyond time, for We have no morning or evening in Our Realm of Absolute Reality. We Are complete and total Love, Perfection, and Light. We Are Strength and Truth. Fear not, My beloved, for the evening shall be followed by morning again.

How shall you spend the night? Are your lamps filled with the oil of your faith, and do you await the bridegroom Who comes to you? Are you ready for the Light, and do you welcome Our Beauty and Truth, Who wait within for you, beyond the shadows? Do you accept Our Strength? Do you know Us within you? Are you ready?

Be made ready through your love for Us, for yourself, for all life, and for all Creation. Have no care, save the care of a loving companion of all life for all other life. Have no fear at all, for the evenings you see are illusions. In the eternal dance of the cycles of time and space, the millions of years in the Sixth Day are nothing. The thousand years in the Seventh Day shall seem longer, and much more glorious to you, for they shall be lived in the more perfect environment of spirits filled with love and emptied of the illusions of time and space.

Evening is the punctuation of time, and evening is always followed by a new sentence of morning. Time shall end in light, not in darkness. Joy shall be the only even remainder when lives are divided by the quotient of time. The integral remainder of the division of light and darkness shall only be light, for the light is real and the darkness is an illusion. You are not alone, for the Light is within you. Find the beauty of Truth, for She is also within you today.

Carry your truth, wrapped in the robe of the beauty of your

life, into the evening of this day and the morning of the next. You are blessed with the power of Creation, you have your truth to release its beauty and freedom to your spirit, and you may have the faith you must have to make this possible for you. Use your freedom to live, selecting the good things and holding fast to them. Their supply is infinite for you. Their promise is eternally for you. You shall not fail if you do not fail to believe. Your belief is the creative power We have given you with your very life.

Turn away from the vain delusions of material values. Have no shade of greed or lust for the things of the world, but have great joy and pleasure in the beauty of time and space. You are in the evening of the Sixth Day, when the dusk is filled with the gentle sounds of lives in tune with the coolness and peace which are to come. The heat of the day is past, the storms are dying in the clouds above you, and a stillness descends upon the Earth. In that stillness, hear the still small voice of Our Truth and Light within you, and sup with the nourishment of Our Strength.

The Scriptures say, 'My beloved is mine, and I am his. He feeds among the lilies.' Enjoy the symbolic poetry of the past, and find its meaning fulfilled in this evening of the Sixth Day. You are surrounded with loving spirits and beings of Light, for you are a life within the Kingdom of Creation, just as the Kingdom of Creation is also within your life. We Are as one, and We Are One. Let your day be filled with joy and peace and beauty, for evening falls and the night is at hand. The time of your resting shall come, for the chambers of the bridegroom of Creation await you.

The day has been beautiful, for its beauty consists of reality among the illusions. The flowers are no less beautiful because they are of time. They are more beautiful because they are immortal bits of life, just as the life of the butterfly which feeds and rests among them. When I see the beauty of these flowers around

Last Days?

me, growing there because my mate loved life enough to plant and nurture them, I am so much exalted through their inner reality. Beauty is so much more real to me than the pursuit of the things of time. Possessions have beckoned me, I have answered, and they have come and gone. Truth is left among the ashes of my materialistic past, and its beauty and freedom are so real. As I write, just now, a humming bird hovers outside the window, looking at me with curiosity for a few seconds, then flitting away. Beauty of all kinds appear and disappear before any eye which desires to see them. All the opportunities I have missed have been missed because of lack of creative desire. Opportunities could have been found through faith and created into being through thoughts and hopes of a better life. So often, while focusing on illusions near to me, I have failed to see the beauty beyond and within them.

"And as you continue to tread the paths of time, look around you with joy. Be aware of the flowers, and enjoy the sight and smell of them. Hear the music of the ages, written by inspired souls of centuries ago and performed by the inspired musicians of your present day. Continue with patience in the life of your choice, and believe you deserve the joy of your progress. Know the perfection of your present stage each day, and forget the cares you might have later while overall perfection is being achieved."

From Book 7 — <u>A New Way of Living</u>

Chapter 38   From Book 33 — <u>A New Way of Living</u>

Regardless

Time and space surround you while you live on Earth. The purpose of living is fulfilled with your progress toward Eternity. Your progress, with all the cycles which attend it, will come. You shall find peace. With peace, you shall find joy. When you are successful, love shall attend your way. How shall you find success? It shall be spiritually found, spiritually enjoyed, and in spirit you shall live. Natural things, being illusions, shall pass away. Spiritual things, being real, shall endure forever.

Time is allowed to mark your progress. Joy is given to mark

your success. In all the changing events of time, joy is possible, and it is a reward for your attainment of truth for the moment at hand. What you do to find a new and better way of living will be done with the immediate reward of joy. Sacrifice for the sake of progress is a man-made and useless habit. You can only sacrifice illusions, which time, in any event, would have taken from you. Reality cannot be sacrificed, for it is neither mortal nor expendable.

If you knew this were to be the last day of the Sixth Day of Earth, what would you do today? Or, if you knew there were a million remaining years, what *then* would you do today? If you have learned the lessons We are teaching you, regardless of time or the demands of life on Earth, your answers would be exactly the same. There is nothing you can do to change the events around you, but the impact of those events upon you is entirely in your control.

Regardless of the illusions of time and space, your joy of living is based on your awareness of the reality of spiritual things. Do you believe you should love one another only in the last few moments of the Sixth Day? If so, you have missed the joy of loving, and you are not yet ready to find it in this life. Love is not conditional, not based upon any consideration of time at all, and is not a matter of expediency. Love is a matter of divine, cohesive, and creative force. Regardless of circumstances, love is the source of all joy.

Joy is enough for your spirit to have, and love is enough to find joy for you. Even before the pain of childbirth is past, mothers enjoy love. Even before the pain of separation or obstacles is over, lovers enjoy love. If this moment were your last on Earth, or if it were to be followed with millions of added moments, the best way of living would be, for you, the same. Truth, appropriately found and practiced by you in any and all circumstances, will lead you to love and to joy. The intangibles of spiritual reality transcend all the demands of time and space. Illusions are not served through denying love and accepting sacrifice for *any* reason. Joy is as natural as freedom of spirit. Without regard for time or the events around you, your life can be a joyful one.

If you are to find joy, reality is always to *first* be sought and found. Regardless of your concern for the things of time and the darkness around you, your best way of living is found in the same way each day. You need not know the outcome of the ominous clouds of war, the place and time of the end, or the intentions of others. You need to know the joy of loving and the confidence of knowing you are loved by Creation.

If you know these things, you are happy when you do them. No need is ever upon you to find the ways of time and space, nor need you know the events that are before you. You might have wondered, 'What would I do if this were to be the last day of this life on Earth?' If your answer would be to go on living just as before, you are very wise and are very happy. If not, you lack the full awareness of the reality of your life.

Knowing the difference between reality and illusions allows you to live happily, regardless of time, of time's events, and of the future. But We do not lay a burden of perfection upon you. If perfection is a journey to you, you have found what you need today. If perfection is a conditional goal, which you hope to find before you find joy, however, you have missed the point of Our lessons.

Regardless of your life until now, your present condition, or your hopes for creative faith, your attainment of perfection is proportional to your attainment of an awareness of reality.

Regardless of circumstances, your joy is proportional to your belief in your own reality and the reality of all the spiritual realms of Creation. Your joy is not dependent upon the relative status of *any, or all, illusions.* Therefore, you are able to be happy on Earth at any moment in which you are aware of reality, aware of the illusions of time and space, and thus, comfortable with that moment.

There is little you can do about the ways of the lives of those around you, or about the events that surround you. There is, however, much you can do about your attitude toward those lives and those events. This is the use you shall find for your truth of each moment, and this is the reason your truth must change in a changing world. Adapt to the events of time, which also continually change.

If only, through knowing the foolishness of your fearful anticipation or of your regrets for the past, you could learn these lessons well. The past and future, being of time, can never exist for you in any real and meaningful way. Regardless of the past and future, which are of time, your life is only a life of the present moment. Even so, you were created before time, shall live after time is gone for you, and can be happy *regardless of time.*

Since time is not a factor in reality, and since reality is only spiritual, your immortality allows you to live in joy and peace whenever you love, are at peace, and are able to maintain a renewed creative faith in Our Kingdom and Our Being. When you love, you have nothing to fear of time and space, so the time and circumstances of the end are of no concern for you. If you feel you need to know the time and circumstances of the end of the Sixth Day, or of the outcome of the events that cause the war clouds to encircle the Earth today, you are not ready.

But if you love one another with unconditional love, *you are ready,* and you are no longer at the mercy of the events which might have troubled you. Too many, through a strong desire to know the nature of the unfolding events of time and space, have lived in fear. Too few have lived in peace and joy, just through finding, without regard for anything of time or space, the creative faith with which they made themselves ready. Judge yourself spiritually, believe in your spiritual immortality, and be satisfied with the illusions which surround you and only *seem* to rule your life on Earth.

Let your illusions go, be quick to release them to the demands of time, and enjoy them only as fleeting symbols of reality, which lasts forever. Let the conflicts come and go, and let the contrasts flicker and change in the intensity of their cycles and their events, for you are above and beyond the impact of the time or space that make events possible, even as illusions. Our Kingdom is only within you. We Are because We Were and shall Be forever. Time is not a part of Our Absolute Reality at all, and neither is it part of your reality. Even on Earth, your joy is not dependent on time or space.

Learn to live and to love, each moment, to the fullest. Your joy and peace shall follow your faith, and your desire to love one another will create the love you desire. Having found this, you have found the key that can unlock the shackles of time and space. Even while you live on Earth, regardless of circumstances, you need not fail to enjoy reality and to live in peace with your reality. Your truth of the moment is sufficient for you. Sufficient to this day are both the life and the illusion of evil. Evil, being opposite of life, can only exist in the past and future. In the reality of life, there are no past and future.

So today, My beloved child, say to yourself, 'I am Light. I and the Father are One. I shall be happy today, regardless of what happened in any previous moment or what might happen in any future moment.' This belief is not in the nature of your physical body or of your mind, but it is in the reality of the life of your spirit. Your reality is your spirit, We Are Spirit, and your desire is sufficient to bring joy to you, if you believe in the reality of All Creation, in which you live as a perfecting part of Us.

Learn to love, *regardless,* and you will instantly find the key that unlocks the shackles of time and space for you. Learning these things, you shall no longer have a need to understand the past or know the future, for the past and future are no longer significant to you. The millions of moments that make up your past can fade into oblivion, for they have no significance at all. They are not real. Neither are the imagined events of the future of any significance for you. If you have found your truth today, are living with the greatest awareness of your reality that you can find, and love one another, that is enough. The world could last another million years, or it could last only one more second of time, and neither need be of concern for you.

But you are human, and you are concerned. Pray for the faith which allows your concern to be replaced with love. Regardless of anything or everything around you, love is enough.

> *But knowing is not enough. Believing and feeling are the things I have found to bring happiness. Emotions bringing spiritual joy, being based on the intangibles of spiritual reality, are enough. For me, truth based on knowledge seems artificial, for knowledge is of time and space. But truth based on faith is enough, for it, being of faith in reality, has nothing to do with time or space at all. All the considerations of 'what if' lose their importance when belief through faith, regardless of time or space, is found.*

"I have told you of your spirit, your mind, your body, and your soul. I have taught you how to love one another and how to love yourself. I have given you words of understanding, which tell you of some of the mysteries of time and space. I have told you that I am a part of all things, and that all things are a part of Me.

You have learned that I do not give you miracles and signs to prove My existence, for it would take away your freedom to choose to live in My love if you were forced by absolute proof to believe in Me. I have told you that you will never be able to understand the vastness of Creation, the greatness of My Power, or the Wisdom and Truth of all things."

From Book 6 — <u>A New Way of Living</u>

Chapter 39   From Book 33 — <u>A New Way of Living</u>

I Am God

I fly upon the wings of eagles. I stand upon the waters. I walk the halls of the morning in the misty dawn. I Am among you, within you, beneath you, above you, below you, and all around you. You are Mine and I Am yours. We Are Lovers, not always acquainted, but always knowing that Our love is Our eternal destiny. I Am God.

When you looked into the eyes of a child and loved it, you loved Me, as well. When you clasped the hand of your lover, you knew, just for a moment, the ecstasy of Our love. When you knew of nowhere else to turn, you found Me and were comforted. If you have not found Me, you have not found fulfillment, and in your heart of hearts, you know it.

The glimpse of perfection once found in the illusion of your youthful body has been converted, by time, into a greater perfection of your spirit. Age has not withered your spirit, variety has not added to the confusion of your spirit, and your knowledge has allowed the expansion of your awareness and love of life far less than has your faith. I Am God. I Am in every living thing, and in every meaning of every symbol of every illusion of time and space. Your eyes are able to only dimly see Me, but your faith sees Me in every blade of grass and in the vast reaches of every ocean, every desert plain, and every mountain range upon the Earth.

If someone asks you, 'How do you know God?' tell that seeking soul that God is known to anyone who lives with faith. I am known more without knowledge than with it. I am known less through understanding than through faith. I am lived through love, found through desire, and kept through faith. When I am discarded, I remain. When I am rejected, I stand and await the one who rejects Me. Time does not lose Me from you, space does not separate Me from you, and the blindness of your anger does not destroy My Reality to you, for I Am beyond any of the means of time or space to sequester Me from you.

How can you love anything without loving Me? I Am revealed to you in everything you love, for I Am within Everything. I Am hidden from you in everything you hate or despise, but I Am still in everything which becomes the object of your anger. If you cannot see Me in your enemy, you have missed a part of Me in your friend, as well. The bird that flies above you has no doubt of its ability to fly, for it is flying. Why should you doubt that you shall live forever in Absolute Reality, for are you not alive in a world of time, which is only an illusion?

I Am God. How, when every instinct of your soul and spirit

constantly tells you that death is impossible for you, can you even dream of death? A belief in death, although it can seem to create death for you, is a learned, but mistaken, belief based on many illusions. The mysterious languages of love and beauty can never teach you of death, for love and beauty are real. They are parts of life, so they are of Me. I Am God.

When you awaken in the early dawn, with a mind washed by sleep and a spirit refreshed through rest in Our Kingdom, believe in Me. I Am God. Reach for Me in every beautiful thing you sense with the senses of your body. Know Me in every desire for faith and for love. Desire Me, desire to love, desire to give, and desire to grow toward the perfection which surely awaits you. There is uncertainty in every illusion, for it is doomed to die or to be translated into something else through the events of time. But you are alive, We Are One, and I Am God. There is no uncertainty in Me.

There is none other than God, for nothing else exists. We Are within you, Our stamp is upon every atom, quark, and electron of Creation, and We Are One with All Things. Size, being of space, is an illusion. Events, being of time, are also illusions. We, Being of Love and of God, are Absolute Reality. You shall not lose Us, you shall not fail to know Us, and you shall find Us within you.

Why, when We Are within you, must you first look for Us around you? Why, when your imagined Heaven is so much farther away from you than Our Kingdom within you, should you wish for Our Kingdom in Heaven? While you are in time, and are restricted through the very vastness of space, look close to yourself for Us. Look within you. I Am God.

When you are graduated from the school of this particular lifetime, you shall have the joy of discovering Us in timeless and spaceless reality, where you cannot now even imagine Absolute Reality. Find all the truth and beauty you can, just for today, and let tomorrow provide its own to you when tomorrow comes. Find Us where you are, in the place and the moment of this breath, for I Am God and We Are within you.

How, until you have found Us within you, can you find Us afar, tomorrow, or anywhere at all? If you cannot see Us nearby in your friend and, even more easily, in yourself, you shall not see Us anywhere at all. And yet, you have the faith available to you through which to know, without knowing, what is real and what is true. Find Us with the simple act of desiring Us. Only a thought is between you and joy. Only a moment is needed to find Us, for We are not far away, not separated from you with time, and not released through knowledge or understanding. Your consciousness is often blocked with your ability to reason, and your faith is often blocked through the illusions you have thought to be true.

Reach out with the simple tools of desire fulfilled and strengthened by love. You need no time, no space, and none of the products of time and space to find Us. We are found beneath the trees and in the deserts and forests of Earth more easily than We Are found among the altars and sanctuaries of the stiff-necked and prejudiced purveyors of man-made versions of absolute truth on Earth. Look for Us in simplicity, remember Us, even in complexity, retain Us through your awareness of life and beauty, and find your truth today. Be set free, and know that I Am God.

What you wish for is what you shall think you find, and what you fear will not, until you replace your fear with love, be a stranger to your consciousness. I Am God. If you love Me, you will need no commandments. If you do not, commandments will not bring joy into your life and peace into your soul. Your need for commandments are in inverse proportion to the quality of your love for Me. I Am God.

When you feel that your lack of safety requires commandments from Us, seek, instead, more to love. I Am God. There is none other. There is nothing else. I Am a God of Love.

To the extent that you know love, you know Me. This is

not a function of reason, of understanding, or of experience. A new-born child knows more of love and of Me than does the learned scholar who has tried for a lifetime to replace the faith of a child with the knowledge, regarding God, of humankind.

Let this day and its beauty, however small, be truth enough for you. Let your life tell you that you live, and let your living spirit testify of Me. I Am God. You prove Me with every breath you take, with every beauty you see, and through the peace of mind that comes to you when you are attuned to beauty and to all the life around you.

If, in the confusion of living on Earth, you cannot see beauty, look within you. Is not a breath of air or a drink of water beautiful to you? Through faith, take blessings and beauty for granted, love them because they are of Me, and know that I Am God. Let the illusions teach you of their purposes as symbols of reality. Learn, through comparison, of your truth, for you are in a relative world. Know that there can be no comparison in Absolute Reality, for, in eternal perfection, nothing of lesser perfection can be found. Knowing this through faith, know also, through faith, that I Am God.

If you know of your heritage, you cannot abase yourself through exalting Me in your heart. When you know that I Am God, you lift yourself up to the eternal status of My child. You do not lose yourself, distance yourself, or humiliate yourself through knowing of My greatness and My power. When you know Me, you walk *only* with Me, for there is nowhere else to walk. On Earth or in the endless realms of Absolute Reality, Only I Exist. I Am God.

Belief in one universal God denies the possibility of any separation of anything from anything else. Separation is an illusion, based on Earth's fundamental illusions of space and time. Space and time are directly involved in every form of judgment, making the act of absolute judgment an act of disbelief. Love is everywhere, binding all life together and making Eternity the reality that it is. Have faith, for there is nothing of disbelief in any faith in God. I Am God, I Am All Things, and We Are One.

> *I have believed, at some time in my life, in my separation from God. I have believed in the commandments of God as means of finding Him. I have believed that God was everywhere, and at the same time, have believed he was not near to me. These beliefs, I now know through faith, contain the seeds of their own destruction. They are impossible beliefs, which I now know from the joyful experience of having found the Kingdom of God within me. Jesus told me that God's Kingdom was within me, that love is the only important commandment, and that the perfect law of liberty was what he brought to Earth when he lived in the flesh.*

"This means that if you believe I do not allow freedom to you, then neither will you allow freedom to those over which you have power in this life. And if you believe I do not forgive all things, you will not be prepared to forgive all things in others around you. And if you believe I am vengeful, you will be quick to seek revenge on others. There is your peace destroyed, and with the destruction of peace, the joy of beauty and love is gone."

From Book 5 — <u>A New Way of Living</u>

Chapter 40 From Book 33 — <u>A New Way of Living</u>

Preparation

The need for preparation increases. This lesson is for you, the reader, and it is to be taken differently by each of you who read it. In an earlier lesson We told of the first call. In a later lesson We told of each call. This is another call. It is a call to prepare. You can ignore it or heed it, for you are free. We love you and Are within you, there is no incentive of fear behind this call, and the desires of your heart will prevail, for you, over the need of all Creation.

In any event, Creation survives and is perfected, for We Who Are within you are Perfect. As you work out your perfection, you will join Creation, Whom We Are, and We shall be One. Whenever you love perfectly, We are One. But perfect love is not sustainable on Earth, nor is your perfection sustainable among the illusions of time and space.

The time to prepare for the last days of Earth, if you wish, is now. The preparation is entirely of your attitude, of your spiritual comprehension, and of your free will. That is the reality of your preparation. It is intangible, and it has no form. But the outward appearance of your life, as shown through the illusions readable with your physical senses, are the things that are the substances revealed through your faith.

Without wanting you to be deceived with the illusions of time, We advise you to learn to play the game of life on Earth more skillfully, today and in the days to come. This game is not for the purpose of gaining material goods, power, fame, or comfort. It is for the purpose of letting your love grow through using it. We have often taught you that love is not diminished through use, but that, each time you feel love and give it, it is expanded. It is a time for love, for peace of mind, and for the *power* of the creative force of love to be expressed and enjoyed by all who will develop it.

Yesterday we taught you of the orphans that will be found among the wreckage of the holocausts of the last days. There are also many other lives who will suffer. This includes the lives of plants and animals, of older people, and of many in the prime of life. The call is for you to develop whatever skills you would wish to use for the unfortunate souls around you. If you like, you will be guided from within, will find and believe your own truth, and will follow the path of your destiny. If you do this, much faith will be required.

You will be guided in directions you do not understand, and each of you, according to your desires and the choices you made while you were last in timelessness, will be guided in different directions.

We will give you a few examples of needed skills that you might choose. Raising food, first aid, preventive medicine with the use of herbs and natural substances, psychological and philosophical help for those confused and disturbed, food preparation and storage, care of domestic animals and food for them, child care and recreation, reading and education, housekeeping, building and carpentry, wood-cutting, game-hunting, and many other things of this nature will require skill and *practice*.

Among all the skills you might be able to use, there are some for which you are best suited. Practice and enjoy these skills while there is time, for there will be a need for them and for your love. The work of your choice might take you to others, might bring others to you, or might even never be needed. Nevertheless, prepare yourself to do what you can, for the time for preparation shall be followed with a time for action.

As your truth comes to you, let yourself go. The Brotherhood of Light reveals these things to you, seemingly without reason. With faith and trust in the Power of Creation, heed the specific call you receive, keep your own counsel, and, if you wish, prepare yourself. There is much contentment and joy in being prepared, even for what might never come, or for what might come in a different way than you had ever imagined. The examples given in this lesson are only small parts of what skills could be needed. Know that your call will come from within you, not from these words. Your purpose will reveal itself to you in due time. Be ready to receive the call, and be ready to heed it.

If you fail in this, there shall be no punishment. If you succeed, there shall be great joy. A few steps taken in faith are far better than many steps guided with the reasoning power of humankind. The majority on Earth will be deceived, the consensus will be confusing and misleading, and the only reality from which your truth shall come is within you. Trust Our Kingdom within you, wherein lives your Inner Self, and follow the calls, which come from Us. We Are beyond time and space, We roam the farthest reaches of the galaxy, and We Are within you. No space and time affect Us, but you are living within the illusions of your environment.

As you prepare, prepare as if for a game. It *is* a game, your reality is beyond it, and only your love is needed to win it. However seriously those around you might take the game of life on Earth, be sure you find the faith to rise above the game and love *all* the players. You are not alone on Earth, but you are alone with respect to the Kingdom of God found in others. Your Kingdom is *only* within you, and from that timeless and spaceless realm of Absolute Reality you can find your truth. Let your truth lead you, in your own unique way, to prepare yourself. The guidance for others is far beyond your need or your ability to understand.

As you prepare, enjoy the company of one another. Know that many others will choose to prepare the way you do, but be slow to judge those who prepare in a different way. Be even slower to judge those who do not seem to prepare at all. Some, in ways you cannot see or do not understand, are already prepared. Give each of your companions the same freedom you have, and be sure to keep your own freedom for yourself. It is a time for preparation, and preparation is a very individual thing.

It might be wise to hone the skills you already have, for those are the things you can prepare most quickly and readily. Do what you enjoy, and if you want to be prepared when the need to be prepared arises, begin to do something. Time does pass, quickly or slowly, and not all will be ready.

Speak to your friends and those around you who have made changes in their ways of living. Ask them if they knew, before they took the first one, what the second step would be. Ask them if their faith was increased through taking one confused and halting step into an unknown direction. Ask them if they have reduced their fears by stepping just one step into the unknown. Ask them if their spirits have been quickened and been made more alive with their moving into the unknown. Ask them if their first step has given them more courage to take the second one when it is time.

Better still, take the next step toward your *own* preparation. If you have taken one step, take another. It is a simple matter to take one short step after the other. You have the Light, the Strength, and the Truth within you. Our Kingdom within you is all you need. You have it. But Our Kingdom does nothing to invade your privacy or your freedom.

Submit yourself as you will, or, if you will, beg and plead with Us to decide for you. It will change nothing until *you* decide to prepare, for We have given you freedom, eternal life and the heritage of a child of God. Nothing you can do will endanger your immortality, and nothing We shall do will endanger your freedom.

If you like, prepare yourself. If you have had an urge to take a class, practice a hobby, or change jobs in order to develop a new or better skill, consider what might be the source of the urge. The source could be Our Source within you, operating through the individual freedom of your Inner Self. The still, small voice you are hearing might be wisely considered, for it comes from Yourself in Our Kingdom. You and We, when you love universally, Are One. Control and balance the perversions of your mind, and have the goodwill for Creation that is guaranteed through the love you have for Us and for All Things.

Consider how you might prepare, in physical and natural ways, to better play the physical and natural game of life in the last days of Earth. Open your mind and your heart to the call of Creation, for We are calling you in specific ways to your unknown, but specific, purposes. The purposes are yours, determined in freedom by your soul before the beginning of time. You have chosen before you were born. Now, if you choose, is the time to prepare for what you have chosen. Listen closely and lovingly to the still, small voice within you. It is from Us and from you.

> *I get many hints of the things for which I am preparing. They come often, being in the form of hunches,*

sudden ideas, and small openings of opportunity in the environment around me. Some I have heeded. Some I have not. No amount of prayer has given me a guarantee, in this lifetime, of the outcome of any step. It seems the step has always been taken with a certain amount of faith and a certain lack of knowledge regarding the results of it. However, the faith was later rewarded through proof in the form of success. This has developed more courage to take added steps. It has been hard for me to stop asking for a decision, but to keep asking for guidance toward the decision I made in freedom. We are preparing as best we can, long before we can know what we are preparing for. I hear many of you saying the same thing. Those of you who are taking steps to prepare, without knowing, seem to be the happiest and the most fulfilled.

"For the Earth will automatically destroy herself and live again as a new and cleansed Earth, because of the moral and physical pollution by mankind. Earth would serve her purpose of being your willing host if your collective consciousness would live in harmony, but she will not be a host of war and misery and sorrow and sin. She was not created for that, and she will naturally oppose it. The gunpowder, the rusting military equipment, the rotting bodies of soldiers, the evil intentions to destroy, the pollution of the air, the nuclear explosions, the destruction of innocent plants and animals, the sterilization of fertile soil by chemicals, and the disruption of all the balances of nature are forcing the Earth to destroy herself."

From Book 4 — <u>A New Way of Living</u>

Chapter 41 From Book 33 — <u>A New Way of Living</u>

Being Prepared

How can you be prepared for the unexpected? How can you be prepared for that which is to come? How can you be prepared without knowing for what you are prepared? My child, My beloved and wandering child, your beauty is found through faith. Your truth is found through faith. Your joy is found through living. Living to the fullest, with the most possible joy and peace on Earth, is living with a full knowledge and a deep awareness of reality.

You have learned to love through loving all Creation. You

have learned to heal in healing yourself and others. You have learned to give by forgiving, first yourself, then others. You have learned of life through living. You have learned of freedom with the use of your own freedom. You have learned of kindness through being kind. You have learned of giving by giving. You have learned of mercy through the feeling and showing of mercy.

You have healed your wounds, many of which have been illusions that you regarded, at one time or another, as truth. You have been wounded emotionally, spiritually, physically, socially, temperamentally, and psychically. Your wounds received in this life on Earth have left scars. But the only scars which you have are scars upon wounded illusions. Your truth shall set you free from all the wounds and scars that deal with things of time and space. All scars shall pass away. The moment you find your truth on a basis of your reality, your scars and wounds shall be healed.

You are taking a most advanced course in reality when you read and study the words of <u>A New Way of Living</u>. From the beginning, these words have dealt with your concept of reality and of illusions. Little by little, step by step, and moment by moment, you have learned that there is no reality at all in things great or small, in steps, or in moments. Reality consists entirely of energy, of life, of being, of truth, and of love. Reality has no form, no time, no space, no illusions, and no residual overtones in the form of scars, unfinished business, remainders of past troubles, or problems. Reality has nothing to hold you to things which are of sin or evil.

We have taught you that sin and evil are only the absence of love and life. We have taught you of the attraction and joy of loving and living. We have taught you of the cohesiveness of love. We have taught you of the creative force of love. We have taught you of Our Presence within you, and of Our Nature, which far transcends the nature of the world in which you now live.

When you have learned to always know and realize the

difference between reality and illusions, you are prepared. This is a hard lesson to learn. When someone says to you, 'Wake up and face reality,' they usually mean things of time and things entirely made up of illusions. How can you face reality until you know what it is?

Be certain of your truth, know your reality, and live joyfully out of danger from your fears. In fears, there is no reality. Be prepared spiritually, for this is the first and last requirement you need in order to cope with the physical illusions which seem to grasp and tear at your faith, love, and goodwill.

We Are Spirits, A Spirit of One God. You who worship Us must worship Us in spirit and in truth. These Realities are not connected with time, with space, with circumstances, or with events. However, you have chosen to live among the events of time and space in a world of humankind who seem to be going mad.

Always, in times such as these now besetting the people of Earth, there are those who despair, become discouraged, and fail to function. There are those who run around in circles in constant fear, saying, 'What shall we do?' Fear devours hope, frustration devours love, troubles devour faith, illusions seem to devour reality, and death stalks among the shadows in the nations of Earth. The only items of news seem to be bad news, for humankind has been deceived and has accepted illusions as reality. They are not. Illusions are, most certainly, not reality.

You are prepared for the refugees, the homeless, the confused, the sick, the lame, the blind, and the suffering that shall be cast off from society as useless shells. You are prepared through your recognition of spiritual reality, of spiritual realms, of spiritual guidance, of spiritual love, and of spiritual truth. You are prepared with every beautiful thing you find and love, every joy you know, and every bit of truth that you receive from Our boundless supply of Strength, Light, and Truth within you. You, of yourself and from within yourself, are prepared in any moment in which you find truth, love, joy, and peace in your heart. These are all eternal and boundless sources of reality for you.

No martyr who has died with faith in Us has died in misery, for he has learned the lessons of reality which so clearly reveal the illusions. This is true for the Muslim, the Buddhist, the Baptist, the Catholic, or for anyone who has found a personal God within. We Are within you, My beloved child, and you are, in the moment you find Us within you, prepared.

You are prepared for anything, anything of either reality or illusion. So long as your faith lasts and your universal love is your desire and your joy, you are prepared. Fear not the lapses in being prepared which come to you with anger, with greed, with lust, with materialism, or with vanity. Forgive yourself for these things. They are not real, not lasting, and not eternal. Forgive all, and desire truth, beauty, and joy. Through your desire, you shall create what you desire. If you desire to be prepared, through faith and love, you are immediately prepared. At that moment, without doubt and without question, you are prepared.

Sustain your condition of being prepared through your continual desire for spiritual reality, faith, love, and peace. Your peace can be so quickly found with a subtle, but real, change in your attitude. If your attitude is one of faith, not skepticism, and if your attitude is based on reality, you are prepared. In that moment, for as long as you can maintain your faith in Our Realm of Absolute Reality within you, you are prepared.

Keep your faith as the skies darken, the war clouds hover over the lands, the standards of living on Earth are shattered, and troubles abound. Keep your faith, and know the love that allows you to keep your freedom from any fear at all of things which are not real. The great test of your faith comes clearly to you when you are forced to choose between the illusions of tangible things and the realities of spiritual things.

When you learn to live your life according to your truth, to love universally and unconditionally, and to preserve and

Being Prepared   245

protect your freedom to believe what you believe by continuing to believe it, you are prepared. When you know that your reality is not measured with time, with space, or with any of their products, you shall suddenly see yourself, without fear and without fail, as a master of time and space.

Know this, and live it with confidence and courage. When you know that your preparation is spiritual, you are prepared. The skills you hone in order to best play the game of life are skills which can be used to express your spiritual love in physical ways. Through healing one another, loving one another, forgiving one another, helping one another, and goodwill toward one another, you are prepared.

You are *not* prepared through judging one another, advising and guiding one another, or assuming the right to control or direct the freedom of one another. Let the guidance of each come freely from within. You are not prepared through seeking a consensus of opinion based on the judgment of the majority. You are not prepared through judging or directing the path of another. You are not prepared by judging the quality of truth found in the preparation of another. You are not prepared through feeling any responsibility to prepare one another.

You walk, with respect to the illusions of space and time, alone among All Creation. But when you are prepared as We have taught you, you are an immortal and functioning part of All That Is. If you are prepared to do what you can do for yourself, of yourself, and yet with full love and awareness of the truth, beauty, and life in all Creation, you are prepared. Be ready, wait, and sharpen your skills for the game of life on Earth, never forgetting the clear and constant Presence of Absolute Reality within you.

> *Nothing, for me, is harder than waiting. This is especially true when I wait impatiently for an unknown event which might or might not happen. We are taught of many ways in which prophecy will be fulfilled during*

the last days of Earth. Will my corner of the world suffer from earthquakes, from war, from plagues, from tempests, from floods, from fires, from pestilence, or from famine? Yet, if I am prepared as this lesson teaches, what does it matter? For all who love and live in faith, a way will open, for the entire Presence of Creation and Absolute Reality Are within Us. If our mind is open, our faith is sustained, and our love stands the tests of time, these tests of time shall be passed with flying colors. The whole purpose of life on Earth seems to be centered around the acceptance of spiritual reality and the awareness of the truth and beauty symbolized through the illusions of time and space. In the moment we are prepared, the way, the time, and the place of the end lose their power over us.

"So love is the victor over doubt, and it is the way to remove doubt. Express love to others and love your own soul as a masterpiece of My Creation, for if your soul is precious to Me should it not also be precious to you? And if you know I love you, can you not love yourself with Me? You are worthy of love, no matter what others have told you. There is no soul who is not worthy of love."

From Book 3 — <u>A New Way of Living</u>

Chapter 42 From Book 34 — <u>A New Way of Living</u>

Conditional Cares

It is so easy now for you to think of time, of events, and of the conditions that might come about. But the clouds of war are no greater than the clouds of negativity that preceded today's crisis. The value of living for the moment at hand is no greater than it has ever been. The foolishness of caring about the past and future is the same. You are still alive, reading this, and learning your truth from within. You are beloved, real, and destined for perfection. What have you to fear?

Among the changing conditions in your world are many rays of hope. Light and truth are being discovered, moment by moment, as ways of coping with problems not seen before on Earth. Now you have the threat of nuclear, biological, and chemical warfare. But before that there were times when hundreds of thousands of people died of tuberculosis, lockjaw, black plague, and gangrene. Even appendicitis was a frequent cause of sudden death during this century.

There is a real cure for every illusionary problem. The conditional cares you might have today, which are based only on changing conditions, can be coped with by your spiritual separation of truth from illusions. Reality demands no care, no changing conditions, and no victims who must suffer and die to no avail. Illusions, if they are seen for what they are, also demand nothing from you except your ability to create an awareness of reality through your faith, your hopes, and your thoughts.

You can find many around you who are filled with anxiety, saying, 'Things have never been this way for me before. I don't know what to expect.' Expect nothing, hope wisely for reality to take the place of your illusions, and let your illusions vanish in the flash of light that reveals your truth to you. Then have the courage to wait, or the strength to act, and the wisdom to know which is appropriate for you. Seek no consensus of opinion from those around you, and share your own counsel and advice only with those who sincerely ask you.

But, even when asked, take no responsibility for others. You are responsible only for yourself. Save yourself from the travail and suffering found on Earth today. The changing conditions, coming so quickly as they are, will not allow you to carry burdens. If you must flee into the hills to survive, leave your prized possessions behind, for your life is all you *really* possess. And you shall not lose it, My beloved. You might change it for a better life by being found with universal love and faith in Us, but you shall not lose it.

If you must consider the possible conditions of the future in order to prepare yourself, consider only the preparation for physical survival for a little while. The threat of Armageddon, which looms over the world, is pervading the consciousness of many. More and more interpret these days as being the last days of Earth, but no one knows the day, the hour, or the way of the coming of Armageddon. You need not know.

If your cares reflect concern for the future, they are not likely to be accurate, for the future changes like the scenes in a fast-moving play. Armageddon, in the event it happens soon, will transpire quickly. If you were to be foolish enough to fear, your fears for the events of Armageddon would still be inappropriate. There would be more to fear, if you fear, from the days and months which follow Armageddon.

To Us, time is nothing. The passing of a few years after Armageddon would see the unraveling of the entire civilizations of Earth. Lawlessness would replace law, as it already has in many of the ghettos of the world. The law of the jungle would prevail again, and the ones who had anything visible and desired by others would have to fight for it, or give it up, and, in the process, probably have their bodies destroyed.

Conditional cares are the only kind there are. No care is possible if it is unconditional. The conditions which surround you can give rise to your anxiety, worry, and care. For those who believe in the illusions and see them as reality, there is no other choice but to care and to fear. However, We would have you to be joyful, knowing that the destruction during the harvest of Earth is limited only to the destruction of some of the illusions of time and space.

So if you care at all, your care is conditional, being related to changing conditions and events of time. Do not care, My child. Be as a little child in a physical body, who plays when there is sunlight and safely sleeps when there are shadows. Let your mind be at peace, and if you like, set yourself up to live in some out-of-the-way place, and let the world go by. Hope for a way of life that might seem boring to some, and fill your moments with hope for timelessness and for the absence of the cares of this life.

Hope for things which are good, in which no opposites are present at all. Instead of worrying about things getting worse or expecting things to get better, just hold fast to that which is good. Ignore the cares of conditions around you as best you can, and learn, a little more each day, to cling to the things of spiritual reality. These things are not tangible, not subject to the ravages of war, and shall not forsake you.

We teach you a better way than to care. Our way is more than better and more than best for you. Our way is the absence of care, of conditions, of threatening events, and of time, itself. Our way is the way of a life in which nothing is conditional, nothing is reserved, nothing is committed, nothing is a prerequisite, nothing is an illusion, and nothing is withheld. Our way is a way of universal love, which holds all good together, sorts the illusions from the reality, allows Creation to continue toward the perfection of all life and all reality, and keeps you safe from any changing condition.

If you learn to forsake all conditional cares, no cares will be left for you. Some conditions do not look good, for they are of illusions, which can be bad. Fear, if you must fear at all, deceiving yourself with illusions. But love, universally and perfectly, as much as you can. Balance the perversions of your mind and put your faith in the things for which you hope. If your faith is in the illusions, your hope shall fail. And if your hope fails, redirect it with faith in the reality of Our Kingdom within you.

When Our Presence within you is the foundation of your hopes and dreams, your faith will not be misplaced. In Us, in Whom there are no changes in events or conditions, you shall be secure and shall not fail. There is no conditional care of any kind to be found in the reality of Our Kingdom within you. With Us, all is peace and love. No conditions are attached.

Learn from the contrasts of the good and bad around you. Learn, from the contrasts revealed in every illusion, where lies the truth for you. The nature of life on Earth is changing, and you cannot know the conditions that are to come. You can, however, know unconditional love, which denies the impact of the conditions and denies your need for any care at all. Unconditional care is not possible. But unconditional love is very real, very possible, and very fulfilling for you.

Hope for peace on Earth and goodwill toward men, but expect nothing. Be, in the present moment, carefree, not careless, and watch the conditions as they change the forms of the illusions of time and space around you. As you watch, smile, and be careless of the future, for the future only stands, for a little while, between you and timelessness. If there are not better days ahead, or better times ahead, there are still unconditional joys ahead for you. These unconditional joys need no certain times, events, or conditions in order to be yours.

When David wrote Psalm 23, he wrote it for you. 'The Lord is my Shepherd. I shall not want.' And you shall not want for anything real or needful, My beloved. Throw your cares away, replace them with hope, and find your hope through finding faith in Our Kingdom within you. We Are of Spiritual Reality, not of your world, and are able to take you away from a place where so many cares seem to surround you. But they only *seem* to surround you, for the conditions in which your conditional cares *seem* so real do not exist. They only appear for a time, giving you a choice to exercise your freedom to believe or not to believe in them.

You have chosen the environment in which you are tested, and you have chosen the tests you are finding. Your truth shall set you free from this, and no conditional cares shall be of help to you. Care not at all, but live in fervent hope for the joy that is yours for the taking. In all your seeking for truth, seek it in the Absolute Reality of Our Kingdom within you.

Today, for the first time, I heard reports of a nation

threatening another nation with nuclear war in retaliation for chemical warfare. Perhaps there is nothing wrong with wondering what will happen, but the ability to wonder without caring is not so easy for me. Nevertheless, A New Way of Living *has taught me to be more aware of what is happening, so I will need to heed the lesson today in order to let that awareness be more comfortable for me. I have never been much to bury my head in the sand, but neither have I been very good at ignoring the future and hoping without expectations. I cannot know when and where time will end for me, but I can know that time and space will be followed with the joy of Absolute Reality, in which there are no cares and no changing conditions.*

"If I had required you to come to Me, there would be no blessing for you. But since, of your free will, you can choose whether or not to come to Me, you will be greatly blessed by the practice of coming to Me daily for the renewal of faith which leads to joy. So come to Me daily. Don't wait until joy is lost and you need to seek Me out again. After you have found Me, never let Me go. Keep Me forever within you by coming to Me daily. I am the source of your life, for your life is enriched by My Spirit within you. Come to Me often, and I will be in you."

From Book 2 — <u>A New Way of Living</u>

Chapter 43   From Book 35 —<u>A New Way of Living</u>

Waiting

If you think of the future often, you often are waiting for something. Time has a way of keeping you involved with the things it gives and takes away from you. Waiting is an illusionary function of time. The things which are good and are of reality are not things for which you need to wait. They are things that are not of time.

So if you must wait, either from force of habit or from strong desire, wait for the illusions of time and its products. Wait only for things that are of time, and know that the good things of life, which are free and timeless, can come to you now as easily as at any other time.

When is not a good time for love? When is friendship not to be expressed and desired? Where is the place that cannot be made better through your awareness of the reality of Our perfect and joyful Creation? Your awareness of time is increased by waiting for things that are not of time. Let your waiting be only for the uncertain events of time and space, for your spirit shall survive in its immortal life and in the goodness of Our gift of eternal love to you.

Let time weigh lightly on your spirit until you have no more need for time at all. Wait with careless unconcern for the things of time. The things for which you wait, if they are of time or space, will not be at all important to you when you find your own reality within you. You are, in reality, separate from the world.

When you wait for anything today, wait with little desire for the illusion for which you wait. If what you wait for is of reality, waiting is needless. Reality is before you, within you, around you, above you, beneath you, and in all the illusions of all times and places. When you are waiting, you are masquerading an illusion by painting it with the brush of reality. The illusion is on the outside, apparent to you in time and space, but the reality is within.

Reality cannot be seen with your eyes, described with your words, or explained within your mind. But reality begins where time and space end, and waiting for reality to come to you is a needless excuse for the procrastination of that which is good for you. The greatest failure you can find in your world of time and space is found by waiting for reality to come to you. You are already real, no waiting is required, and to wait for reality to appear to you only relegates the reality you seek into an illusionary form.

Relative truth only *seems* to change. Waiting for truth, however appropriate, will cause it to seem to elude you. What you seek in truth is to be for this moment, just for now. The truth you need for tomorrow is not obvious to you today, so your truth for today is enough. Seek not so much to reconcile your truth with that of others as to reconcile it with what you need in just this moment of time.

Be satisfied that the truth you find today brings joy to your spirit and life to your awareness of Creation. The things for which you wait will be different from what you might expect. The last days of Earth will be entirely different than you might imagine, for they will be many things to many people. The way of the life and death of physical illusions can take many forms. But the renewal of life after physical death is more similar, for all renewal starts in a new framework of timelessness.

What are you waiting for today? Are you waiting for death so that life may begin again for you. If you are, focus on the rebirth that will follow the death, for the rebirth is the reality of what you are waiting for. That reality of rebirth will not come to you at a predictable time or place, for it is of spiritual reality.

And if you are waiting for your life to begin in this lifetime, why wait? You are alive, you are conscious, you are aware, and you have many choices before you in this day. Take the choice that moves you nearer to your truth, cling to the good things of life, and let time and space go on with their illusions of beauty for some and pain for others. You intensify your ability to create through the things you choose to wait for. The act of waiting for gloom and doom will make them seem to come to you. But if you seek your truth, hope for good, desire to be joyful, and live in peace, what is there to wait for?

The last days of Earth are no more significant to your reality and truth than any of the other illusions of time and space. Your spirit shall survive, your body shall be renewed, and your hope for eternal joy shall be justified. But when shall your spirit survive, when shall your body be renewed, and how will your hope be justified? As you think, so shall it be for you. The things of time and space, as they affect you, are under the control of your creative power.

So the physical survival of your body in the last days of Earth is as much an illusion as your body, itself. The survival of your spirit is as much a reality as is the reality of your spirit, itself. How you think of survival is the key to the effect survival shall have upon you. Your experience will be different, in terms of the illusions of time and space, and the last days of Earth will go according to the expectations of those who live in the last days.

If you are inclined to wait and see what happens without preparation, you are only preparing in a different way. The open mind and the peaceful heart filled with faith and hope for happiness and joy will find them. Beauty is found in death for those who know of death as only an illusion. Death is only the door to renewed life and new truth. Your emphasis on survival is determined by the degree of faith and hope your mind can develop during these last days of Earth.

So your attitude toward last day survival is the key to its effect on you. Waiting for it with little care or concern will cause it to be of little or no concern for you. But if you are fearful of the impact of the physical death of Earth on the reality of your spirit, you have some truth to find. Your body and your spirit are the illusion and the reality of your being. Your life is immortal, your body is dispensable, and time and space are only the means you have chosen to find your truth today.

What are you waiting for? Are you waiting for a better time to live, to love, and to seek beauty and joy? There is no better time than today. And if you are waiting for the exact moment to begin preparation for what you fear in the last days of Earth, there is no exact moment for you. The preparation that is of reality is the spiritual preparation for the last days, which is the entire essence of your reality. Food and shelter and clothing to use in times of need are enough for your physical comfort. They are useful if you can forget about them when you have prepared them for the times to come.

But if the preparation is made in fear, in belief in the illusions, in ignorance of the reality of your life and your spirit, and in anxiety, your waiting will only be more painful after you are prepared. The key to survival is the key found through sorting the reality from the illusions. Last day survival is a spiritual reality for every one. It is also a physical illusion for everyone. There will be no difference, in the events of the last days, for one than for another, but the impact will be entirely different for some than for others.

Your waiting will seem a heavy burden for you if you are not prepared. And if your preparation is entirely physical, the passage of time will only add to the burden of your waiting. Keep reality and illusions separate in your mind. The illusion of Earth and of many of the physical lives upon it will seem to be destroyed so that many new beginnings may take place. If these illusions seem real to you, and if you are unaware of your own spiritual reality, you shall find it a heavy burden to wait for the events of the last days.

So prepare yourself to make the waiting a joy and a comfort to you. Prepare by praying and meditating upon the reality, the good, and the beautiful parts of Creation. These are not of time or space, are not withheld until a certain time or place are reached, and can be realized and accepted by your spirit whenever you are ready. The time for waiting is only found in waiting for the things of time. There is no effectiveness in waiting for the things of love, of joy, of peace, of mercy, and of goodwill. These are timeless. If you cannot find them today, they will be just as elusive for you tomorrow.

The mind can seem to imagine horrible things when an indefinite time of waiting comes. The many ways in which the last days of Earth might come could be as varied and depressing as your imagination might allow. I have noticed that the things for which I have realistically prepared never seem to bother me very much. After being prepared, it doesn't seem to matter whether my preparations are needed or not. So often, the trouble for which I prepare never comes, and I never think much about it while I wait for it. Being ready, the consciousness of time is lessened and peace is more easily found.

"The only limit, as you reach out to Me and to others, is your conception of what is possible. As your concept grows and accepts and believes, so does the process of the word, the thought, the action, and the adoption of a new Life transpire. This is the unfolding I told you of yesterday. I will speak to you of days, time, and life as if they exist for you, but they are only a bit of what will be for you when time does not exist for you — it has never existed for Me. I am beyond time, and space, and purpose of Being. I Am because I Am; I live forever, as a circle, with no beginning, no end, and not the slightest hesitation of existence. My Fullness is all Powerful, all Glorious, and all Merciful to humankind and to you. I am beyond the comprehension of any of My beings."

From Book 1 — <u>A New Way of Living</u>

Chapter 44   From Book 36 — <u>A New Way of Living</u>

Best is Last

If time seems to be leading you nowhere at all, what is the use of time? You are in command of it, and time always has a first and last, formed by your creative hopes and dreams. There are no restrictions in time or space that can stop you from fulfilling your destiny. Time belongs to you. How are you using your time?

When you feel time is using you, there is a gap in your faith. The purpose of your life is chosen by you, can be controlled by you, and will be fulfilled by you. Growing older is of little comfort if growing happier and better is not a part of it.

Last Days?

Good is the aftermath of the best that life has to offer you. If your last moment today is not better than the first, you have missed the point of living in the day at hand.

Small changes lead to large ones, for the events of time are always taking you in one direction or another. If you have adopted the habit of waiting for things to get better, you have missed the joy of creative hope and its fulfillment. Go on with your life today in peace, having the hope you need to create hope's own fulfillment. Your dreams can come true if they are dreams of this step and this moment. If, however, they are of a distant future, with drudgery and toil in between, the trend you find will not take you where you want to go.

While you are in a world of time, make the best of it. Make time last and make it best for you. Time is yours to control, and it will last as long as you need it. Your choices can lead to better and better ways of living.

The last days of your life are the best ones for you. This is equally true of the last days of Earth. They are better because they are closer to a new beginning. The best is yet to come, your last use of the times that are with you is now, and it can become very good. When you look for the best, it will come to you, it will last, and good will follow.

Even the negativity of the world will help to develop the positive good things that are to follow. The contrary opinion theory is used by traders in the stock market to know when the market is ready to turn. If a small majority believes things will get better, they will, If a very large majority comes to believe this, however, the market will turn against them, for they have created a market that is overbought. The opposite is equally true in the case of a market expected to get worse.

There are uses for all things, including negativity. Creation uses every illusion, every reality, and every truth to find Our Harmony. There is nothing that can be lost, as far as purpose is concerned, and your greatest efforts to avoid it will not allow you to escape final perfection. The last days are best. They take you to a new beginning on the other side of that era of time.

The process cannot be hurried. It does no good to invite the illusion of death in order to advance the reality of the life which is renewed thereafter. Illusions are not the stepping stones to reality. They are only the visible means of seeing reality's symbols and finding reality's truth in a physical world. Neither haste nor waiting will change the steady steps of time on Earth. Only the attitude of hurry or of delay will change things by making time appear to change its impact on your life.

Break the habit of regrets for times past. Your youthfulness led to many problems you have forgotten. Your wishes to grow older and more independent has led, in many ways, to better things. The last days of any life, if it is a life with purpose and with fulfillment, are better. Retirement and rest, before the end of any physical life on Earth, is not a punishment filled with boredom and futility.

Time is meaningless, and good is better than best. The last days and first days are of equal value, for they are only different stages of illusions in the same cycles of time that lead you to reality and truth. Compared either little or much, the waves of time are of small value in your assessment of the purpose of life. But time is an incremental measuring tool, a yard-stick, a milestone, and a mark of your progress. If things seem to be going your way, getting better and better, time becomes a welcome ally. If, on the other hand, things seem to be getting worse, time then seems to be working against you.

But time is always on your side, and the last is always better than the first in the overall picture of your truth and reality. You are not able to see this from the troughs of the cycles of your life in time, nor can the crests of your waves of progress show you the many troughs in the waves beyond. But the last is best, even though it might be found in the trough of a wave in a cycle of time.

Withdraw, in spirit, from time for a while. Use this day to

reminisce and to enjoy the best that has, thus far, come to you. The life you now live can be neither all good nor all bad, for such is life in the cycles and waves of time. Other troughs and waves are ahead of you, and your joy will seem to come and go in proportion to your faith in Our Kingdom within you. Your grasp of reality will slip from time to time, causing the illusions to shake you more and more as you believe more and more in them.

When this happens, retreat, retrench, reconsider, and renew your faith. There is a time to move on and a time to pause. Digest the food for thought that comes with your truth today. Press on when you are filled with new courage and confidence gained through faith. Make the last days the best you find in this life, for they can be the best for you. You are not at the mercy of time.

Love and feel loved, for so you are. The love of Creation abounds all around you, being expressed in the beauty of every illusion you see. That symbolic revelation of beauty in an illusion is not an accident. You need not feel that only real things can be enjoyed. The illusions are equally enjoyable, though changeable and fleeting. You have chosen illusions as an environment. Make the best of it, and know that the last days of your life, like the last days of the life of Earth, can be very good.

This goodness will not be found by those whose firm grasp on illusions has no end. If held tightly, the illusions will pull you down into their seeming death before you can let go of them. Hold fast, instead, to that which is good, for that will carry you across the waves of time and keep you near the surface, where reality is found and truth is enjoyed. You have, in every moment, the freedom to choose your beliefs. If illusions continue to deceive you in the last days, truth will not interfere, and your last days will not seem the best for you.

But learning truth, using it, and enjoying it can be the indirect and happy final result of the pain of deception. If the illusions overcome your mind and gain a victory over your spirit, you will come to know the freedom of the truth you shall later discover. Each experience of failure leads to a later experience of success, so failure is one way of finding the best the last days have to offer you. Your state of mind, your attitude, and the health of your living spirit will determine how the last days affect you.

Never doubt that you have the freedom, the choice, and the ability to make your last days the best. In any lifetime, and especially now that so many lifetimes coincide with the rare end of a lifetime of Earth, you can be a witness to last days and best days. These can be seen all around you and in yourself. The last, being of time, is an illusion. Good, being of Us, is reality. The best is only a step on the pathway of the journey to good. There is nothing better than good.

Goodness shall prevail. Truth shall prevail. Love shall prevail. Life shall prevail. Reality shall prevail. Creation shall prevail. And you, being created with an immortality beyond time, shall have all the good things that prevail. Goodness is the sum of the reward of all immortality. Life remains when all the illusions are gone for you. But while you are in time, you shall find your last days, and shall see the last days of many lives around you. Make your last days the best, for that is your privilege and lies within the scope of your ability.

You might wonder, 'How, with all the negativity and the natural results of that negativity around me, can this be?' Wonder, if you like, but know that the natural result of any physical event in time is as much an illusion as the events which led up to it. The last days are illusions, and the best is an illusion, but these things lead inevitably to the timeless goals of good and of immortal and Absolute Reality.

> *I do wonder how this can be. But experience shows me, more and more, that concern for survival in the last days of Earth seems more real if it is directed toward*

the illusionary side of this life. If, however, I live one day at a time and think more of the spiritual reality of that day, the illusions become more beautiful, my cares drop away, and the best I have found in this life becomes clearly the last day of it. The trend reveals a hint of what is to come, and my attitude reveals the state of my spiritual health. When that is good, what else matters to me? Nothing!

Glossary

Absolute Reality
Life in the absence of time, space, or any other illusion at all.

Brotherhood of Light
Beings who manipulate the illusions of time and space according to God's perfect plan of freedom and liberty. See **Christ**.

Christ
A Member of the Trinity.

Cosmic Telepathy
"Cosmic Telepathy provides truth filtered from the Perfect Being, Whom We Are. While you are on Earth you shall never see Us, nor shall you truly comprehend how We Are One while We Are All. You are blinded to Our Absolute Reality by your relative environment and by your imperfection. And yet, you are in total contact with Us when your faith allows you to expose Our Perfect Part of your Inner Self to your conscious mind. Cosmic Telepathy allows this exposure to be attainable for you from within."

Creation
Since God is everywhere in the illusions of time and space, and in all the realms of Absolute Reality, as well, God is Creation and Creation is God.

Eternity
The absence of time or space -- timelessness. A realm where Absolute Reality exists, and where nothing is relative at all.

Father
A Member of the Trinity.

Mind Perversions
Anger, lust, greed, vanity, and materialism.

God
The Creator, Creation, All That Is. The I Am That I Am, Everything, All Life.

Inner Self
The timeless realm within your being where Absolute Reality, the Kingdom of God, and the heart of Creation exist.

Light
There are, according to these Books, hundreds of thousands of realms and vibrations of light. If capitalized, the word refers to Christ, a Member of the Trinity of God. The Light is synonymous with life.

Mother of Truth
See **Spirit of Truth**.

Our Kingdom
The Realm of Timelessness, Eternity, and Absolute Reality. This is the Kingdom of God that lies in a realm beyond time and space within each of our Inner Selves.

Path to Perfection
While on Earth we are learning to perfect ourselves. This path, which is an illusion involving time and space, allows us to sort and find our truth from among the illusions, and to perfect ourselves freely as, if, and when we choose. However, the joy of living is found when we move along this path in time toward Eternity.

Seventh Day
The Seventh Day of the creation of our Earth. It is prophesied to last one thousand years. It will begin at the end of the Sixth Day. See **Sixth Day**.

Sixth Day
We now live in the Sixth Day of ongoing Creation. It is described in the Book of Genesis as having been completed. However, time and space are not reality, so the passage of time is an illusion. The Sixth Day has lasted approximately ten million years, making one human lifetime seem infinitely small. But we live forever.

Source & Strength
See **Father**.

Spirit of Truth
A Member of the Trinity.

Workers of Light
Members of the Brotherhood of Light who help with the things of time and space in our physical realm. Some of them are in spirit form in other planes, while others are living in physical bodies among us.

Trinity
The Father, the Christ, and the Spirit of Truth, Who Are the three Beings composing the One God of All Creation.

Other Books from ANWOL Publishers

Each of the 36 Books from the Series of A New Way of Living was published in limited quantities in the month it was completed. Each Book in the Series, consisting of about 150 pages in 6" X 9" GBC binding, is available from ANWOL Publishers in limited quantities until the volume of sales justifies mass printing. Until now, no effort has been made to advertise or sell the original Books to the public.

Order additional copies of Last Days? or any of the 36 Books of the Series called A New Way of Living from your Book Dealer or from

ANWOL Publishers
P. O. Box 525
Jasper, AR 72641
SAN 297-309X

ORDER BLANK

MAIL TO _____

ADDRESS _____

STATE _____ ZIP _____

_____ Copies of Last Days?

_____ Copies of A New Way of Living Book ___

Price $9.95 each plus $1.50 postage and handling.

ANWOL Publishers books are available for bulk purchases with quantity discounts for educational, business, or sales promotional use. For information, please write to ANWOL Publishers.